Bartending

6th Edition

by Ray Foley and Jackie Wilson Foley

dummies
A Wiley Brand

Bartending For Dummies®, 6th Edition

Published by: **John Wiley & Sons, Inc.**, 111 River Street, Hoboken, NJ 07030-5774, www.wiley.com

Copyright © 2022 by John Wiley & Sons, Inc., Hoboken, New Jersey

Published simultaneously in Canada

For general information on our other products and services, please contact our Customer Care Department within the U.S. at 877-762-2974, outside the U.S. at 317-572-3993, or fax 317-572-4002. For technical support, please visit www.wiley.com/techsupport.

Wiley publishes in a variety of print and electronic formats and by print-on-demand. Some material included with standard print versions of this book may not be included in e-books or in print-on-demand. If this book refers to media such as a CD or DVD that is not included in the version you purchased, you may download this material at http://booksupport.wiley.com. For more information about Wiley products, visit www.wiley.com.

Library of Congress Control Number: 2022942418

ISBN 978-1-119-90044-3 (pbk); ISBN 978-1-119-90046-7 (epub); ISBN 978-1-119-90045-0 (epdf)

SKY10059345_110623

Contents at a Glance

Table of Contents

Introduction

Back when I (Ray) started bartending in the 1970s, the most adventurous that many people got with their cocktails was ordering a Harvey Wallbanger or a Grasshopper. (Nothing against Harvey Wallbangers and Grasshoppers!) We've come a long way from those days, and as someone who has proudly spent decades behind the bar, it's so exciting to see how much people's interest in cocktails and learning to bartend at home has grown over the years (this 6th edition is evidence of that!).

Bartending is a lot of fun — at its core, it's all about making people happy — but to do it right, and to do it well, it does take some work. That's the aim of this book, to provide you all the information, tips, tools, and skills you need to not only learn how to mix great drinks, but to arm yourself with the knowledge required to become a true bartender.

Before you step foot behind a bar, however, we advise you to have some knowledge of the most called-for beers, wines, and cocktails as well as the equipment you need to successfully create the drinks you and your guests like the most.

Lucky for you, this edition of *Bartending For Dummies* serves up all that info and more!

About This Book

This book is a reference that you can read now and refer to for years to come. To make the content more accessible, we divided it into four parts:

>> Part 1, Getting Started with Bartending

>> Part 2, Distilling the High Points of Various Spirits

>> Part 3, Drink Recipes: Creating Classic Cocktails and More

>> Part 4, The Part of Tens

We guess that you'll mostly use this book for the recipes in Part 3, which is by far the largest section of the book for that reason! The drinks are also listed by their ingredients in the recipe index at the back of this book.

Foolish Assumptions

You don't need any special knowledge of liquor or mixology to understand this book. Having an interest in creating crowd-pleasing cocktails is definitely a plus, and having the patience to get recipes just right doesn't hurt either. Good bartenders are always trying new things in the interest of serving the tastiest beverages.

A bartender can't be made overnight and a head full of recipes and facts will get you only so far. You need experience, and you must respect and like people. If you aren't a people person, all the great information in this book won't make you a bartender.

As a bartender for more than 20 years, I (Ray) always enjoyed the atmosphere and people in bars and restaurants. They're there to relax and have fun. My job was to serve and be a part of the entertainment, to make the guests feel at home and relaxed, never to be overbearing or intrusive or to overserve. A good attitude, practice, and willingness to learn are key. From here on in, I'm going to assume that you have the former and are working on the latter. You're a good person, especially because you bought this book. Please enjoy — and cheers!

Icons Used in This Book

Scattered throughout the book are little pictures, which our publisher calls *icons*, in the margins next to certain blocks of text. Here's what they mean:

This icon lets you know that we're presenting a neat hint or trick that can make your life easier.

This icon flags information that will keep you out of trouble.

When you see this icon, tuck that bit of info away for future reference.

This icon indicates that we're about to tell a story or provide a little interesting background information.

FABLES AND LORE

We use this symbol in Part 3 to indicate classic drinks that every bartender should know.

Beyond the Book

In addition to the material in the print or e-book you're reading right now, this product also comes with some free access-anywhere goodies on the web at Dummies.com. Check out this book's online Cheat Sheet. Just go to www.dummies.com and search for "Bartending For Dummies Cheat Sheet." There, you find some classic cocktail recipes plus a list of must-have liquors to buy if you're just getting started with stocking your bar. You also find a list of essential mixers, garnishes, and seasonings.

Where to Go from Here

Look up some recipes. Read about the spirits that intrigue you. Check out our list of recommended hangover cures. This book was designed so you can jump around. Simply use the Table of Contents at the front and the Indexes at the back as your guides.

Our best advice is to practice making drinks. That said, get reading and start pouring!

1

Getting Started with Bartending

Start with the tools and glassware you'll need to be a successful bartender.

Discover the proper techniques for mixing drinks, find out how to open wine and champagne bottles, and create popular garnishes.

Buy the right kinds and quantities of supplies so you have what you need for a successful party.

Get the facts about measurements and calories.

Chapter **1**

For Openers: Gathering the Tools and Glasses You Need

To bartend, you need a few essentials: good people skills, knowledge about the products you're pouring, a collection of cocktail recipes, and the proper equipment. This chapter covers the equipment part of the equation. (Part 2 can help you with product knowledge, and Part 3 gives you the recipes. As for people skills, you're on your own.)

Covering the Basics: Bar Tools to Have at the Ready

The most important assets for any profession are the right tools. You need basic bar tools to open, mix, serve, and store your drinks. Whether you're stocking a home bar or working as a professional, your basic tools are a wine opener, cocktail shaker, and strainer.

Wine opener

The most common wine opener used in bars and restaurants is a *waiter's corkscrew* sometimes called a *wine key* (shown in Figure 1-1). It has a sharp blade for cutting foils around corks and a corkscrew (also known as a *worm*) for extracting the cork. This tool also includes a bottle opener for removing caps from beer bottles and the like. You can find this opener online or in most liquor stores and bar supply houses.

Another nifty option is an electric wine opener (refer to Figure 1-1). It's electric *and* ergonomic so it makes your life easier. It also automatically lets go of the cork so there's even less work for you. While more expensive than a waiter's corkscrew, electric wine openers like the Rabbit are easier to use making it great for your home bar or for using in a busy restaurant behind the bar. (When it comes to tableside openings, only the traditional waiter's corkscrew should be used.)

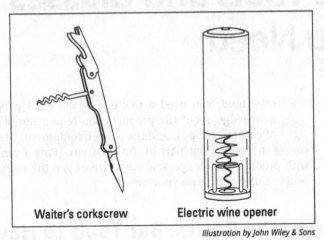

Waiter's corkscrew	Electric wine opener

Illustration by John Wiley & Sons

FIGURE 1-1: A waiter's corkscrew and an electric wine opener.

Cocktail shaker

The cocktail shaker is the most common bar tool used. Get to know it, as you will use it often! Figure 1-2 shows two types of shakers.

>> The *Boston shaker,* also known as a *two-piece shaker,* is the shaker that most professional bartenders use because of its

versatility. It most commonly consists of a mixing/pint glass on top (which can be used to serve the cocktail you're about to make) and a stainless-steel core that overlaps the glass to contain the liquid. This type of shaker requires a separate Hawthorne strainer be used, as described in the following section.

>> The *cobbler shaker,* also known as a *three-piece shaker,* consists of at least two stainless-steel parts and a built-in strainer, making it a good option for your home bar given its ease of use.

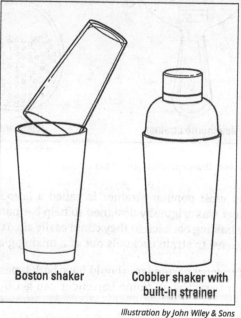

Boston shaker   Cobbler shaker with built-in strainer

Illustration by John Wiley & Sons

FIGURE 1-2: A Boston shaker and a cobbler shaker.

Strainer

A *strainer* is used to strain the liquid out of a shaker or mixing glass catching and keeping any ice or muddled ingredients from getting into the final product.

There are a couple different types of strainers available, but the most popular is the *Hawthorne strainer,* shown in Figure 1-3. The Hawthorne is a flat, spoon-shaped utensil with a spring coil around its head. Place it on top of the stainless-steel half of a Boston shaker or directly into a bar or mixing glass to strain cocktails.

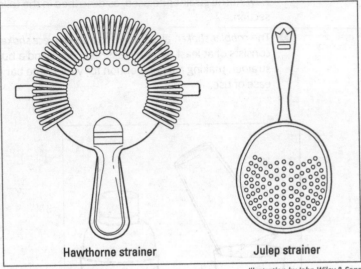

Hawthorne strainer   Julep strainer

Illustration by John Wiley & Sons

FIGURE 1-3: A Hawthorne strainer and a Julep strainer.

The second most popular strainer is called a *Julep strainer.* The Julep strainer was originally designed to help bar patrons drink a cocktail by holding back ice so they could easily sip. It's now more commonly used to strain cocktails out of a mixing glass.

While professional bartenders should have both types of strainers behind their bars, the at-home bartender can get by with just a Hawthorne.

Adding Other Helpful Tools

TIP

Most if not all of the tools in this section should be found at a restaurant or bar. For at-home bartenders, a cocktail shaker, jigger, bar spoon, and mixing glass are most key.

Many of the following tools are shown in Figure 1-4:

>> **Bar towels:** Keeping bar towels behind the bar is always smart to wipe up spills, overpours, or sweat from glasses.

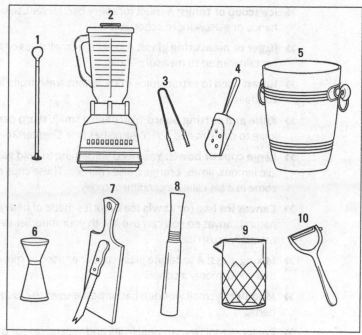

Illustration by John Wiley & Sons

FIGURE 1-4: A collection of bar tools: (1) bar spoon, (2) blender, (3) tongs, (4) ice scoop, (5) ice bucket, (6) jigger or measuring glass, (7) knife and cutting board, (8) muddler, (9) mixing glass, and (10) peeler.

>> **Bar spoon:** A long spoon for stirring cocktails.

>> **Blender:** Used to do just that — mix or blend ingredients.

TIP

When making a drink, always add liquid into the blender jar before switching on the unit; doing so will save your blade and avoid spills. Also, don't assume your blender can be used to make crushed ice. Check with the manufacturer or owner's guide first or buy an ice crusher to be safe.

>> **Bottle opener or church key:** A tool used to open bottles or cans.

>> **Coasters or bar napkins:** Coasters prevent rings from developing on your bar and tables. Napkins help do the same and also help your guests hold their drinks.

>> **Grater:** Use a grater for garnishing drinks with a dusting of grated nutmeg, chocolate, and so forth.

>> **Ice bucket:** Pick one that's large enough to hold at least three trays of ice.

>> **Ice scoop or tongs:** A must for every bar. Never use your hands or glassware to scoop ice.

>> **Jigger or measuring glass:** A *jigger* is a small glass or metal container used to measure liquid.

>> **Juicer:** Used to extract juice from various fresh fruits for cocktails.

>> **Knife and cutting board:** You need a small, sharp paring knife to cut fruit and other garnishes (see Chapter 2).

>> **Large cups or bowls:** You need something to hold garnishes like lemons, limes, oranges, and cherries. These cups often come in a set called a *condiment caddy*.

>> **Canvas ice bag (or Lewis Ice Bag):** It's made of heavy grade natural canvas so you can use it with your muddler to manually crush ice.

>> **Mixing glass:** A separate glass container used to mix drinks that contain only alcohol.

>> **Muddler:** A small wooden bat or pestle used to crush fruit or herbs.

>> **Peeler:** A tool used to peel fruits and vegetables for drink garnishes.

>> **Pour spout:** This device gives greater control to your pouring. Many different types are available, including some with a lidded spout that prevents insects and other undesirables from entering the pourer.

>> **Stirrers and straws:** Used for stirring and sipping drinks.

Pour It Out: Giving Some Thought to Glassware

People generally expect certain drinks to be served in certain kinds of glasses. The problem is that there are more standard bar glasses than most people (and many bars) care to purchase. In any event, Figure 1-5 shows most of the glasses that you're ever likely to use to serve drinks.

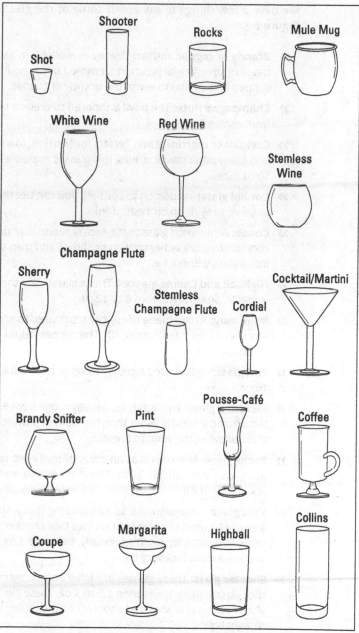

Shooter

Rocks

Mule Mug

Shot

White Wine

Red Wine

Stemless Wine

Champagne Flute

Sherry

Stemless Champagne Flute

Cordial

Cocktail/Martini

Pousse-Café

Brandy Snifter

Pint

Coffee

Coupe

Margarita

Highball

Collins

Illustration by John Wiley & Sons

FIGURE 1-5: Glasses, glasses, glasses.

We have a few things to say about some of the glasses shown in Figure 1-5:

>> **Brandy or cognac snifter:** These are available in a wide range of sizes; the large, short-stemmed bowl should be cupped in the hand to warm the brandy or cognac.

>> **Champagne flute:** The bowl is tapered to prevent bubbles from escaping.

>> **Cocktail or martini glass:** Perfect for Martinis, Manhattans, and many other classic drinks, this glass is available in 3 to 10 oz. sizes.

>> **Cordial glass:** In addition to cordials, you can use this glass to serve straight-up or "neat" drinks.

>> **Coupe:** A stemmed glass that typically serves "up" drinks or cocktails that are either shaken or stirred and then strained into a glass without ice.

>> **Highball and Collins glasses:** These glasses are the most versatile. Sizes range from 8 to 12 oz.

>> **Mule mug:** A mug made of copper that's used to serve Moscow mules (see Chapter 20). The copper helps keep the drink cold.

>> **Pint glass:** A glass used typically to serve beer, usually 12 to 16 oz.

>> **Red wine glass:** These glasses usually range from 8 to 22 oz. Note that the bowl is wider than the bowl of a white wine glass, allowing the wine to breathe.

>> **Rocks glass:** Also known as an *old fashioned glass,* sizes of this glass vary from 5 to 10 oz. Use the 5 or 6 oz. variety and add plenty of ice.

>> **Shot glass:** Originally used as a measuring tool, a shot glass also can be used to serve shot recipes (see Chapter 21) or shots of straight liquor. Traditionally, these are 1 to 1.5 oz. and are a must for every bar.

>> **Shooter glass:** These glasses are taller and skinner than a shot glass, usually measuring 1.5 to 3 oz. These glasses are also used to serve shot and shooters recipes along with straight liquor.

>> **Stemless glasses:** Becoming popular in recent years, stemless glasses usually hold red or white wine but also can be used to serve a variety of cocktails.

» **White wine glass:** These glasses are typically smaller than red wine glasses, usually holding 8 to 12 oz. The U-shape not only helps with temperature but also helps preserve aromas.

TIP

Overall, the most standard glasses are pint, highball, red and white wine, rocks, champagne, and shot. However, if you're planning on creating a bar at home or serving cocktails at a party, keep your glass selection smaller to save space. You can simplify by using two types of glasses: a white wine glass and a red wine glass. Both are shown in Figure 1-5. You can use these two glasses for every type of cocktail (including shots, even though a shot glass is essential for every bar), plus beer and wine. Also, if you use these two glass shapes, cleaning and storing your glasses is less complicated.

IN THIS CHAPTER

» Mixing, stirring, and muddling drinks with style

» Exploring types of ice

» Prepping some great garnishes

» Conjuring up some simple syrup

» Popping the champagne and wine bottles

Chapter **2**

Methods to the Drink Making Madness

Making good cocktails takes more effort than just pouring ingredients into a glass. This chapter shows you how to make drinks and pull off some of the little touches that make both you and your drinks look and taste better, with the ultimate result of happier guests.

Shaking a Drink

The main reasons for shaking drinks are to chill a cocktail, to mix ingredients, or to put a *head* or froth on some cocktails.

TIP

As a general rule, you should shake all cloudy drinks (cocktails with citrus, milk, or cream). Never shake a cocktail that has carbonated water or soda. For some drinks, such as the Stinger or Martini, ask your guests whether they prefer them shaken or stirred.

To shake a cocktail in a Boston shaker (described in Chapter 1), follow these steps:

1. **Put some ice cubes (if called for in the recipe) in the glass container.**

2. Add the cocktail ingredients.

3. Place the metal container over the glass container.

4. Hold the metal and glass containers together with both hands and shake with an up-and-down motion.

5. Use your Hawthorne strainer (see Chapter 1) to strain your shaken cocktail into the desired glassware.

WARNING

Make sure you always point the shaker away from your guests. That way you avoid spilling anything on them if the shaker isn't properly sealed.

WARNING

The two pieces of the shaker may stick together after you shake a drink. Never bang the shaker against the bar or any other surface or object. Instead, gently tap it a few times at the point where the glass and metal containers come in contact to separate them and allow you to pour your cocktail.

Stirring a Drink

Stirring cocktails allows you to mix, dilute, and chill the drink. In general, you should stir cocktails that are spirit or liquor forward, meaning cocktails that are more spirit than mixer. A lot of classic cocktails like the Old Fashioned, Manhattan, and Negroni should be stirred.

To stir cocktails, follow these instructions.

1. Add the cocktail ingredients and ice into the mixing glass.

2. Insert your bar spoon into the mixing glass and stir in a circular motion for around 30 to 45 seconds.

3. Use your Julep strainer (see Chapter 1) to strain the cocktail into a glass.

Every Day I'm Muddling

Muddling, or more simply put, crushing or breaking down an ingredient, helps release the flavors of fresh ingredients such as fruits and herbs. This technique is often used in making drinks like a Caipirinha, Mint Julep, Mojito, and Smashes.

The following steps walk you through how to muddle mint, but you can use these same simple steps for any herb or fruit.

1. Add the mint leaves into a glass or cocktail shaker.

2. Take your muddler and press firmly into the mint and twist.

3. Do this a few times till you can smell the essences from the mint (or see the juices from fruit) being released.

Do your best not to over muddle ingredients. You should only need two to four presses. You'll know you over muddled if the muddled ingredient is shredded apart.

4. Use the muddled mint to finish making the cocktail per recipe instructions.

Chillin' on Ice

Ice is very important in making cocktails because it makes the drink cold and helps with dilution. Bars and bartenders use a few different types of ice; here are the most common ones.

» **Standard (1-inch square):** This is the most common type of ice used in bartending.

» **Rocks ice:** When you hear someone say "on the rocks" or "on one rock," this is the ice you most commonly think of. Usually, this is one larger square but can be a circle as well.

» **Crushed ice:** Smaller ice pieces that are ideal for frozen drinks. Pebble and Julep ice fall into this category. You see this ice a lot in tiki, frozen, and julep cocktails.

There are other types of ice as well, such as collins spears, which are long spears that are used for highballs and long drinks, and dry ice, which is used more for show than for actual drink making.

WARNING

Be *very* careful when using dry ice in cocktails because it can seriously harm a guest, employee, or even yourself! Dry ice should be used more for show and display, as touching dry ice can burn your skin, and ingesting dry ice is an even bigger no-no!

Making the Cut: Common Garnish Shapes

Many drinks require garnishes. Your guests expect the garnish, so you can't forgo it, and presentation counts, big time, so you need to have a solid garnish game. You may mix the best drinks on the planet, but if they don't look good when you serve them, no one's going to want to drink them.

Garnishes are generally made from fruits and vegetables. Most commonly used are lemons, limes, oranges, and cucumbers, all of which we cover in the following sections!

The next few sections show you how to cut the most common garnishes. Of course, wash your fruits and veggies thoroughly first!

Slices

Time to slice and dice! This is an easy cut that gives your cocktails a nice pop! The next few steps and Figure 2-1 show you how to cut lime slices, but you can use the same technique to cut lemons, oranges, grapefruit — you name it.

1. **Cut off both ends of the lime.**

2. **Slice the lime in half.**

3. **Lay each half down and cut it into half-moon slices.**

4. **Lay each half-moon slice down and cut into the flesh at the fruit's middle point, being careful to slice only halfway into the wedge.**

   This slot will hold the garnish in place on the rim of your glass.

Wedges of all sizes

Wedges are the most common garnish, as they're used in many standard drinks like Vodka & Soda and Rum & Coke, so get used to cutting this garnish!

Small citrus wedges

The following steps for cutting wedges are shown in Figure 2-2, but you can use the same technique to cut lots of fruits like limes and oranges into small wedges.

1. With the ends removed, slice the lemon in half the long way.
2. Lay the cut halves down and halve them again.
3. Cut wedges from the quarters.

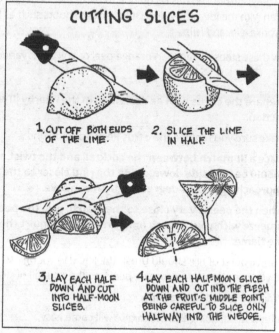

CUTTING SLICES

1. CUT OFF BOTH ENDS OF THE LIME.

2. SLICE THE LIME IN HALF.

3. LAY EACH HALF DOWN AND CUT INTO HALF-MOON SLICES.

4. LAY EACH HALF-MOON SLICE DOWN AND CUT INTO THE FLESH AT THE FRUIT'S MIDDLE POINT, BEING CAREFUL TO SLICE ONLY HALFWAY INTO THE WEDGE.

Illustration by Elizabeth Kurtzman

FIGURE 2-1: Cutting slices.

CUTTING SMALL WEDGES

1. SLICE THE LEMON OR LIME IN HALF THE LONG WAY (WITH ENDS CUT OFF).

2. LAY THE CUT HALVES DOWN AND CUT AGAIN.

3. CUT WEDGES FROM THE LEMON OR LIME QUARTERS.

Illustration by Elizabeth Kurtzman

FIGURE 2-2: Cutting small wedges.

FLAMING AN ORANGE PEEL

Flaming the oil of an orange peel enhances the orange flavor in a cocktail, especially one made with Lillet, an orange-based aperitif. After I (Ray) introduced this technique to bartenders in New York City, they ran with the idea and added it to various liquors such as bourbon, vodka, gin, and rum.

Follow these steps to flame an orange peel or any other variety of citrus.

1. **Prepare the citrus peel as described in the nearby "Twists" section.**

   Make sure you remove the citrus flesh from the rind.

2. **Place a lit match between the cocktail and the twist, which should be rind-side down; bring the rind closer to the flame, approaching at a 45-degree angle from above.**

3. **When the peel is very close to the match, give the peel a good squeeze with your thumb and forefinger to squirt the oil into the flame.**

   A small burst of fire should brush the liquid in your glass. After it's lit, you can choose to drop the peel into the cocktail or discard.

4. **Practice, practice, practice.**

   After a while, doing this technique will come easy.

Medium pineapple wedges

Feeling tropical? Figure 2-3 and the following steps show you how to cut pineapple wedges. These garnishes are most commonly used in tropical drinks like a Pina Colada.

1. Cut off the top and bottom of the pineapple.
2. From top to bottom, cut the pineapple in half.
3. Lay the half pineapple down and cut it in half again.
4. Remove the core section of the pineapple quarters.
5. Cut wedges.

CUTTING MEDIUM WEDGES

1. CUT THE BOTTOM AND THE TOP OFF OF THE PINEAPPLE.

2. FROM TOP TO BOTTOM, CUT THE PINEAPPLE IN HALF.

3. LAY EACH HALF PINEAPPLE DOWN AND CUT EACH IN HALF AGAIN.

4. REMOVE THE CORE SECTION OF THE PINEAPPLE QUARTERS.

5. CUT WEDGES.

Illustration by Elizabeth Kurtzman

FIGURE 2-3: Cutting pineapple wedges.

Long cucumber ribbons

Long cucumber ribbons make great floating garnishes for Bloody Marys, some Martinis, and Collins cocktails. Here's how you make them (see Figure 2-4):

1. Cut off the ends of the cucumber.

2. Holding the cucumber lengthwise, use a vegetable peeler to create long ribbons.

3. Repeat this process until you reach the seeds. Then do the opposite side.

Wheels

Wheel garnishes are great for adding a pop of citrus to a drink. These garnishes can be placed on the side of the glass or floated on top of a cocktail. You're likely to see wheels on drinks like Cosmopolitans and Daiquiris (see the recipes in Chapter 20).

Here's how to make a fun lemon wheel garnish (see Figure 2-5):

1. Cut off both ends of the lemon.

2. Stand the lemon up on one end and cut about a quarter of the way down. This will allow the formed wheels to

have a small slit in them for garnishing on the side of the glass.

3. Lay the lemon on the side and then thinly cut each slice.

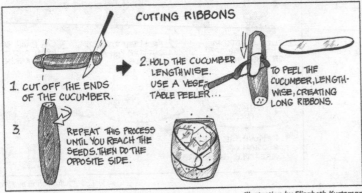

Illustration by Elizabeth Kurtzman

FIGURE 2-4: Cutting cucumber ribbons.

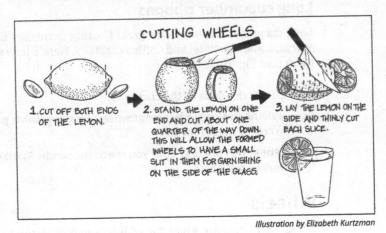

Illustration by Elizabeth Kurtzman

FIGURE 2-5: Cutting lemon wheels.

Twists

It's time to twist! Figure 2-6 illustrates the procedure for cutting twists from a lemon.

1. Cut off both ends of the lemon.

2. Insert a sharp knife or spoon between the rind and meat of the lemon and carefully separate them.

DON'T FORGET THE OLIVES AND MARASCHINO CHERRIES

When you start bartending you may think the olive is the most common garnish, but they are usually only used for martinis. Olives are great to eat and add a brininess to Martinis. You usually skewer them and place them on the side of the glass or in the Martini itself. You can also stuff olives for added flavor, the most common being blue cheese stuffed olives.

All kinds of drinks are garnished with Maraschino cherries, including the kid-friendly Shirley Temple and the more adult Manhattan. You can find Maraschino cherries in small jars at any food store, and the best thing about them is that you don't have to cut them before serving.

3. Cut the rind into strips.

4. Twist your strip to form the garnish

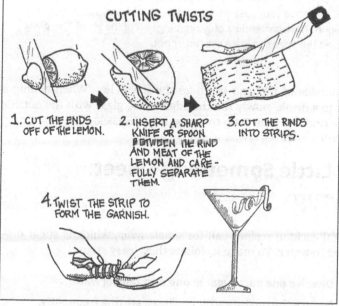

CUTTING TWISTS

1. CUT THE ENDS OFF OF THE LEMON.

2. INSERT A SHARP KNIFE OR SPOON BETWEEN THE RIND AND MEAT OF THE LEMON AND CAREFULLY SEPARATE THEM.

3. CUT THE RINDS INTO STRIPS.

4. TWIST THE STRIP TO FORM THE GARNISH.

Illustration by Elizabeth Kurtzman

FIGURE 2-6: Cutting twists.

RIM A COCKTAIL GLASS

To help balance flavors and add a bit of flare to your cocktails, you can rim the glass with salt, sugar, or a spice mixture, most commonly seen in the Margarita. To rim a glass, follow these steps:

1. Cut your citrus wedge in half. Note this can also be done with water or simple syrup, so if using that, skip this step.

2. Prep your rim mixture in a dish or bowl.

3. Rub the citrus flesh up against the outside rim of the glass. If you're using liquid, place the rim of the glass into the liquid, coating the entire rim.

4. Place the glass into the mixture bowl, coating the outside rim in the mix.

5. Let the rimmed glass rest and then pour your cocktail into the glass and serve!

Tip: If you work in a bar that has a lot of rimmed cocktails, you can prep the rims in advance. This will give the rim time to dry and stick to the glass better. This will also save you time so you can make more drinks and serve your customers quicker. In addition, some modern techniques have bartenders only rimming half of the glass. This gives the guest the option to taste the rim or not.

TIP

The outside of the rind is where the flavor lies. When adding a twist to a drink, slowly *rim* the edge of the glass with the outside of the rind and then drop the twist into the cocktail.

Adding a Little Something Sweet: Simple Syrup

Several cocktail recipes call for *simple syrup*, which is sugar dissolved in water. To make it, follow these easy steps:

1. Dissolve one part sugar in one part boiling water.

2. Reduce the mixture over low heat, stirring frequently, until it thickens.

It shouldn't take more than a couple of minutes. Basic simple syrups can last 3 to 4 weeks in the fridge, and flavored syrups can last 1 to 2 weeks.

TIP

You can make a variety of flavored syrups using the same measurements. Add in fresh fruits or herbs to make unique syrups and test them in different cocktails to make your own twist.

Opening Wine and Champagne Bottles

Opening bottles doesn't take much skill — just a little practice. The more you practice, the more wine or champagne you have to drink. Score!

Wine bottles

To open a wine bottle, use a waiter's corkscrew, as shown in Figure 2-7. Here's how:

1. Using the blade on the opener, cut the lead foil or capsule at the middle of the bulge near the bottle neck.

2. Remove the foil and wipe the bottle top with a cloth to remove any mold or foreign particles.

3. Line up the corkscrew or worm directly over the bottle, and with gentle downward pressure, screw the worm clockwise into the cork.

Don't break the end of the cork; screw in just enough to extract the cork.

WARNING

4. Attach the lever of the opener to the lip on top of the bottle, and while holding the bottle firmly, slowly lift the cork straight up.

5. Wipe the neck of the bottle to keep it clean.

6. Present the cork to your guest and pour a small amount of wine into their glass for tasting.

If the wine is to your guest's satisfaction, pour more. Keep your towel handy to wipe the neck of the bottle as you pour the wine for other guests.

OPENING A WINE BOTTLE

1. USING THE BLADE ON THE OPENER, CUT THE FOIL OR CAPSULE AT THE MIDDLE OF THE BULGE NEAR THE BOTTLENECK.

2. REMOVE THE FOIL AND WIPE THE BOTTLE WITH A CLOTH TO REMOVE ANY MOLD OR FOREIGN PARTICLES.

3. LINE UP THE CORKSCREW OR WORM DIRECTLY OVER THE BOTTLE, AND WITH A GENTLE, DOWNWARD PRESSURE, SCREW THE WORM CLOCKWISE INTO THE CORK.

4. ATTACH THE LEVER OF THE OPENER TO THE LIP ON TOP OF THE BOTTLE, AND WHILE HOLDING THE BOTTLE FIRMLY, SLOWLY LIFT THE CORK STRAIGHT UP.

5. WIPE THE NECK OF THE BOTTLE TO KEEP IT CLEAN AS YOU POUR WINE FOR YOUR GUESTS.

Illustration by Elizabeth Kurtzman

FIGURE 2-7: Opening a wine bottle.

Champagne and sparkling wine bottles

You don't use a corkscrew when opening sparkling wine bottles — you simply use your hands (see Figure 2-8).

1. **Remove the wine hood and foil capsule.**

2. **Hold the bottle at an angle and point it away from you and anyone else (and anything valuable).**

3. **While holding the cork in one hand, twist the bottle with the other hand and gently remove the cork.**

   Twist the bottle, not the cork, to help stop the cork from breaking.

REMEMBER

4. **Just before the cork is about to pop, place a bar towel over the cork and bottle and loosen it the rest of the way.**

   The towel will catch the cork and prevent it from becoming a UFO.

OPENING A CHAMPAGNE BOTTLE

1. CUT THE FOIL, REMOVE THE WIRE HOOD FROM OVER THE CORK.

2. HOLD THE BOTTLE AT AN ANGLE, POINT IT AWAY FROM YOU AND ANYONE ELSE (AND ANYTHING VALUABLE).

3. WHILE HOLDING THE CORK IN ONE HAND, TWIST THE BOTTLE WITH THE OTHER HAND AND GENTLY REMOVE THE CORK.

4. JUST BEFORE THE CORK IS ABOUT TO "POP", PLACE A BAR TOWEL OVER THE CORK AND BOTTLE AND LOOSEN IT THE REST OF THE WAY.

Illustration by Elizabeth Kurtzman

FIGURE 2-8: Opening a champagne bottle.

TIP

Keep another towel handy in case the champagne bottle bubbles over after you remove the cork. To avoid the bubbling, don't shake the bottle before opening.

Chapter **3**

Setting Up Your Home Bar

When you're doing any sort of entertaining, one of the biggest mysteries is figuring out how to set up your bar and how much liquor you need to buy. If you like to throw parties all the time, are planning a big party, or are just looking to start a nice home bar, this chapter can help.

Preparing for a Party

Before we get into what and how much to buy, here are some pointers on how to set up a bar for a party.

Situating the bar

When setting up a home bar for personal use, find an area that makes sense with the flow of the room. It can be in your living or dining room. But when setting up a bar for a party, you want the bar to be close to running water or a sink to help with rinsing glassware and tools and cleaning up any spills.

>> Keep the bar as far as possible from your food and snacks. Doing so prevents large groups of people from staying in one area.

>> If possible, base a self-serve wine and beer bar in one area and a cocktail bar in another.

>> Cleaning up spills is much easier if the cocktail bar is in your kitchen. What's more, you do less running around when you're close to the sink and refrigerator.

>> If you have to set up your bar in a location other than your kitchen, put a small rug or mat under and behind the bar to protect the floor or carpet.

>> And no matter where your bar is, use a strong, steady table to avoid tipping or collapsing.

Serving smartly

TIP

Your party will run smoothly and your guests will be happy if you take the following suggestions to heart:

>> When you're hosting a party with 20-plus guests, your best bet is to hire a professional bartender.

>> Use nothing larger than a shot glass for shots, and don't serve doubles to your guests. You aren't doing anyone any favors by overserving. If a recipe calls for 1½ oz. of vodka, use just that amount. No mixed drink should exceed 2 oz. of liquor.

>> Use lower-proof products if they're available. (See Chapter 8 for an explanation of proof.)

>> Have alcohol-free drinks available, including coffee, tea, and even nonalcoholic beer and spirits (find options in Chapter 24).

>> Use only fresh ice and fresh fruit for garnishes.

>> If possible, chill glasses and don't put them out until 5 minutes before the party begins.

>> When serving hot drinks, make sure that the cups or glasses have handles.

>> Use a scoop, tongs, or a large spoon to serve ice. Never use your hands.

>> If you don't have bottle pourers (or pour spouts discussed in Chapter 1), rub waxed paper over the tip of liquor bottles to prevent dripping.

>> Use a champagne bucket or any type of small bucket to dump out any extra liquid or ice from your shakers if you don't have a sink nearby.

>> Close the bar an hour to an hour and a half before the end of the party.

Stocking Your Bar

When setting up your home bar, try to use the more popular premium brands. These brands are usually made with the best quality and tend to be the most recognizable.

The following sections present three different levels of bar stocking: basic, more complete, and the ultimate bar.

We recommend that you stock and use mostly premium brands. You don't want your guests thinking that you'd serve them anything but the best. There are also some options for spirits here; we recommend you work with someone at the liquor store to help guide you on what's best for the type of bar you're looking to build. Also, if you have an affiliation for one brand or type of spirit over another, purchase that!

If you purchase in bulk from one store, ask the manager for a case discount (usually 6 or 12 bottles). This type of discount can save you some bucks!

TIP

The basic bar

A basic bar setup for your home and for spur-of-the-moment entertaining should consist of the following:

>> One 750 ml bottle of vodka

>> One 750 ml bottle of gin

>> One 750 ml bottle of rum (light or dark)

>> One 750 ml bottle of blended scotch

>> One 750 ml bottle of bourbon

>> One 750 ml bottle of blanco tequila

>> One 750 ml bottle of dry or sweet vermouth (dry is used for Martinis and sweet is used for Manhattans)

>> One 750 ml bottle of brandy or cognac

>> One 750 ml bottle of sparkling wine or champagne

>> One 750 ml bottle of white wine (Suggestion: Chardonnay)

>> One 750 ml bottle of red wine (Suggestion: Cabernet Sauvignon)

>> Twelve 12 oz. bottles of beer (domestic or imported)

>> Twelve 12 oz. cans of hard seltzer

>> One bottle of angostura bitters

>> Nonalcoholic drinks (could include nonalcoholic spirits or beer)

The estimated cost to set up this bar is between $400 and $500 if you stock basic or call liquors, meaning brands that are good quality but not at the premium or ultra-premium quality level. Examples of call brands include Jack Daniels and Captain Morgan. If you level up and stock premium brands, add 20 to 30 percent to this total.

A more complete bar

If you plan to serve more than the basics at your bar, add the following items to the ones outlined in the preceding section:

>> One 750 ml bottle of flavored vodka (such as lemon or orange)

>> One 750 ml bottle of single malt scotch

>> One 750 ml bottle of rye whiskey

>> One 750 ml bottle of Irish whiskey

>> One 750 ml bottle of reposado or añejo tequila

>> One 750 ml bottle of V.S. or V.S.O.P. cognac

>> One 750 ml bottle of Irish cream liqueur

>> One 750 ml bottle of Italian liqueur

>> Two 750 ml bottles of red wine (Suggestion: Pinot Noir and Merlot)

>> Two 750 ml bottles of white wine (Suggestion: Pinot Grigio and Sauvignon Blanc)

>> Twelve 12 oz. cans of hard seltzers

The estimated cost of these items is an additional $500 to $600 to the basic bar setup in the previous section.

The ultimate bar

If money is no object and you want the most complete home bar, or if you have the basics covered and are ready to expand, then add the following items to those in the preceding two sections:

>> Two 750 ml bottles of super-premium vodka

>> One 750 ml bottle of super-premium gin

>> One 750 ml bottle of dark rum

>> One 750 ml of light or flavored rum

>> One 750 ml bottle of Japanese whiskey

>> One 750 ml bottle of Canadian or Tennessee whiskey

>> One 750 ml bottle of reposado tequila

>> One 750 ml bottle añejo tequila

>> One 750 ml bottle of mezcal

>> One 750 ml bottle of triple sec/orange liqueur

>> One 750 ml bottle of sherry

>> One 750 ml bottle of absinthe

>> One bottle of orange bitters

The estimated cost of the ultimate bar is roughly $600 to $700 in addition to the basic and complete bar setups outlined previously.

Picking up mixers and other important supplies

Here are the typical mixers and supplies you should have on hand. Check out the following section, "The Party Charts: Calculating Liquor and Supply Needs," for recommended amounts.

>> Cola or diet cola

>> Cranberry juice

>> Energy drinks (Red Bull and Monster in original and sugar-free varieties)

>> Ginger ale

>> Ginger beer

>> Grapefruit juice

>> Lemon juice or lemon mix

- Lemon-lime soda
- Lime juice
- Orange juice
- Pineapple juice
- Pomegranate juice
- Seltzer water or club soda
- Tomato juice
- Tonic water

You also need the following fruits and garnishes (see Chapter 2 for cutting instructions):

- Lemon twists
- Lime and lemon wedges
- Maraschino cherries
- Olives
- Orange slices

Don't forget these items:

- Angostura bitters (if not already purchased)
- Grenadine
- Salt and pepper
- Superfine sugar
- Simple syrup (Chapter 2 provides a simple recipe)
- Tabasco sauce
- Worcestershire sauce

Finally, bar tools. Here is a list of the must-haves (refer to Chapter 2 for full descriptions):

- Bar spoon
- Cocktail shaker
- Jigger
- Mixing glass
- Muddler

>> Peeler

>> Strainer

>> Wine opener/corkscrew

You can get a full cocktail set from online vendors like Cocktail Kingdom for a reasonable price.

TIP

The Party Charts: Calculating Liquor and Supply Needs

Say that you're throwing a party and don't know how much is enough for the number of guests you've invited. The tables in the following sections have all the answers when it comes to stocking up on liquor and supplies for any size get-together.

How much liquor should you buy?

Table 3-1 shows the amount of liquor you should buy for the number of guests at your party. The left column lists the products, and the remaining columns list the number of bottles of that product you should purchase, depending on how many guests you're having. The last row of the table lists the total estimated cost.

With the exception of beer and wine, Table 3-1 is based on 1¾ oz. of liquor per drink. Cost totals are in U.S. dollars.

TABLE 3-1 How Much Liquor to Purchase for a Party

Product (750 ml Bottles)	10–30 Guests	30–40 Guests	40–60 Guests	60–100 Guests
White wine, domestic	5	5	6	8
White wine, imported	2	2	2	3
Red wine, domestic	1	2	3	3
Red wine, imported	1	1	2	2
Blush wine	1	2	2	2
Champagne or sparkling wine	2	3	4	4

(continued)

TABLE 3-1 *(continued)*

Product (750 ml Bottles)	10–30 Guests	30–40 Guests	40–60 Guests	60–100 Guests
Champagne, imported	2	2	2	2
Vermouth, extra dry	1	1	2	2
Vermouth, red	1	1	1	1
Vodka	3	3	3	4
Rum	2	2	2	2
Gin	1	2	2	3
Scotch	1	2	2	3
Whiskey, American or Canadian	1	1	2	2
Bourbon	1	1	1	1
Irish whiskey	1	1	1	2
Tequila	2	2	2	3
Brandy/cognac	1	2	2	3
Aperitifs (your choice)	1	1	2	2
Cordials (your choice)	3	3	3	3
Beer (12 oz. bottles)	48	72	72	96
Estimated Total Cost	**$500–$600**	**$600–$650**	**$650–$725**	**$725–$800**

REMEMBER

The size of a crowd isn't the only factor to consider when buying liquor:

>> The number of products you purchase varies depending on the age of the crowd. If people between the ages of 21 and 35 dominate a crowd, increase the amount of vodka, whiskey, tequila, and beer by one half.

>> You should also think about the time of year. In the fall and winter, maybe serve less gin and more beer or whiskey. In the spring and summer, we suggest more hard seltzers, vodka, gin, and tequila.

>> Geographical location is also an important consideration when it comes to selecting your liquor stock for your guests. Consult a local bartender or liquor clerk to find out what the most popular products are in your area. For example, if you're located in an area with a lot of wineries, then you should consider carrying their products. If you're located in Kentucky, then you should consider having more bourbons on hand for locals and tourists to enjoy.

How many supplies should you buy?

Your bar needs more than just liquor. Table 3-2 lists the other supplies that you want to purchase. Again, the total costs (in U.S. dollars) are listed in the bottom row.

TABLE 3-2 **Other Bar Supplies**

Product	10–30 Guests	30–40 Guests	40–60 Guests	60–100 Guests
Soda (2-liter bottles)				
Club soda/seltzer water	3	3	4	5
Ginger ale	2	2	2	3
Cola	3	3	3	4
Diet cola	3	3	3	4
Lemon-lime soda	2	3	3	4
Tonic water	2	2	3	3
Juices (quarts)				
Tomato	2	2	3	3
Grapefruit	2	2	3	3
Orange	2	2	3	3
Cranberry	2	2	3	3
Miscellaneous Items				
Ice (bags)	10	15	20	30

(continued)

TABLE 3-2 *(continued)*

Product	10–30 Guests	30–40 Guests	40–60 Guests	60–100 Guests
Napkins (dozen)	4	4	6	8
Stirrers (1,000/box)	1	1	1	1
Angostura bitters (4 oz. bottle)	1	1	1	2
Cream of coconut (cans)	1	2	2	2
Grenadine (12 oz. bottles)	1	1	1	2
Energy drink	6	6	12	12
Horseradish (small jars)	1	1	1	2
Lime juice (12 oz. bottles)	1	1	1	2
Lemons	3	4	5	6
Limes	2	3	3	4
Maraschino cherries (jars)	1	1	1	1
Olives (jars)	1	1	1	1
Oranges	1	2	2	3
Milk (quarts)	1	1	1	2
Mineral water (1-liter bottles)	2	3	4	5
Superfine sugar (boxes)	1	1	1	1
Tabasco sauce (bottles)	1	1	1	1
Worcestershire sauce (bottles)	1	1	1	1
Estimated Total Cost	**$60–$80**	**$80–$100**	**$100–$120**	**$120–$140**

Chapter 4

Keeping Tabs: Helpful Charts and Measures

So how many ounces are in a jigger? How many calories are in a shot of bourbon? The tables in this chapter answer these and many other burning bartending questions.

Bottle-Related Measurements

Table 4-1 has some handy information about the capacities of standard distilled spirit bottles. Refer to this table when you need to purchase the right bottle(s) for your home bar or event.

TABLE 4-1 Standard Distilled Spirit Bottles

Bottle Size	Fluid Ounces	Bottles/Case	Liters/ Case	Gallons/Case
1.75 liters	59.2	6	10.50	2.77
1 liter	33.8	12	12.00	3.17
750 ml	25.4	12	9.00	2.38
500 ml	16.9	24	12.00	3.17
200 ml	6.8	48	9.60	2.54
50 ml	1.7	120	6.00	1.59

Wine bottles come in different sizes from distilled spirit bottles. Table 4-2 lists the capacities of standard wine bottles for quick reference.

TABLE 4-2 **Standard Wine Bottles**

Bottle Size	Fluid Ounces	Bottles/Case	Liters/Case	Gallons/Case
4 liters	135.0	N/A	N/A	N/A
3 liters	101.0	4	12.00	3.17
1.5 liters	50.7	6	9.00	2.38
1 liter	33.8	12	12.00	3.17
750 ml	25.4	12	9.00	2.38
375 ml	12.7	24	9.00	2.38
187 ml	6.3	48	8.98	2.38
100 ml	3.4	60	6.00	1.59

Bar Measurements and Their Equivalents

You're likely to run across many of the measurements listed in Table 4-3. Some may be listed in recipes; other measurement terms are handy to know when you're buying alcohol. Walk into your local liquor store and tell the clerk you want to buy a jeroboam of wine. See whether they ask which brand you want four bottles of.

TABLE 4-3 **Standard Bar Measurements**

Measurement	Metric Equivalent	Standard Equivalent
1 dash	0.9 ml	1/32 oz.
1 teaspoon	3.7 ml	1/8 oz.
1 tablespoon	11.1 ml	3/8 oz.
1 pony	29.5 ml	1 oz.
1 jigger/shot	44.5 ml	1.5 oz.
1 miniature (1 nip = 50 ml = 1.7 oz.)	59.2 ml	2 oz.

Measurement	Metric Equivalent	Standard Equivalent
1 wine glass	119.0 ml	4 oz.
1 split	187.50 ml	6.34 oz.
1 half pint	200 ml	6.8 oz.
1 tenth	378.9 ml	12.8 oz.
1 "pint" (½ bottle of wine)	375 ml	12.68 oz.
1 pint	472.0 ml	16 oz.
1 "quart" (1 bottle of wine)	750 ml	25.4 oz.
1 fifth	750 ml	25.4 oz.
1 quart	946.40 ml	32 oz.
1 imperial quart	1.14 liters	38.4 oz.
Magnum	1.50 liters	51 oz.
1 half gallon (or *handle*)	1.75 liters	59.20 oz.
Jeroboam (4 bottles of wine)	3.00 liters	101 oz.
Tappit-hen	2.25 liters	76 oz.
1 gallon	3.79 liters	128 oz.
Rehoboam (6 bottles of wine)	4.50 liters	152 oz.
Methuselah (8 bottles of wine)	6.00 liters	203 oz.
Salmanazar (12 bottles of wine)	9.00 liters	305 oz.
Balthazar (16 bottles of wine)	12.01 liters	406 oz.
Nebuchadnezzar (20 bottles of wine)	15.01 liters	507 oz.

Beer Measurements

Ever wonder how much beer is in a barrel? Table 4-4 tells you that and a whole lot more.

TABLE 4-4 Some Handy Beer Measurements

Barrel Size	Gallons	Equivalent Measurement
1 barrel of beer	31.0 gallons	13.8 cases of 12 oz. cans or bottles, or 2 kegs
½ barrel of beer	15.5 gallons	1 keg
¼ barrel of beer	7.75 gallons	½ keg
⅛ barrel of beer	3.88 gallons	¼ keg

Drinks per Bottle

How many glasses can you get out of a standard spirit or wine bottle? Check out Table 4-5.

TABLE 4-5 Number of Servings from Standard-Size Bottles

Serving Size	750 ml Bottle	1-Liter Bottle	1.75-Liter Bottle
1 oz.	25	33	59
1¼ oz.	20	27	47
1½ oz.	17	22	39
3 oz.	8	11	19
4 oz.	6	8	14
5 oz.	5	6	11
6 oz.	4	5	9

Calories and Carbohydrates

Most people watch what they eat, but many dieters sometimes forget to watch what they drink. Alcohol is a form of sugar, so it's high in calories. If you're counting calories or trying to keep tabs on your carbohydrate consumption, check out Table 4-6.

REMEMBER

Proof is the strength of an alcoholic beverage. In the United States, the scale is 200 degrees, with each degree equal to 0.5 percent alcohol by volume. So a 100-proof spirit is 50 percent alcohol.

A NOTE ABOUT GLUTEN

Many people have a problem consuming anything with gluten. If you're one of those people, you need to watch what you drink. *Gluten* is a protein in spelt, wheat, rye, kamut, triticale, and barley. Many beverages, especially rye, bourbon, and scotch, are made from these products. Ninety five percent of all beers contain gluten. Your best bet is to consult the label. Most products that don't contain gluten, particularly beers and spirits like vodka, will say that they're gluten-free. For more information on making gluten-free selections, check out *Living Gluten-Free For Dummies* by Danna Korn (Wiley).

TABLE 4-6 The Number of Calories and Carbohydrates in Many Drinks

Drink	Calories	Carbohydrates (Grams)
Beer (12 oz.)		
Light beer	110	6.9
Typical beer	144	11.7
Bourbon (1 oz.)		
80 proof	65	trace
86 proof	70	trace
90 proof	74	trace
94 proof	77	trace
100 proof	83	trace
Brandy (1 oz.)		
80 proof	65	trace
86 proof	70	trace
90 proof	74	trace
94 proof	77	trace
100 proof	83	trace

(continued)

TABLE 4-6 *(continued)*

Drink	Calories	Carbohydrates (Grams)
Champagne (4 oz.)		
Brut	92	2.1
Extra Dry	97	2.1
Pink	98	3.7
Coffee Liqueur (1 oz.)		
53 proof	117	16.3
63 proof	107	11.2
Gin (1 oz.)		
80 proof	65	0.0
86 proof	70	0.0
90 proof	74	0.0
94 proof	77	0.0
100 proof	83	0.0
Rum (1 oz.)		
80 proof	65	0.0
86 proof	70	0.0
90 proof	74	0.0
94 proof	77	0.0
100 proof	83	0.0
Scotch (1 oz.)		
80 proof	65	trace
86 proof	70	trace
90 proof	74	trace
94 proof	77	trace
100 proof	83	trace

Drink	Calories	Carbohydrates (Grams)
Tequila (1 oz.)		
80 proof	64	0.0
86 proof	69	0.0
90 proof	73	0.0
94 proof	76	0.0
100 proof	82	0.0
Vodka (1 oz.)		
80 proof	65	0.0
86 proof	70	0.0
90 proof	74	0.0
94 proof	77	0.0
100 proof	83	0.0
Whiskey (1 oz.)		
80 proof	65	0.0
86 proof	70	0.0
90 proof	74	0.0
94 proof	77	0.0
100 proof	83	0.0
Wine (1 oz.)		
Aperitif	41	2.3
Port	41	2.3
Sherry	41	2.3
White or red table	29	1.2
Other		
Hard seltzer	100	2

SEEING STANDARD SERVINGS

Here's a helpful visual of how the amount of alcohol in standard servings of beer, spirits, and wine compares.

A STANDARD SERVING OF BEER, DISTILLED SPIRITS, AND WINE CONTAINS THE SAME AMOUNT OF ALCOHOL, APPROXIMATELY 0.6 OZ.

STANDARD SERVINGS FOR BEVERAGE ALCOHOL ARE:

BEER 12 OZ. = SPIRITS 1½ OZ. = WINE 5 OZ.

Illustration by Elizabeth Kurtzman

2

Distilling the High Points of Various Spirits

Get an overview of just about all the liquor categories out there, including where they come from and how they're made.

Shop lists of popular spirit brands.

Find out how to store each type of alcohol and get some serving suggestions.

Chapter **5**

Vodka

Vodka, a clear, almost flavorless spirit, is historically thought of as the national spirit of Russia and other Slavic nations. Both Russia and Poland claim the invention of vodka and explain that the name is a diminutive of the word *voda*, meaning "little water." Slavic countries have been producing vodka for more than 600 years. Vodka is one of the most mixable and versatile of spirits and is used in hundreds of recipes, including some famous cocktails such as the Vodka Martini and Bloody Mary.

How Vodka Is Made

Vodka was originally distilled only from potatoes, but today, it's also made from grains — mostly wheat, rye, and corn. But distillers don't seem at all hindered by tradition; in Turkey, they use beets! Some vodkas use other base ingredients such as sorghum, rice, and fruits.

Vodkas are distilled at a very high proof (190 or higher), and most are filtered through activated charcoal. (Flip to Chapter 8 for an explanation of proof and the distillation process.) Certain charcoals are so important to the making of vodka that distillers patent them. High-end vodkas are triple- and even quadruple-distilled or more, and some are even filtered through fine quartz sand.

Popular Vodka Brands

Vodka is now produced in almost every country in the world, and each location tends to put its spin on the classic. You may want to sample some of the following brands to see whether you can find differences:

>> **360 Vodka:** An eco-friendly, green-packaged vodka that's six-times-distilled.

>> **Absolut:** Introduced in 1979 and produced in Sweden, this vodka has become one of the most popular brands in the world.

>> **Beluga:** Produced in Russia and named after the most expensive caviar.

>> **Belvedere:** Polish rye vodka.

>> **Boru:** Made in Ireland from grain and pure Irish water.

>> **Chopin:** From Poland and made with potatoes.

>> **Cîroc:** Made from snap-frost grapes in South of France and distilled five times.

>> **Crystal Head:** Made with water from a deep aquifer in Newfoundland and sold in a cool skull-shaped bottle.

>> **Danzka:** From Denmark and made with whole grain.

>> **Double Cross:** An award-winning, seven-time distilled vodka produced in the Slovak Republic.

>> **EFFEN:** A Dutch vodka made from 100 percent wheat.

>> **Finlandia:** Classic Finlandia is imported from Finland. It's made from spring water and barley.

>> **Gordon's:** Has been distilled in the United States since 1957.

>> **Grey Goose:** From France, made from soft winter wheat and Gensac spring water.

>> **Hangar One:** An American vodka made from Midwestern grain and California grapes.

>> **Iceberg Vodka:** Made from the waters of Canadian icebergs.

- **Ketel One:** From Holland, Ketel One is handmade in small batches according to the techniques and secret family recipe developed by the Nolet family more than 300 years ago.

- **Rain Vodka:** A super-premium vodka that is distilled seven times.

- **Reyka:** From Iceland and distilled from glacial spring water.

- **Russian Standard:** Russia's number-one premium vodka. Employing a unique blend of century-old tradition and a passionate attention to detail, it's made using only the finest Russian ingredients.

- **Seagram's Vodka:** A very popular American-made vodka.

- **SKYY:** An American vodka made with water enriched by minerals.

- **Smirnoff:** Produced in the United States, the largest-selling vodka in the world.

- **Snow Queen:** Made with organic wheat from Kazakhstan.

- **Sobieski:** Made with Dankowski rye from Poland.

- **Square One:** A certified organic vodka made with organically grown America rye.

- **Stoli:** A popular Russian vodka produced in Latvia.

- **Svedka:** Imported from Sweden.

- **Tanqueray Sterling:** An English vodka from the makers of Tanqueray gin.

- **Three Olives Vodka:** Imported from England.

- **Tito's Handmade Vodka:** Produced in Texas's first and oldest legal distillery, Tito's Handmade Vodka is corn-based and certified gluten-free.

- **UV Vodka:** A four-time distilled corn vodka made in the United States.

- **Vincent Van Gogh Vodka:** From Holland, handcrafted using small batches of the finest grains.

- **VOX:** Distilled five times in the Netherlands from 100 percent wheat.

Flavored Vodkas

Flavored vodkas, which have become quite popular, are made with the addition of natural flavoring ingredients. Scores of flavored vodkas are available, anything from citrus flavors such as lemon and orange to unique flavors like jalapeño and cake. New flavors of vodka come out seemingly every day. The following is a list of just some of the most popular flavored vodkas:

- **360 Vodka** offers a wide variety of flavors, including Double Chocolate, Huckleberry, Watermelon, Pineapple, Mango, Sorrento Lemon, Grape, and Red Raspberry.
- **Absolut** offers many flavors, including Berri Açaí, Citron, Lime, Grapefruit, Mango, Mandrin, Pears, Peppar, Raspberri, Watermelon, and Vanilia.
- **Bakon Vodka** is a bacon-flavored vodka made from potatoes and the essence of bacon.
- **Cîroc** offers Mango, Apple, Pineapple, Red Berry, Coconut, Peach, French Vanilla, Summer Citrus, White Grape, Summer Watermelon, and Pomegranate.
- **EFFEN** offers Black Cherry, Cucumber, Yuzu Citrus, Raspberry, Green Apple, Blood Orange, and Rosé.
- **Finlandia** offers Grapefruit and Raspberry.

- **Firefly** offers Sweet Tea Vodka, Lemonade, and Ruby Red Grapefruit.

- **Grey Goose** offers Le Citron, L'Orange, and La Poire.

- **Ketel One** offers Citroen and Oranje. Ketel One also offers a product line called Ketel One Botanical, which is vodka distilled with botanicals and infused with natural fruit essences.

- **New Amsterdam** offers Orange, Grapefruit, Peach, Pineapple, Lemon, Raspberry, Red Berry, and Watermelon.

- **Seagram's** offers Apple, Lime, Mango Pineapple, Strawberry Lemonade, Watermelon, Peach, and Sweet Tea.

- **SKYY** offers Blood Orange, Citrus, Pineapple, and Watermelon.

- **Smirnoff** offers an extensive list of flavors, including Blueberry, Cranberry, Coconut, Green Apple, Kissed Caramel, Raspberry, Spicy Tamarind, Strawberry, Watermelon, and Whipped Cream, plus others.

- **Sobieski** offers Cytron, Orange, Raspberry, and Vanilla.

- **Stoli** offers Blueberi, Citros, Hot, Lime, Ohranj, Peachik, Razberi, Salted Karamel, Strasheri, Cucumber, and Vanil.

- **Three Olives** offers Berry, Citrus, Cherry, Cucumber Lime, Espresso, Peach, Pineapple, Pomegranate, Mango, Strawberry, Coconut Water, Vanilla, Blueberry, Fresh Watermelon, Apples & Pears, Pink Grapefruit, Loopy, Orange, Grape, Rosé, and Raspberry.

- **UV Vodka** offers Raspberry, Ruby Red, Apple, Blue, Cake, Cherry, Pink Lemonade, Chili Pepper, Grape, Orange, and Vanilla.

- **Vincent Van Gogh** offers Acai-Blueberry, Citroen, Double Espresso, Dutch Chocolate, Dutch Caramel, Espresso, Mango, Melon, Oranje, Pineapple, Pomegranate, Raspberry, Cool Peach, and Wild Appel.

Storing and Serving Vodka

Store at least one bottle of vodka in the freezer or refrigerator. (Don't worry, it won't freeze because of the high alcohol content.) Storing any spirit in the freezer increases the *viscosity* or thickness which will add a nice texture in cocktails like a Martini or straight shots.

Serve vodka *neat* (straight up) in a small cordial glass, especially paired with caviar, smoked fish, salmon, sardines, steak tartare, and spicy foods.

Vodka is the base for cocktail recipes such as Screwdrivers, Cosmopolitans, Moscow Mules, and White Russians. Vodka takes on whatever flavors you mix with it. Therefore, try making your own spin on cocktails.

When an opened bottle is refrigerated or stored in a cool, dry place, it should last up to three years.

Chapter 6
Gin

G*in* is basically a distilled grain spirit flavored with extracts from different plants, mainly the juniper berry. The Dutch were the first to make gin and have been doing so since the late 1500s.

A LITTLE HISTORY

Gin is said to have been invented by Professor Sylvius de Bouve, a chemist and academic at Leiden University in the Netherlands. Why? Who knows but Mrs. Sylvius?

Sylvius used a juniper berry elixir known as *genlevere* — French for "juniper." He thought that juniper berries could assist in the treatment of kidney and bladder ailments. British soldiers sampled his elixir when returning from the wars in the Netherlands and nicknamed it "Dutch courage." When they brought the recipe back to England, they changed the name to *gen* and later to *gin,* which soon became the national drink of England.

Quality Gin and How It's Made

Although gin has been produced and consumed for centuries, the methods for making the quality gin that you drink today have been around only since the turn of the 20th century.

Gin comes in many types; the most popular include the following:

>> **London dry gin (English)** is distilled from a grain mixture that contains more barley than corn. It's distilled at a high proof and then redistilled with juniper berries or other botanicals.

>> **Dutch gin or Holland gin (also known as genever)** contains barley, malt, corn, and rye. It's distilled at a lower proof and then redistilled with juniper berries in another still at low proof. Dutch gins are usually slightly sweet.

>> **Flavored gin** is a newer product. It's basically gin to which natural flavorings (lime, lemon, orange, and so on) have been added. The flavoring always appears on the bottle.

Popular Gin Brands

Each of the gin brands in the following list has its own distinctive flavor that comes from a carefully guarded recipe.

>> **Aviation:** A gin distilled in the U.S. from an adventurous blend of spices from around the world.

>> **Beefeater:** A gin that dates back to 1820, now made in the Kennington district of South London.

>> **Bluecoat:** An American gin distilled in Philadelphia.

>> **Bols Genever:** A gin from Holland made with high-quality malt wine. (Gins from Holland are also called genever.)

>> **Bombay Sapphire:** A gin made from ten hand-selected botanicals from all over the world.

>> **Boodles:** A gin made in Britain from English wheat.

>> **The Botanist:** The first Islay Dry Gin made in Scotland from 22 local botanicals.

- **Bulldog:** A London dry gin infused with 12 botanicals, including white poppy and dragon eye.

- **Citadelle:** Made in Southwest France, with 19 exotic botanicals.

- **Cork Dry Gin:** An Irish gin distilled in County Cork.

- **Damrak:** A high-quality gin from Amsterdam.

- **Gordon's:** First distilled in 1769 in London by Alexander Gordon, who pioneered and perfected the making of an unsweetened gin with a smooth character and aromatic flavors known as London Dry.

- **Hendrick's:** A Scottish gin with juniper, coriander, rose petal, citrus, and an infusion of cucumber.

- **Magellan:** A French gin handcrafted in small batches, using natural exotic botanicals from around the globe.

- **Martin Miller's:** A London dry gin, considered the world's first super-premium gin.

- **Monkey 47 Schwarwald Dry Gin:** A dry gin made with 47 botanicals.

- **Plymouth:** Legend has it that a surgeon in the Royal Navy invented this gin to help the sailors make their Angostura bitters more palatable (pink gin). You can read more about Angostura bitters in Chapter 15.

- **Seagram's Extra Dry:** A citrus-tasting golden gin.

- **Tanqueray:** Its unique green bottle is said to be inspired by an English fire hydrant.

- **Tanqueray No. Ten:** A super-premium gin from Tanqueray with a blend of fresh botanicals, including grapefruit and chamomile. It's distilled four times.

Storing and Serving Suggestions

As you peruse the recipe section of this book (Part 3), you'll probably notice that gin appears in many cocktails, so choosing the right gin — that is, your favorite — can really affect your enjoyment of a given drink. Try to avoid using cheap, nonpremium gin when making a drink. The results will be a disaster. Quality gin has an herby, spicy, organic flavor, so do your best and try the premium London dry gin brands such as those we list in the previous section.

TIP

When you're at a bar, don't order simply a Gin & Tonic because you'll end up with some cheap, awful bar (or *well*) gin. The *well* is the easiest-to-reach place behind the bar and usually contains the most widely used — and cheapest — bottles of alcohol. If you don't request a brand by name, the bartender will reach for whatever is in the well. Order a Tanqueray & Tonic or a Sapphire & Tonic, and you'll get a decent drink. The same goes for gin Martinis: Always specify what brand of gin you want.

Store an unopened bottle of gin in a cool, dry place out of direct light. After you open a bottle, it should last about two years.

FABLES AND LORE

FAMOUS GIN-RELATED LINES

From one of the most romantic movies of all time, after Ingrid Bergman comes into Rick's bar in Casablanca, what does Humphrey Bogart say? "Of all the gin joints in all the towns in all the world, she walks into mine."

Eliza Doolittle, in the movie *My Fair Lady,* makes this remark about someone's drinking at a fashionable horse race: "Gin was mother's milk to her."

Finally, a little poem:

I'm tired of gin

I'm tired of sin

And after last night

Oh boy, am I tired.

—Anonymous

Chapter **7**

Tequila and Mezcal

A gave-based spirits, such as tequila and mezcal, have been enjoyed since the time of the Aztecs, when drinkers would down a milky white concoction known as *pulque*. Though you can still find pulque served in Mexican towns, its stronger sister spirit, tequila, is the most popular alcohol coming from the agave fields.

Mezcal is originally famous for the worm in the bottle (though less likely to be found today) and is now rapidly growing in popularity.

One Tequila, Two Tequila . . .

Since the 17th century, and now by Mexican law, all tequila must come from one of the five authorized states in Mexico. These states are Guanajuato, Jalisco, Michoacan, Nayarit, and Tamaulipas. Jalisco is home to tequila's largest producers and is where most tequila comes from (the actual town of Tequila is located in Jalisco). Anything produced outside of these five states may not be called tequila.

Tequila is produced from the heart of one species of agave plant, the *Agave tequilana weber*, or the Weber Blue Agave. Its heart is known as the *piña*, and it usually weighs between 80 and 150 pounds. The piña is steamed and shredded until the *aguamiel* (juice) runs off. This juice is then mixed with yeast and fermented for two to three days. The fermented juice is double-distilled in traditional copper pot stills to 90 proof or higher. Tequila must contain a minimum of 51 percent distillate from the blue agave plant, though most popular tequilas today are made from 100 percent agave.

Types of tequila

Tequila comes in five categories:

>> **Tequila blanco (white, silver, or platinum tequila):** This tequila comes fresh from the still and may be brought to *commercial proof* (salable proof or for sale commercially) with the addition of demineralized water.

>> **Tequila joven (gold tequila):** This is blanco tequila with added colorings and flavorings to mellow the flavor.

>> **Tequila reposado ("reposed" or "rested" tequila):** This tequila is aged for at least two months but no more than one year in oak tanks or barrels. Flavorings and coloring agents may be added, as well as demineralized water, to bring the tequila to commercial proof.

>> **Añejo (aged tequila):** This tequila is aged for at least one year, but not more than three, in government-sealed oak barrels. Flavorings and coloring agents may be added, as well as demineralized water, to bring it to commercial proof. When tequilas of different ages are blended, the youngest age is designated.

>> **Extra añejo:** This tequila is aged in barrels for at least three years.

READING A TEQUILA LABEL

The Mexican Government established NORMA (Norma Oficial Mexicana de Calidad) in 1978 to set standards of quality for tequila production. On every bottle, the letters *NOM* must appear, followed by four numbers designating the distillery where the tequila was produced. Besides the brand name and NOM, the label must state the category of tequila, the proof, "made in Mexico," and whether the tequila is 100 percent agave.

Several tequila brands now offer flavored tequilas. Whether this trend catches on remains to be seen. Lemon, orange, and other citrus flavors are common, and you can also find such diverse flavors as chili pepper and chocolate if you're feeling adventurous.

Popular tequila brands

You're likely to find these brands at your local liquor store:

- **1800 Tequila:** The world's first premium tequila was born in the year 1800. This brand offers silver, reposado, añejo, extra añejo, and a luxury line featuring a cristalino tequila, which is an aged tequila filtered to remove any color.

- **Avión:** Comes in silver, añejo, reposado, and Reserva 44, which is a small batch extra añejo.

- **Cabo Wabo:** Sammy Hagar's tequila. It was introduced to the United States around 1996.

- **Casamigos:** A tequila inspired by George Clooney and friends. Casamigos comes in blanco, reposado, and añejo, as well as a mezcal.

- **Cazadores Tequila:** This tequila has a seven-step fully sustainable and zero waste production process.

- **DELEON Tequila:** Launched in 2009, this tequila has a blanco, reposado, and añejo.

- **Don Julio:** Starting in the year 1942, this 100 percent Weber Blue Agave tequila was founded by Don Julio González. Available in blanco, reposado, añejo, 1942, and primavera.

- **El Tesoro:** Meaning "the treasure," this tequila was created by Don Felipe Camarena in 1937, and today his grandson is the Master Distiller.

- **Espolòn:** Created by Maestro Cirilo and offers a blanco, reposado, añejo, and a cristalino.

- **Ghost Tequila:** This is a 100 percent agave spicy tequila that was made especially for spicy margaritas and other spicy cocktails.

- **Gran Centenario:** Handcrafted from 100 percent Weber Blue Agave, this ultra-premium tequila is available in these varieties: plata, reposado, añejo, and extra añejo.

- **Herradura:** The name is Spanish for "horseshoe." It's available in silver, reposado, añejo, and a few high-end varieties.

- **Jose Cuervo:** The world's oldest and largest tequila maker, and the oldest spirit company in North America. Available in these versions: especial silver, especial gold and a tradicional plata, reposado, and añejo, as well as several high-end varieties.

- **Margaritaville Tequila:** Premium 80-proof tequila that comes in gold and silver.

- **Milagro Tequila:** Founded in 1998, Milagro makes a silver, a reposado, and an añejo.

- **Ocho:** Meaning "eight" in English, Ocho produces a plata, reposado, añejo, and an extra añejo.

- **Olmeca Altos:** Created by bartenders in partnership with Maestro Tequilero Jesus Hernandez. This brand produces tequila in the Destileria Colonial de Jalisco in Los Altos.

- **Partida:** An authentic estate-grown tequila, available in blanco, reposado, añejo, and extra añejo.

- **Patrón:** One of the most popular premium tequilas. Its core line is available in silver, reposado, añejo, and extra añejo.

- **Sauza:** It's available in these versions: hacienda silver, hacienda gold, and conmemorativo añejo.

Messin' with Mezcal

The process of making mezcal hasn't changed much since the Spanish arrived in Mexico in the early 1800s and brought with them distillation technologies. The Aztecs near the mountaintop settlement of Monte Alban in Oaxaca had cultivated a certain species of agave plant for juice, which they fermented into what they called pulque. The Spaniards, wanting something much more potent, began to experiment with agave.

REMEMBER

Mezcal, like tequila, is made from the agave plant, but the process is different. The key difference between tequila and mezcal is that the heart of the agave plant is roasted before distilling, which is why mezcals have a smoky flavor. Whereas tequila is produced only from Weber Blue Agave, mezcal is made from several different varieties of agave.

Mezcal has a high potency and a strong, smoky flavor. Most mezcal is produced in the Mexican state of Oaxaca.

The famous worm

Worms live in the agave plant and are hand-harvested during the rainy summer season. They're stored in mezcal, drained and sorted, and placed in bottles near the end of the process. The worm is what makes mezcal unique; it's added as a reminder that it comes from the same plant from which the alcohol is made.

The worm is increasingly rare as mezcal has become more seriously regarded. These days, worms are still common in low-end brands, but higher-end producers and craft distillers have gone wormless.

FABLES AND LORE

Apocryphal legends note that the worm gives strength to anyone brave enough to gulp it down. Some even believe it acts as an aphrodisiac. Like the drink itself, the worm is something of an acquired taste.

A few brands

The number of mezcal brands is much smaller than the number of tequila brands. Here are a few:

- >> Dozal Mezcal
- >> Del Maguey (current most popular brand)
- >> Ilegal Mezcal
- >> The Lost Explorer
- >> Mezcal Rey Campero
- >> Monte Alban
- >> Pierde Almas
- >> The Producer

Storing and Serving Suggestions

Tequila appears in many popular cocktails, including the Margarita and Paloma. Many higher-end tequila brands are meant to be sipped neat or enjoyed on the rocks like scotch. Or you may enjoy tequila the traditional way: as a shot. To take a shot of tequila requires a little coordination and a steady hand.

1. Place salt on the web of your hand between your thumb and forefinger.

2. Hold a wedge of lime or lemon with the same two fingers and have a 1-oz. shot glass filled with tequila in the other hand.

3. In one quick, continuous motion, lick the salt, drink the tequila, and bite the lime or lemon wedge.

You can drink mezcal straight, without the salt or citrus. Some folks drink it with a glass of water on the side.

An opened bottle of tequila or mezcal has a shelf life of many years if kept in a cool, dry place.

Chapter **8**

American and Canadian Whisk(e)y

This chapter explores several kinds of whiskies: bourbon, Tennessee whiskey, rye whiskey, Canadian whisky, blended whiskey, flavored whiskey, and wheat and corn whiskies. These spirits are key ingredients when making some timeless cocktails.

How Whiskey Is Made

Whiskey is a spirit that's distilled from grain. The type of grain or grains used determines the type of whiskey.

After the grain is harvested, it's inspected, stored, and then ground into *meal* (a coarse powder) and cooked to separate the starch. Malt is added, changing the starch to sugar. This mixture, called *mash*, is cooled and pumped into fermenters. Yeast is added to the mash and allowed to ferment, resulting in a mixture of grain residue, water, yeast cells, and alcohol. This mixture is then pumped into a *still*, where heat vaporizes the alcohol. The alcohol vapors are caught, cooled, condensed, and drawn off.

This new, high-proof spirit is stored in large holding tanks. Water is added to lower the *proof* or strength of the alcohol, and the whiskey is drawn into barrels, which are stored in a *rickhouse*, also called a rackhouse or barrel house, for aging. After aging, the barrels of whiskey are drained into the tanks that feed the bottling line.

DISTILLING THE DISTILLATION PROCESS

When you read about the production of alcoholic beverages, you see terms like *proof* and *distillation* thrown around.

Proof is the strength of an alcoholic beverage. In the United States, the scale is 200 degrees, with each degree equal to 0.5 percent alcohol by volume. So a 100-proof spirit is 50 percent alcohol. A 200-proof spirit is after-shave, or 100 percent alcohol.

Distillation is the process of converting a liquid by heating it into a gas or vapor that is then condensed back into a liquid form. In the case of liquor production, the liquid is a blend of ingredients that have been fermented so that it contains some alcohol. When you heat this liquid, the alcohol it contains vaporizes first (because alcohol has a lower boiling point than, say, water). So the vapor that's trapped and later condensed back into a liquid has a much higher alcohol content than the original liquid.

Distillation is usually performed by a *still*. Stills come in two basic types:

- **The pot still:** A *pot still* is a copper or copper-lined vessel with a large bottom and a long, tapered neck connected by a copper pipe to a cooling spiral tube, which is the *condenser*. As the liquid boils, it evaporates. The vapor rises up to the condenser, cools, and returns to a liquid state with alcohol. Often, this process is repeated to achieve the right alcohol level.

- **The continuous still:** Also known as a *column still, patent still,* and *Coffey still,* the *continuous still* has tall copper columns that continually trickle liquid down over many steam-producing plates. The vapor is drawn into vents and condensed. A continuous still performs under the same principles as a pot still but can work with a constant flow of materials coming in and going out, which is great for mass production.

In the case of blended whiskey (including Canadian), different whiskies are mixed together, and the grain spirits or other whiskies are added. (Check out the nearby sidebar "Distilling the distillation process" for details on, well, distillation.)

Bourbon

Bourbon is the best-known and probably the most popular whiskey produced in the United States. It has an amber color and a slightly sweet flavor.

By law, straight bourbon must be made from at least 51 percent corn, and it must be aged in *brand-new*, charred oak barrels for at least two years. Although Tennessee whiskey doesn't have to be made this way, both Tennessee distilleries — George Dickel and Jack Daniel's — also follow these guidelines.

After aging, only pure water can be added to reduce the barrel proof strength to bottling (selling) proof. Scotch whiskies, Canadian whiskies, and Irish whiskies can have added caramel coloring, but bourbon can't.

A BIT OF BOURBON HISTORY

Settlers on the East Coast of North America began making rye whiskey in the 1700s. They were mostly immigrants from Scotland, England, and Northern Ireland and weren't familiar with corn. In the 1790s, when the U.S. government imposed a tax on distilled spirits, the whiskey makers of Pennsylvania revolted, culminating in the Whiskey Rebellion of 1794. President Washington called out federal troops to put down the rebellion, and many distillers fled west to Kentucky, where the law wasn't imposed quite so strictly.

In Kentucky, early settlers had already begun making whiskey from corn, and the newcomers quickly learned how to use this American grain to make what would become known as bourbon. Its name came about because it was shipped from Bourbon County in Kentucky to places such as St. Louis and New Orleans, where it soon became known as whiskey from Bourbon and eventually bourbon whiskey. Other theories note that the name originated from New Orleans's famous Bourbon Street!

Popular bourbon brands

All bourbon is whiskey, but not all whiskey is bourbon. Why? It's all in the makeup! (Bourbons need to be mostly distilled from corn, aged in charred-oak barrels, and no less than 80 proof.)

When purchasing bourbons, look for brands that are popular for their flavor and wide availability. That way your guests are likely to recognize the brands or may be more willing to try something new. We include some of the most popular brands in the following list:

>> **Baker's:** Aged for 7 years and bottled at 107 proof.

>> **Basil Hayden's:** Aged for 7 years and bottled at 80 proof.

>> **Booker's Bourbon:** Produced in a variety of proofs and ages.

>> **Buffalo Trace Bourbon:** 90 proof and produced in a variety of ages.

>> **Bulleit Bourbon:** 90 proof.

>> **Elijah Craig Bourbon:** 12 years old and 94 proof.

>> **Evan Williams Black Label Kentucky Straight Bourbon Whiskey:** 7 years old and 86 proof.

>> **Evan Williams Single Barrel Vintage Kentucky Straight Bourbon Whiskey:** Vintage-dated and 86.6 proof.

>> **Four Roses Bourbon:** Available in a variety of different proofs.

>> **I.W. Harper Kentucky Straight Bourbon Whiskey:** Born in 1872.

>> **Jim Beam:** 80 proof, one of the most famous Kentucky straight bourbon whiskies in the world.

>> **Jim Beam Black:** Extra-aged and 86 proof.

>> **Knob Creek:** Aged at least 9 years and bottled at 100 proof.

>> **Lexington:** 86 proof.

>> **Maker's Mark Kentucky Straight Bourbon Whisky:** 90 proof

>> **Old Charter Kentucky Straight Bourbon Whiskey:** 8 years old and 80 proof.

>> **Old Crow Bourbon:** Aged for 3 years and 80 proof.

- **Old Fitzgerald Kentucky Straight Bourbon Whiskey:** 86 and 90 proof.
- **Old Grand-Dad:** 80 proof. Bottled in Bond, 100 proof. 114 Barrel Proof.
- **Very Special Old Fitzgerald (Bourbon Heritage Collection):** 8 years old and 100 proof; very limited distribution.
- **Wild Turkey:** 80 proof. Wild Turkey Rare Breed, a blend of 6-, 8-, and 12-year-old stocks that's usually around 108 proof. Wild Turkey Old Number 8 Brand, 101 proof. Kentucky Spirit, 101 proof.

Specialty bourbons

As you discover bourbon whiskey, you come across several different types within the category, including small batch and single barrel, which are more expensive and harder to find. Try to pick up one or two bourbons mentioned in the following sections to continue your flavor journey!

Small batch

A *small batch* bourbon is produced and distilled in small quantities of approximately 1,000 gallons or fewer. In other words, it's made in small batches, but you probably figured that out. The following are small batch bourbons:

- Baker's
- Basil Hayden's Small Batch
- Blanton's Single Barrel Bourbon
- Booker's Small Batch
- Eagle Rare
- Elijah Craig
- Four Roses Small Batch
- Knob Creek
- Michter's Small Batch Bourbon
- Old Rip Van Winkle and Pappy Van Winkle's Family Reserve
- 1792
- Woodford Reserve

Single barrel

Single barrel bourbon also has a self-explanatory name. Each bottle contains bourbon whiskey from just one barrel, with no blending. Some single barrel bourbons include

>> Benchmark Single Barrel Kentucky Straight Bourbon

>> Blanton's Single Barrel Kentucky Straight Bourbon

>> Elijah Craig Single Barrel Kentucky Straight Bourbon

>> Evan Williams Single Barrel Vintage Kentucky Straight Bourbon

>> Four Roses Single Barrel Bourbon

>> Henry McKenna Single Barrel Kentucky Straight Bourbon

>> Jack Daniel's Single Barrel

>> Wild Turkey Kentucky Spirit Single Barrel Kentucky Straight Bourbon

WARNING

A limited number of distilleries produce a whiskey bottled at *barrel proof*, which enters the barrel at 125 proof and gains strength during aging, so it sometimes exceeds the 125-proof legal limit. Pretty potent stuff — drink at your own risk.

Flavored American bourbons

You can find flavored bourbons from American distillers. It seems that bourbon has developed a sweet taste of its own. Here's a list of popular flavors; most are honey flavored, with a few cinnamon and fruit flavors thrown in for variety:

>> **Bird Dog Whiskey:** Blackberry, Peach, Hot Cinnamon, and several others

>> **Evan Williams:** Honey, Fire, Apple, Peach, Cherry, and others

>> **Knob Creek Smoked Maple**

>> **Jim Beam:** Peach, Apple, Vanilla, and Fire

>> **Wild Turkey American Honey**

Rye Whiskey

Distilled at no more than 160 proof, *rye whiskey* is a fermented mash or grain containing at least 51 percent rye. It's matured in new charred-oak barrels for a minimum of two years. Rye has a strong, distinctive flavor. For quite some time, rye has taken a backseat to bourbon with American whiskey drinkers, but rye has seen a resurgence lately leading more brands to make more rye products. The spice notes coming from the rye grains allow for more complexity in cocktails.

Here's a sampling of what's available on the market today:

>> **Basil Hayden Dark Rye:** 80 proof

>> **Bulleit 95 Rye:** 90 proof

>> **High West Double Rye:** 92 proof

>> **Jim Beam Rye:** 80 proof

>> **Koval:** Created from rye locally sourced in Minnesota; 80 proof

>> **Michter's Straight Rye:** Aged in new American white oak barrels

>> **Old Overholt:** One of the early brands of American straight rye; 4 years old and 80 proof

>> **Redemption Rye:** 92 proof

>> **Rittenhouse:** 100 proof

>> **Russell's Reserve Rye:** 90 proof

>> **Templeton Rye:** Produced in Iowa; 80 proof

>> **Thomas H. Handy Sazerac:** 125.7 proof whiskey

>> **Van Winkle Family Reserve Rye:** 95.6 proof and aged for 13 years

>> **WhistlePig:** Available in a variety of ages and proofs

>> **Wild Turkey Rye:** 81 proof

Tennessee Whiskey

Tennessee whiskey differs from bourbon in that it's mellowed (altered) through sugar-maple charcoal before it's aged. Although both whiskies are usually filtered before bottling, the sugar-maple charcoal adds a different flavor to Tennessee whiskey.

Here are some popular brands of Tennessee whiskey:

>> **George Dickel Tennessee Whisky:** Foundation Recipe No. 1, 91 proof; Classic No. 8, 80 proof; Superior No. 12, 90 proof. Barrel Select, at least 9 years old and 86 proof. Bottled in Bond, 100 proof; and single barrel whiskies.

>> **Jack Daniel's Tennessee Sour Mash Whiskey:** Old No. 7, 80 proof. And flavored whiskies include Honey, Apple, and Fire.

>> **Uncle Nearest:** Premium Aged Whiskey is a blend aged between 8 and 14 years old and is 100 proof.

Canadian Whisky

Canadian whisky (spelled without the *e*) is a blend of aged grain whisky and heavier-flavored blended whiskies; it's aged in oak casks (usually white oak barrels) for a minimum of three years. No rules limit the grain, distilling proof, formula, or type of barrels used. Each distiller is allowed to make its own type of whisky. Canadian whiskies sold in the United States are blends bottled at a minimum of 80 proof and are generally 3 years old or older. Popular brands include the following:

>> **Black Velvet:** 80 proof and 3 years old.

>> **Canadian Club:** Made since 1858.

>> **Canadian Mist:** 80 proof and 3 years old.

>> **Crown Royal, Crown Royal Special Reserve, and Crown Royal XR:** All 80 proof.

>> **Forty Creek:** Highly awarded Canadian whiskies.

>> **J.P. Wiser's:** Deluxe 80 proof.

>> **Seagram's VO:** 80 proof, aged for 6 years (the *VO* means "Very Own" or "Very Old").

>> **Tangle Ridge:** 100-percent rye whisky aged for 10 years in oak barrels, blended with sherry and other natural flavors, and then re-cased before bottling.

There are also some great Canadian Rye whiskies — give one of these a try:

>> **Crown Royal Northern Harvest Rye:** 90 proof

>> **J.P. Wiser's Triple Barrel Rye Whisky:** 90 proof

>> **Lot 40:** 86 proof

Finally, if you're looking for a flavored Canadian whisky, try one of these:

>> **Crown Royal Apple, Peach, Vanilla, and Salted Caramel:** 70 proof

>> **Fireball Cinnamon Whisky:** 66 proof

Blended Whiskey

American blended whiskey is required to contain at least 20 percent straight whiskey. The rest can be a neutral spirit or other proof whiskey. Sometimes, additional coloring and enhancers are added. Blends are bottled at no less than 80 proof.

Whiskies blended with neutral spirits have a label on the back of the bottle that states the percentages of straight and neutral spirits. The most famous and biggest seller of blended whiskey is Seagram's 7 Crown Blended Whiskey. It, of course, is part of the famous drink, the Seven and Seven, which is 1½ oz. Seagram's 7 Crown Blended Whiskey and 5 oz. 7UP, garnished with a lime.

Other brands of blended whiskey include the following:

>> Barton Reserve

>> Carstairs

>> Fleischmann's

>> Heaven Hill

>> Imperial

>> Mattingly & Moore

>> Rebecca Creek

>> Tin Cup

Wheat and Corn Whiskies

Wheat whiskey must contain 51 percent of a single type of grain and must be aged a minimum of two years in a new, charred, white oak barrel. As a commercial product, this type of whiskey is not very common. For all we know, some wheat farmers could have been making this stuff for a couple of centuries, but you couldn't buy it at the local liquor store until recently.

There are a few popular brands currently including Bernheim Original Straight Wheat Whiskey (90 proof), Cedar Ridge Wheat Whiskey (80 Proof), and Dry Fly Washington Wheat Whiskey (120 proof). More brands are likely to follow.

Corn whiskey is similar to bourbon except that it must be made of a mash consisting of at least 81 percent corn. It's still called moonshine or white lightning in the southern United States. Available brands include the following:

>> George Dickel #1 White Corn Whisky

>> Georgia Moon Corn Whiskey

>> Mellow Corn

>> Midnight Moon (available in various flavors)

>> Ole Smoky Moonshine

>> The Original Moonshine

>> WL Weller

Storing and Pouring the Most Popular Serves

American whiskey and Canadian whisky can be served straight, on ice, with water or seltzer, or mixed as a cocktail. Some of the most popular cocktails for the category include Boulevardier, Manhattan, Mint Julep, Old Fashioned, Toddy, Whiskey Smash, and Whiskey Sour. See Chapter 20 for recipes.

Store an unopened bottle in a cool, dry place. After opening, a typical bottle should have a shelf life of at least two years.

IN THIS CHAPTER

» Discovering where Irish whiskey's distinctive flavor comes from

» Checking out some Irish whiskey brands

» Preserving Irish whiskey's flavor

Chapter 9
Irish Whiskey

The Irish have been distilling whiskey for at least 600 years, if not longer. Though it's safe to say that Irish whiskey has a distinct character, it's also equally true that each brand of Irish whiskey is a unique product.

What Makes Irish Whiskey Taste So Good?

Irish whiskey is triple-distilled from barley and other grains in pot stills and aged between five and ten years. One major difference between scotch and Irish whiskey is that when drying the barley malt from which the whiskey is distilled, the Irish use coal rather than peat, which prevents the smoky flavor found in scotch whisky.

What's more, Irish whiskey also gains a great deal of flavor from the casks in which it's aged. Depending on the brand, Irish whiskey is aged in casks that have held sherry, rum, or bourbon.

FABLES AND LORE

For centuries, the Irish produced an illegal distilled spirit called *potcheen* (po-cheen), a colorless, unaged spirit that's high in alcohol content and similar to white lightning or moonshine in the southern United States. (You may know it by another name such as Poitín, uisce betha, or water of life.) But as of 1997, it's legal and being produced and sold in Ireland and the rest of the world.

Popular Irish Whiskey Brands

You may be surprised at the variety of flavors among the brands of Irish whiskey:

» **2 Gingers** is a blended Irish whiskey, distilled twice and aged four years in the mild climate at the Cooley Distillery.

» **Bushmills** produces Bushmills Original, Black Bush, Red Bush, and single malts aged 10, 12, 16, and 21 years.

» **Connemara** makes Pot Still Peated Single Malt Irish Whiskey, a unique product because it's the only widely available peated single malt.

» **Danny Boy** is a 15-year-old Irish malt whiskey matured in the finest American white oak casks.

» **Jameson Irish Whiskey** is the world's largest-selling Irish whiskey. It's aged in oak casks for a minimum of four years. It's available in a variety of styles, including Cold Brew, Black Barrel, Caskmates, Orange, and 18 Years.

» **Kilbeggan** is Gaelic for "little church." What's now an idyllic village in the center of Ireland was for many years an active religious community built around a monastery. The first licensed whiskey distillery in the world was established in Kilbeggan in 1757.

» **Knappogue Castle Irish Single Malt Whiskey** is pot-stilled using only malted barley and bottled on a vintage basis.

» **Midleton** produces its Very Rare Irish Whiskey, a blend of triple-distilled whiskies ranging from 12 to 21 years old. It's matured exclusively in special, individually selected, bourbon-seasoned American oak casks. Midleton is a credit to the old sod.

» **Paddy's Old Irish Whiskey** is named for Paddy Flaherty, a salesman for the Cork Distilleries Company in the 1920s.

» **Powers** was the first to introduce bottling in Ireland.

» **Proper No. Twelve** is a blend of single malt and grain whiskies.

- **Redbreast Irish Whiskey** is a single, unblended whiskey, triple-distilled in oak casks for no less than 12 years.

- **Roe & Co** is a premium blended Irish whiskey named in honor of George Roe, an Irish whiskey pioneer.

- **Teeling Whiskey** has a deep route in distilling, dating back to 1782. It has a single grain, single malt, single pot still, and a peated single malt Irish whiskey.

- **Tullamore D.E.W.** is the original triple blend Irish whiskey. It's named after the town of Tullamore in Ireland and a great Irish distiller, Daniel Edmund Williams (DEW).

- **The Tyrconnell Single Malt Irish Whiskey** is made from a mash of pure malted barley produced at a single distillery. (In contrast, other whiskies blend a variety of malt and grain products from several distilleries.)

- **The Wild Geese** is produced using a special extended double distillation process to remove impurities and to achieve optimal alcohol content for maturation.

Storing and Serving Suggestions

While drinks like Irish coffee are common, usually guests like Irish whiskey served with mixers instead, such as colas and ginger ale.

Storing Irish whiskey is very simple. An unopened bottle will last indefinitely because Irish whiskey doesn't mature after it's bottled. After a bottle is opened, it has a shelf life of about two years.

Chapter **10**

Scotch Whisky

Scotch whisky (spelled without the *e*) is a malt or grain whisky that is made in Scotland. All scotch must be distilled and matured for at least three years. Similar to champagne or cognac, all scotch must be made in Scotland to be called scotch. Scotland has more than 100 distilleries that produce more than 2,000 different scotch whiskies. Lucky for you, we help narrow down your options and provide our recommendations in this chapter.

Types of Scotch Whiskies

Two kinds of scotch whiskies are distilled: *malt whisky* (from barley) and *grain whisky* (from cereals). Malt whiskies are divided into four groups according to the geographical location of the distillery in which they're made (see Figure 10-1):

» **Lowland malt whiskies:** Made south of an imaginary line drawn from Dundee in the east to Greenock in the west.

» **Highland malt whiskies:** Made north of the aforementioned line.

>> **Speyside malt whiskies:** Made in the valley of the Spey River. Although these whiskies come from within the area of the Highland malt whiskies, the concentration of distilleries and the specific climatic conditions in Speyside produce whiskies of an identifiable character, which is why they're classified separately.

>> **Islay malt whiskies:** Made on the island of Islay.

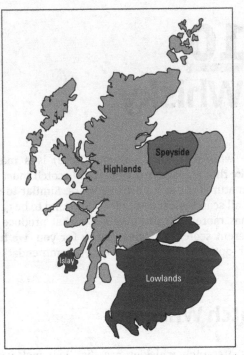

Illustration by Lisa Reed

FIGURE 10-1: The four main scotch-producing regions.

Each group has its own clearly defined characteristics, ranging from the gentle, lighter-flavored Lowland whiskies to those distilled on Islay, which are generally regarded as the heaviest malt whiskies.

Grain distilleries are mostly found in the central belt of Scotland, near the cities of Glasgow and Edinburgh. Single-grain whiskies display individual characteristics in the same way as malts, although the geographical influence isn't the same.

Married together, malt whiskies and grain whiskies create *blended* scotch whisky, which accounts for 95 percent of world sales. A blended whisky can have many (up to 50) different types of malt whiskies blended with grain whisky (from cereals).

As you may expect from the name, a *single-malt* scotch whisky is made from one type of malt, and it's not blended with other malts or grain whiskies.

How Scotch Is Made

Making scotch whisky from malts dates back to 1494 to Friar John Cor and his fellow friars. Until the mid-1800s, nearly all scotches were single-malt. Then Andrew Usher came up with the idea of mixing malt whisky and grain whisky to create blended scotch whisky. Here's how the process works:

1. The barley is *malted,* or soaked and dried for germination. During this period, the starch in the barley converts to fermentable sugar.

2. To stop the germination, the malted barley is smoked, usually over peat fires in open malt kilns, giving scotch whisky its smoky taste.

3. The barley is mixed with water and yeast. Fermentation takes place, and alcohol is the result. This liquid is then usually pumped into stills and double-distilled until the correct proof is attained.

4. After distillation, the whisky is typically placed in used American oak wine or bourbon barrels (some distillers use sherry casks or wood from other countries); these are then aged by law for a minimum of three years. Most scotch whiskies age from five to ten years, sometimes much longer. It's said that the longer a whisky ages in the barrel, the smoother it becomes.

After the whisky finishes aging in the barrel, each distiller then completes its own blending, filtering, and bottling.

TIP

The numbers on the bottle refer to the youngest whisky in the bottle used to produce the product. Therefore, when you see Lagavulin 16, for example, the youngest liquid in that bottle is 16 years old.

Dispelling Myths about Scotch Whisky

There are a few myths to scotch whisky, and we cover two in this section. First is that all scotches are smoky. The smoky character that some scotches have comes from burning peat, which is partially decayed vegetation or organic matter and looks like and is often referred to as turf. Not all scotches have this smoky quality. Many scotches have little to no smoke at all and make for a great introductory scotch such as OBAN.

The second myth is that the older the scotch is, the better it tastes. Not true at all! The longer the whisky sits in a barrel, the more oak and wood influence it takes on. So, while some old scotches are delicious, some just don't age that well!

Popular Blended Scotch Whiskies

These are the brands of scotch whisky that you're most likely to find at your local bar or liquor store.

TIP

Some of these brands have a product that they label "reserve," which usually is just a marketing term but can mean a variety of things depending on the brand. Be sure to look into the offering before purchasing to determine if the bottle is high-end scotch or actually entry level with a fancy name, for example.

>> **Ballantine's** is available in such varieties as Ballantine's Finest, 12 Year Old, and 17 Year Old.

>> **Bell's** is available in Extra Special and Special Reserve Blended Malt.

>> **Black & White** is a blend of some of the finest whiskies in Scotland. A majority of the blend is grain whisky and founded by James Buchanan.

>> **Chivas Regal** is available in 12-, 15-, 18-, and 25-year-old varieties, as well as other specialty expressions.

>> **Cutty Sark** is a popular brand that was introduced in 1923 and wears a distinctive yellow label.

>> **Dewar's** offers these varieties: White Label, 12 Year Old, 15 Year Old, 18 Year Old, and 25 Year Old. Dewar's also offers a

"Cask Series," which has a variety of blended scotches aged in different casks.

>> **The Famous Grouse** is available in its classic bottling along with a cask series that features a Ruby and Bourbon cask.

>> **Grant's** is available in Triple Wood and Triple Wood 12.

>> **Johnnie Walker** offers these varieties: Red, Black, Double Black, High Rye, Green, Gold Blue, and King George V, along with special editions like Jane Walker.

>> **J&B (Justerini & Brooks)** offers its flagship J&B Rare, blended from Speyside malt whiskies, along with Jet J&B and Reserve J&B.

>> **Monkey Shoulder** is a blend of single malts from three Speyside distilleries and was created with a focus on cocktails.

>> **Royal Salute** is available in 21 Year Old and 62 Gun Salute, as well as limited edition varieties.

>> **Vat 69** is available in Finest and Reserve de Luxe varieties.

>> **White Horse** is available in its standard blend and Extra Fine 12 Year Old.

Taking a Closer Look at Single-Malt Scotch

Single-malt scotch whisky is unblended malt whisky from a single distillery. The water and malted barley, the raw materials of scotch whisky, differ from distillery to distillery and region to region. In addition, the production methods, variations in topography and climate, and size and shape of the pot stills all contribute to the uniqueness of each distillery's single malt.

Scotland has more than 100 single-malt distilleries, so if you're a fan of single-malt scotch whisky, you likely won't run out of whiskies to sample and enjoy. The following is a listing of just a few brands worth trying:

>> Aberlour

>> Ardbeg

>> Auchentoshan

>> Balvenie

- » Blair Athol
- » Bowmore
- » Brora
- » Bruichladdich
- » Bunnahabhain
- » Cardhu
- » Dalmore
- » Deanston
- » Glenfiddich
- » Glenlivet
- » Glenmorangie
- » Glenrothes
- » Highland Park

- » Isle of Jura
- » Lagavulin
- » Laphroaig
- » Ledaig
- » The Macallan
- » Oban
- » Port Ellen
- » Scapa
- » Singleton
- » Speyburn
- » Springbank
- » Talisker
- » Tobermory

Storing and Serving Suggestions

Scotch can be served over ice, straight up, with water or club soda, or in a variety of cocktails. Some popular cocktails for scotch are Penicillin, Blood & Sand, Rob Roy, Godfather, and Rusty Nail (find recipes for these cocktails in Chapter 20).

Single malts and aged scotch whisky can be served straight up or on the rocks with a splash of water, which opens up the spirit.

After opening, store a bottle of scotch whisky in a cool, dry place out of direct light. It should have a shelf life of approximately two years.

REMEMBER

Whisky doesn't improve with age after it's bottled.

Chapter **11**

Japanese Whisky

onnichiwa! And welcome to your tour of Japanese whisky, which is a growing category. Many guests and bartenders love these brands and flavors, so dive right in!

A BRIEF HISTORY OF JAPANESE WHISKY

Production of Japanese whisky dates back to the early 1870s, but the first commercial malt whisky distillery in Japan, Yamazaki, was founded by Shinjiro Torii in 1923. Torii originally sold and produced wine but wanted to make a variety of liquors. He later partnered with Masataka Taketsuru, and the two are known as the godfathers of Japanese whisky. Taketsuru spent years in Scotland learning the production process and wanted to create a similar style of whisky in Japan. While the two worked together for some time, they later broke off to start their own companies. In 1940, Taketsuru made his first whisky called Nikka.

There's still a lot of history to discover, but from what we already know, it makes sense that the more popular Japanese whiskies come from the Nikka and Yamazaki houses.

How Japanese Whisky Is Made and Aged

The flavors of Japanese whisky are most similar to scotch (see Chapter 10) because it uses a majority of malted barley and is distilled twice in pot stills. As a whole, Japanese whisky is softer, milder, more mellow, and more floral than other styles of whisk(e)y.

When it comes to aging, Japanese whisky uses the typical wood-aging method, meaning they use oak barrels and age for at least three years. The category has been seen to use woods such as American oak, sherry, and Japanese mizunara oak, which is quite rare and expensive. The price points are most similar to a scotch or bourbon as well.

Popular Brands

While this category is still growing, here are a few brands to check out. The most popular and available brands come from the Suntory or Nikka houses and should be available at most liquor stores.

>> Akashi

>> Chita

>> Chichibu

>> Hakushu

>> Hatozaki

>> Hibiki

>> Karuizawa

>> Kirin

>> Kurayoshi

>> Nikka

>> Ohishi

>> Shinshu

>> Suntory Toki

>> Tenjaku

>> Tokinoka

>> Yamazaki

Storing and Serving Suggestions

Storing Japanese whisky is very simple: Keep it out of the light and unopened, and it will last indefinitely. After a bottle is opened, it has a shelf life of about two years.

Like scotch, you can drink this spirit neat or on the rocks. For cocktails, Japanese whisky is mostly seen in highball cocktails.

TIP

Japanese whisky with soda or in tea is a delicious and easy cocktail. It can also be used in an Old Fashioned, Sidecar, or really anything that works with bourbon or scotch, though the flavors, depending on the brand, are more subtle.

Chapter **12**

Rum

R um is a spirit distilled from sugarcane. It comes in light and dark varieties and is an ingredient in hundreds of cocktail recipes. This chapter sets you up with everything you need to know about this popular spirit.

How Rum Is Made

Rum is distilled from *molasses,* a sticky syrup that results when sugarcane is boiled down. When first distilled, the crude rum is between 130 and 180 proof. This rum is then aged for two to ten years to mellow it. This aging process determines whether the rum is light or dark: Rum aged in charred oak casks becomes darker (caramel and other agents are added to affect its color), and rum aged in stainless steel tanks remains colorless.

Most light rum comes from Puerto Rico. Most dark rum comes from Jamaica, Haiti, and Martinique.

RUMMAGING THROUGH RUM HISTORY

Caribbean rum has been exported out of the islands for hundreds of years, linked to the tropical and subtropical climates where sugarcane thrives. But the origins of rum are far more ancient, dating back, most experts say, more than 2,000 years. Here are a few key points on the timeline:

- The Islamic people from the Middle Ages, known as the Saracens, passed on their knowledge of distilling sugarcane to the Moors, who made arak (a cane-based proto-rum) and planted sugarcane in Europe sometime after AD 636.

- Christopher Columbus brought sugarcane to Puerto Rico on his second voyage in 1493. Later, Ponce de León, the first Spanish governor of the island, planted the first cane fields in Puerto Rico, which were soon to become vital to the local economy and to the world's palate for fine spirits.

- The first sugar mill, a precursor to the Puerto Rican rum industry, was built in 1524, when the product of cane distillation was called *brebaje,* the word *rum* later introduced by crusading English seamen.

- In 1893, the first modern column still was introduced to Puerto Rico. With this innovation, the foundation was laid for the island to produce a more refined, smoother-tasting rum at a dramatically increased pace.

- The first Puerto Rican rum for export to the continental United States was shipped in 1897 — some 18,000 gallons.

- During World War II, manufacturers of U.S. distilled spirits were ordered to limit their production. However, because the territorial mandate didn't apply to Puerto Rico, demand for Puerto Rican rum increased. Sales were phenomenal throughout the war years, with Rum and Coke being the national drink.

Popular Rum Brands

Rum is produced throughout the Caribbean and beyond. Here are several popular brands and where they're produced:

>> **Admiral Nelson's Spiced Rum** (United States)

>> **Angostura** (Trinidad and Tobago)

>> **Appleton Estate** (Jamaica)

>> **BACARDÍ** (Mexico and Puerto Rico)

>> **Captain Morgan Original Spiced Rum** (U.S. Virgin Islands)

>> **Cruzan Rum** (U.S. Virgin Islands)

>> **Diplomático** (Venezuela)

>> **Don Q Rums** (Puerto Rico)

>> **Flor de Cana** (Nicaragua)

>> **Gosling's** (Bermuda)

>> **Havana Club** (Cuba and Puerto Rico)

>> **Mount Gay Rum** (Barbados)

>> **Myers's Original Dark Rum** (Jamaica)

>> **Oronoco** (Brazil)

>> **Plantation** (blend of Caribbean rums)

>> **Rhum Barbancourt** (Haiti)

>> **Ron Zacapa** (Guatemala)

>> **Sailor Jerry** (U.S. Virgin Islands)

>> **The Kraken Rum** (Trinidad and Tobago)

>> **Whaler's** (Hawaii)

>> **Wray & Nephew** (Jamaica)

Getting Familiar with Flavored and Spiced Rums

Rums are available in several different flavors with new flavors of rums coming out yearly. Here are some popular options:

>> **BACARDÍ** flavors include Bacardi Limón, Lime, Tropical, Coconut, Dragon Berry, and others.

>> **Captain Morgan** offers Sliced Apple, Cherry Vanilla, and others.

>> **Cruzan Rum** has the following flavors: Banana, Coconut, and others.

>> **Malibu** is a coconut-flavored rum that also comes in Strawberry, Mango Passion Fruit, and others.

Spiced rums are different from flavored rums. Flavored rums obtain their flavors through additives, while spiced rums are more similar to gin and made with the addition of things such as botanicals.

Cachaça: The "Brazilian Rum" That Isn't

Cachaça (pronounced kah-*shah*-sah) is a Brazilian sugarcane-based liquor. Brazil consumes more than 600 million liters of cachaça per year, making it the most popular spirit in Brazil.

REMEMBER

Even though we include cachaça in this chapter on rum, you shouldn't confuse it with rum, which is made from the molasses left over after sugar refinement. Cachaça imported to the United States is taxed as rum and thus is often called Brazilian Rum.

Here are some popular cachaça brands:

>> Boca Loca

>> Cabana Cachaça

>> Sagatiba Cachaça

>> Samba

The most common cocktail made with cachaça is the Caipirinha. Check out the recipe in Chapter 20.

Storing and Serving Rum

While there are a ton of popular rum cocktails, the Rum and Coke, or Cuba Libre, is always a popular choice. Other popular cocktails include Piña Colada, Daiquiri, and Mai Tai.

Store an unopened bottle of rum in a cool, dry place. After opening, a typical bottle should have a shelf life of at least two years.

RUM FOLKLORE

FABLES AND LORE

Legend has it that Paul Revere ordered a mug of rum before his famous ride from Boston to Lexington. And the Rum Flip, a Benjamin Franklin invention made with rum and beer, was raised in 1773 in celebration after the Boston Tea Party.

Chapter **13**
Brandy

Brandy is a spirit made from fruit juice or wine that comes in several varieties. It's made in most countries that produce wine.

Brandy is derived from the Dutch term *brandewijn*, meaning "burnt wine." The term was known as *branntwein* or *weinbrand* in Germany, *brandevin* in France, and *brandywine* in England. Today, the word has been shortened to brandy.

Making Brandy

Brandy is made by distilling wine or fruit and then aging it in oak barrels. The difference in brandy varies from country to country. Soil, climate, grapes, production methods, and blending give each brandy its own unique flavor and style.

When brandy is produced, it undergoes four basic processes: fermentation of the grape, distillation to brandy, aging in oak barrels, and blending by the master blender.

Brushing Up on Brandy Varieties

Each brandy has its own unique flavor. Check out the following list of varieties including where each one is made around the world.

American brandy

Spanish missionaries introduced brandy to California more than 200 years ago. Taking advantage of the healthy soil, good climate, and water, American brandy production primarily occurs in the San Joaquin Valley. California produces the largest percentage of American brandy and has to be aged a minimum of two years.

Here are some popular American brandy brands:

» **Christian Brothers:** This brandy is processed and aged in Napa Valley.

» **E. & J. Gallo:** Gallo produces E. & J. V.S. Brandy, E. & J. V.S.O.P. Brandy, and E. & J. XO Brandy and flavors such as Peach, Apple, and Vanilla.

» **Germain-Robin:** Another excellent alambic brandy (see the nearby sidebar for an explanation of this term) from California.

» **Korbel:** A California brandy from the Korbel Distillery.

Pisco

Pisco is a South American brandy with a long history dating back to the 16th century. It's a colorless or amber-colored grape brandy. Pisco is imported from both Peru and Chile. Here are a few brands:

WHAT THE HECK DOES ALAMBIC MEAN?

Alambic, the French word for "still," is the word approved for label use by the U.S. Bureau of Alcohol, Tobacco, and Firearms (ATF). It denotes brandy distilled on a batch-process pot still rather than on a continued-column still. Cognac, armagnac, and high-quality fruit brandies are distilled on various types of pot stills. The major American alambic brandy producers use cognac stills.

>> BarSol

>> Caravedo/Pisco Portón

>> Kappa

Fruit brandy

Fruit brandies are produced from all kinds of — guess what? — fruits. The fruit is washed and ground into a mash. Water and yeast are added and allowed to ferment. After the sugar metabolizes, the mash is pressed and the liquid is then distilled. Some fruit brandies are aged in oak barrels.

When shopping for fruit brandies, you may see the term *eau-de-vie*, which refers to any fruit brandy or any brandy not qualified as armagnac or cognac.

Some of the major fruit brandy types are:

>> **Applejack:** An apple brandy produced in the United States

>> **Calvados:** An apple brandy made from a variety of apples from northwestern France

>> **Framboise:** Made from raspberries

>> **Kirsch** and **Kirschwasser:** Made from cherries

Fruit-flavored brandies and pomace brandy

In the United States, fruit-flavored brandies are classified as *cordials* and are usually bottled at more than 70 proof. (Chapter 4 has more on proof.) Sugar, natural coloring, fruit, and other flavorings are added. You can find brandies flavored with such diverse ingredients as apricots and peaches.

Pomace brandies are produced by the fermentation and distillation of grape seeds, stems, and anything that remains after grapes have been pressed and their juices extracted. Pomace brandies are neither aged nor colored. The most popular are grappa (Italian), marc (French), and orujo (Spanish).

Sampling Brandy Brands from Around the World

Check out the following list to find the names of just a few brands that are worth trying:

>> **Asbach Uralt (Germany):** A top-selling brandy in Germany.

>> **Azteca DeOro (Mexico):** A 12-year-old brandy made using the solera method. (See the nearby sidebar "The solera aging method" for details on this technique.)

>> **Carlos I (Spain):** Ranked among the finest in the world.

>> **Felipe II (Spain):** A top-selling Spanish brandy in the United States.

>> **Metaxa (Greece):** The most famous Greek brandy.

>> **Presidente (Mexico):** The largest-selling brandy in Mexico.

Cognac and armagnac are two special types of French brandies. They're so special that we cover them in a separate chapter — Chapter 14, to be exact.

THE SOLERA AGING METHOD

The *solera* method of aging brandy is comprised of three stages:

1. The wine spirits are blended and placed for some months in barrels.

2. Half of the brandy in each barrel is then blended in another barrel containing older brandy.

3. Finally, half of that barrel is placed in yet another barrel containing even older brandy.

Enjoying Brandy: Storing and Serving Suggestions

Brandy is traditionally served straight up in a snifter after dinner, but it's also mixed with soda and can be found in some famous cocktails, including the delicious Brandy Alexander. The Pisco Sour is the most famous Pisco cocktail.

Store an unopened bottle out of sunlight. After opening, a bottle of brandy can last up to three years. Brandy doesn't improve with age while it's in the bottle, so open and enjoy!

IN THIS CHAPTER

» **Finding out where cognac and armagnac are made**

» **Deciphering the designations on labels**

» **Getting familiar with the well-known brands**

» **Finishing a meal with something neat**

Chapter **14**
Cognac and Armagnac

rance produces two kinds of brandy: cognac and armagnac. Both are named after the region in which they're made, and both are delicious. (See Chapter 13 for more on brandy.)

Cognac

Cognac can be produced only in the legally defined region of Cognac, France, located between the Atlantic and Massif Central — specifically, at the junction between the oceanic and continental climate zones. The region also straddles the dividing line between northern and southern climates. These four influences create a multitude of microclimates. In addition to the unique climate, the soil characteristics also foster a range of wine and, consequently, the cognac of each region. In 1909, the French government passed a law that only brandy produced in the "delimited area" surrounding the town of Cognac can be called cognac.

How cognac is made

The arduous, time-honored distilling and aging process is what makes cognac so special. The cognac you drink today was produced using methods dating back to the 17th century.

The distillation of cognac is a two-stage process:

1. A first distillate, known as *brouillis,* is obtained, with an alcoholic strength of 28 to 32 percent.

2. The brouillis is returned to the boiler for a second heating, which produces a liquid known as *la bonne chauffe.* The beginning and the end of this second distillation (the head and tail) are discarded, leaving only the heart of the spirit, which becomes cognac.

The cognac is then sent to rest in oak casks made from wood from the Limousin and Tronçais forests.

Maturing slowly over long years in cellars, the cognac acquires a smoothness and flavor beyond compare. The wood and the dark, saturated atmosphere of the cellars work together to develop the aroma of the cognac to its full potential. All cognac is aged a minimum of 30 months.

What are all those letters on the label?

When you shop for cognac, you see all kinds of designations on the labels of various brands — for example, Courvoisier V.S., Martell V.S.O.P., and Remy Martin X.O. The letters and phrases after the brand name are a general indication of the age (and, in turn, price) of the cognac.

Every major brand produces cognacs of different ages. When one of the following designations is used, it indicates the age of the youngest cognac used in the blend that makes up what's in the bottle.

>> **V.S. (Very Special) or Three Stars:** Cognac aged less than 4½ years.

>> **V.S.O.P. (Very Superior Old Pale):** Cognac aged between 4½ and 6½ years. Sometimes called V.O. (Very Old) or Reserve.

>> **X.O. (Extra Old), Napoleon, Hors d'age, V.S.S.O.P., Cordon Bleu, Grand Reserve, and Royal:** Cognac aged at least 5½ years and up to 40 years.

Generally speaking, each cognac producer uses blends that are much older than the minimum required. In the most prestigious cognacs, some of the blends may have matured over several decades.

You're also going to see some of these names on the labels:

>> **Grand Fine Champagne or Grande Champagne:** These identify cognacs made exclusively from grapes grown in the Grande Champagne region of Cognac.

>> **Petite Fine Champagne or Petite Champagne:** These names mean that the cognac is a blend made from grapes grown in the Grande Champagne and Petite Champagne sections of Cognac. At least 50 percent of the blend must be from grapes grown in the Grande Champagne region.

The terms *fine cognac* and *grande fine*, which may also appear on cognac labels, have no legally defined meaning. The designations *extra old* (E.O.) and *very old pale* (V.O.P.) aren't officially recognized by the Bureau du Cognac, which makes up all the names and rules.

Note: You won't see vintage dates on cognac labels because in 1963, the French passed a law prohibiting the placement of vintage labels on cognac bottles. Go figure.

Popular cognac brands

Even though all cognacs are produced in the same region, and even though every brand seems to have the same jumble of age designations on its labels, you may be surprised at the degree of distinctiveness among the brands. Some brands have a strong, room-filling aroma; some have a mild grape flavor; others have hints of caramel and vanilla. If you're a fan of cognac, our advice is that you not only try several different brands but also try some of the variations within each brand.

TIP

If you're curious to find out what an older cognac (X.O. or better) tastes like, visit a decent bar and order a glass (and be prepared to pay $20 or more) before you decide to invest in an expensive bottle of cognac.

THE ANGELS' SHARE

Aging cognac and armagnac is very expensive, not only because it ties up capital but also because millions of bottles per year disappear into the air through evaporation as the spirit sits in its oak casks. To make fine cognac and armagnac, you can't avoid this loss, and producers refer to it as the *angels' share*.

In the following list, the available styles for each brand are listed from the least expensive to the most expensive. All cognacs are 80 proof.

>> **Camus** produces a range of cognacs, including V.S., V.S.O.P., X.O., and Borderies X.O.

>> **Courvoisier** produces V.S., V.S.O.P. X.O., Initiale Extra, and L'Essence De Courvoisier.

>> **Delamain** produces Pale and Dry X.O., Vesper, and Le Trés Vénéré.

>> **D'USSÉ** is masterfully crafted at the prestigious Château de Cognac, one of the oldest cognac houses in France. It produces a V.S.O.P. and X.O.

>> **Hardy** produces V.S., V.S.O.P, Organic, Legend 1863, X.O., X.O. Rare, and a line of prestige brands.

>> **Hennessy,** the most popular brand of cognac in the U.S., produces several styles of cognac.

>> **Hine** has been producing cognac for more than 250 years.

>> **Martell** produces V.S., V.S.O.P., Blue Swift, Cordon Bleu, and X.O.

>> **Remy Martin** produces V.S.O.P., 1783 Accord Royal, Tercet, X.O., Louis XIII de Remy Martin, and a variety of others.

Armagnac

Armagnac, though less well known than cognac, is France's oldest brandy and has been produced continuously since the 15th century (as early as 1422). It's distilled from premium white wine grown in the Armagnac region of southwest France.

How armagnac is made

Armagnac is a distillate produced from the *continuous*, or single, distillation process. Neutral white wine registering about 9 to 10 percent alcohol is heated in a traditional copper alambic pot still at a relatively low temperature. The vapors pass through the swan neck coils and produce a spirit of no more than 63 percent alcohol. This combination of low temperature and lower alcohol produces a spirit that retains more flavor and aroma elements in the brandy.

The clear brandy is then put into casks traditional to the region — handcrafted 400-liter barrels made from Armagnac or Limousin oak. The aging process begins and can last from 1 to 50 years. The spirit takes on flavors of the wood and other special nuances as it matures, creating a brandy of complexity and distinction. It's then up to the cellar master to blend the separate barrels into a harmonious whole to create the full range of armagnacs.

How to read the label

The French government regulates armagnac labeling. The following designations are used:

>> **V.S. or Three Stars:** The youngest brandy in the blend is at least 3 years old.

>> **V.O. (Very Old), V.S.O.P. (Very Superior Old Pale), and Reserve:** The youngest brandy in the blend is at least 4½ years old.

>> **Extra, Napoleon, X.O., and Vieille Reserve:** The youngest brandy is at least 5½ years old.

Unlike cognac, armagnac products may carry a vintage date. All nonvintage armagnacs contain much older brandies than indicated on the labels. Vintage armagnacs are the unblended product of a single year's production.

Popular armagnac brands

There are a wide variety of armagnac brands, but the ones listed here are the most popular and accessible:

>> **Armagnac Lapostolle X.O.** is matured for more than 30 years.

>> **Chateau de Laubade Bas Armagnac X.O.** is a blend of more than 40 brandies.

>> **Janneau** produces V.S., V.S.O.P., X.O., and other armagnacs aged up to 25 years.

>> **Sempe** produces 6-year-old and 15-year-old varieties. Its Xtra Grand Reserve is a blend of brandies aged from 35 to 50 years.

Storing and Serving Suggestions

Cognac and armagnac are typically after-dinner drinks. Cognac is seldom mixed, but some fine cocktails are made with cognac (such as the Sidecar and the French 75; see Chapter 20 for these recipes). Both cognac and armagnac are excellent companions to coffee, tea, and cigars. They should be served at room temperature and in clear, crystal brandy snifters. Like all fine brandies, cognac and armagnac should be gently swirled in the glass and then sipped and savored.

If stored in a cool, dry place, an opened bottle of either brandy should last for two years.

Chapter **15**
Aperitifs, Cordials, Digestifs, and Liqueurs

This chapter is a catchall for a handful of different liquor categories. Aperitifs were developed specifically as premeal beverages, while digestifs are meant to be served after the meal. Cordials and liqueurs have a variety of purposes. Some are great mixers, others are good after-dinner drinks, and a few make good aperitifs as well. Go figure!

Whetting Your Appetite with Aperitifs

Aperitif comes from the Latin word *aperire*, meaning "to open." An aperitif is usually any type of drink you'd have before a meal. Most aperitifs are usually low in alcohol and mild-tasting. You will most likely recognize Aperol and Campari as some of the more popular aperitifs.

You can drink many of the cordials and liqueurs listed later in this chapter as aperitifs as well. Here's a helpful list of aperitif products on the market today:

» **Aperol (Italian):** An Italian bitter liqueur made from oranges, herbs, roots, and other ingredients and has an ABV of 11 percent. Most commonly used in an Aperol Spritz (shocker!).

>> **Amer Picon (French):** A blend of African oranges, gentian root, quinine bark, and some alcohol. Usually served with club soda or seltzer water with lemon.

>> **Campari (Italian):** A unique combination of fruits, spices, herbs, and roots.

>> **Dubonnet (American):** Produced in California and made from a red wine base. Serve chilled.

>> **Lillet (French):** Made in Bordeaux from a blend of 85 percent fine Bordeaux wines and 15 percent fruit liqueurs. Lillet Blanc is made from sauvignon blanc and semillon and has a golden color. Lillet Rouge is made from merlot and cabernet sauvignon and has a ruby-red color. They also make a Lillet Rosé.

>> **Pernod (French):** Comes from the essence of badiane (anise star) and from a spirit made from natural herbs, such as mint and balm.

>> **Punt e Mes (Italian):** Vermouth with bitters and other botanicals added.

>> **Ricard (French):** Made from anise, fennel (green anise), licorice, and other Provençal herbs.

>> **Suze (French):** French bitters distilled from gentian root. *Gentian* is a large, originally wild flower with golden petals that's grown in the Auvergne and Jura regions.

Digesting Digestifs

Digestif is a French word meaning "digestive." These are any type of drink you'd have after a meal. Most digestifs are usually high in alcohol and reduce the hunger hormone, which helps give a sense of closure to the meal.

Digestifs are usually served neat (like brandy, aged rum, and scotch), but they can be cocktails as well. While fortified wines (like port and sherry) and bitter and herbal liqueurs are most popular, here are some other products and serves:

>> **Amaro:** Italian herbal liqueur with a bitter-sweet flavor with an alcohol content of 16 to 40 percent.

>> **Fernet-Branca (Italian):** A bitter, aromatic blend of approximately 27 herbs and spices (including myrrh, rhubarb, chamomile, and saffron) in a base of grape alcohol. Mint-flavored Fernet-Branca is also available, called Branca Menta.

>> **Jägermeister (German):** Composed of 56 botanicals, including citrus peel, aniseed, licorice, poppy seeds, saffron, ginger, juniper berries, and ginseng.

Tea and coffee cocktails, like a Hot Toddy or Espresso Martini, make for nice after-dinner drinks; here are some other popular examples (see Chapter 20 for the recipes):

>> Boulevardier

>> Old Fashioned

>> Rob Roy

>> Rusty Nail

Cordials and Liqueurs

Cordial comes from the Latin word *cor*, meaning "heart," and *liqueur* is derived from a Latin word meaning "melt or dissolve." Both words are interchangeable, although cordials are more popular in the United States, and liqueurs are more popular in Europe. From this point on, we use the word *cordial* to describe both.

Cordials are made by infusing the flavor of fruits, herbs, spices, and other plants with a spirit, such as brandy or whiskey. As you find out later in this chapter, cordials come in many varieties. Most are sweet. In fact, cordials sold in the United States contain up to 35 percent sugar and must contain a minimum of 25 percent sugar by weight.

Within the cordial category are crèmes and fruit-flavored brandies. Crèmes have a high sugar content, which makes them, well, creamy. Usually, the name of such a cordial indicates what it tastes like. Crème de banana tastes like bananas, and apricot brandy tastes like apricots.

WHAT'S ANGOSTURA?

**FABLES
AND LORE**

Angostura aromatic bitters are a blend of rare tropical herbs and spices used to flavor and season a great variety of food dishes and certain alcoholic and nonalcoholic drinks.

Dr. Johann Siegert, surgeon-general in the army of the great liberator of South America, Simón Bolívar, first compounded the formula in 1824. Siegert's headquarters were in the Venezuelan port of Angostura, a city now known as Ciudad Bolívar. The doctor experimented for four years before finding the exact formula that he was after. He wanted to use the bitters to improve the appetite and well-being of his troops. Sailors pulling into the port discovered the bitters and bought bottles to carry away with them. Soon the fame of angostura bitters spread around the world. Angostura bitters are used in many cocktails, including the Manhattan, the Old Fashioned, and the Rob Roy.

Another label is Peychauds Aromatic Cocktail Bitters from New Orleans, which is quite popular. There are a ton of interesting and fun bitters for you to check out and experiment with!

The world has more cordials than any one person can list. Here, we describe the most common cordials, ones that you're most likely to see in recipes (such as those in Chapter 20):

>> **99 Bananas** is a rich-flavored, 99-proof banana cordial. (See Chapter 8 for an explanation of proof.)

>> **Absente** is a product from France that's similar in flavor to absinthe but without the bad reputation or toxic side effects (see the following bullet).

>> **Absinthe** is often called the Green Muse because of its pale greenish color and the dreamy state it induces in imbibers. Absinthe is 65 percent alcohol, or a whopping 130 proof. Because it contains wormwood (a plant that many believe is a narcotic and also toxic, causing death and/or madness), absinthe was for many years outlawed in most of the world. The fears over absinthe's alleged lethality were probably overstated, and absinthe is now widely available.

- » **Akvavit** is a barley-and-potato distillate that's clear, color-less, and potent. It's a Scandinavian drink originally made in Aalborg, Denmark.

- » **Alizé** is a blend of passion fruit juices and cognac. It's available in several varieties.

- » **Amaretto** is an almond-flavored cordial.

- » **Anisette** gets its name from the aniseed, which imparts its rich, licorice-like flavor to this cordial. Practically every Mediterranean country has a variation of the anise liqueur, such as sambuca in Italy, ouzo in Greece, and so on.

- » **Applejack** is distilled from the mash of apples and is the best-known and most typical fruit brandy in the United States.

- » **Baileys Irish Cream** is made from fresh dairy cream, Irish whiskey, and natural flavorings. The Irish whiskey acts as a preservative for the cream, which is why Baileys doesn't need to be refrigerated. It also comes in a wide variety or flavors such as Almande, Salted Caramel, and Vanilla Cinnamon.

- » **Bénédictine** contains more than 27 herbs and spices, including cardamom, nutmeg, cloves, myrrh, and vanilla. **B&B**, which stands for Bénédictine & Brandy, is a blend of Bénédictine and French brandy.

- » **Blue Curaçao** is essentially the same as Orange Curaçao except that a deep blue color has been added, and it's slightly lower in proof.

- » **Bunratty Meade** is a blend of honey, selected herbs, and wine.

- » **Calvados** is an applejack made in Normandy and aged about four years.

- » **Chambord** is made with framboise (small black raspberries) and other fruits and herbs combined with honey. It has a dark purple color.

- » **Chartreuse** comes in green and yellow varieties and is made with more than 130 herbs and spices. It's normally sold at 4 years of age (aged in the bottle), but 12-year-old labels are also produced.

- » **Cointreau** is a clear cordial made from a blend of sweet and bitter oranges.

>> **Crème de cacao** is made from vanilla and cacao beans. It comes in white and brown varieties.

>> **Crème de cassis** is made from black currants imported from France and other selected fruits and berries.

>> **Crème de framboise** is a raspberry-flavored liqueur.

>> **Crème de menthe** is made from mint and spearmint. It comes in green and white (clear) varieties.

>> **Licor 43** is a Spanish liqueur made from a secret formula containing vanilla beans, citrus, and other fruits found in the Mediterranean, as well as carefully selected aromatic plants.

>> **DeKuyper Schnapps** comes in several flavors, including Peachtree, Melon, and Razzmatazz.

>> **Domaine de Canton** is fresh baby ginger married with fine eau de vie (a clear, colorless fruit brandy), V.S.O.P., and X.O. Grande Champagne cognacs crafted with fresh Tahitian vanilla beans and Tunisian ginseng.

>> **Drambuie** is made with aged scotch whisky, honey, and herbs and spices that are prepared in secret.

>> **Frangelico** is made from wild hazelnuts blended with berries and flowers.

>> **Galliano** is a golden-colored liqueur made with lavender, anise, and juniper and blended with exotic flavors, such as vanilla and fragrant balm. Available in a variety of flavors and styles.

>> **Godiva Liqueur** is flavored with the same chocolate used in Godiva chocolate.

>> **Goldschläger** is an 87-proof cinnamon schnapps liqueur imported from Switzerland. It features real flakes of 24-karat gold.

>> **Grand Marnier** is made from wild oranges and cognac.

>> **Hpnotiq** is a blend of cognac, triple-distilled vodka, and natural tropical fruit juices.

>> **Irish Mist Liqueur** is an Irish whiskey–based liqueur.

>> **Kahlúa** is made from coffee and the alcohol distilled from cane sugar. People also discern a chocolate flavor, but the original recipe contains no chocolate. Its origin is a mystery. Some say Arabia; others say Turkey or Morocco. Today, as indicated by the sombrero on the label, it's made in Mexico

with Mexican coffee beans and available in a variety of flavors.

» **Kirschwasser or Kirsch** is a true fruit brandy or eau de vie distilled from fermented cherries and cherry pits. It's clear and dry.

» **Limoncello** is made from the finest grain spirits infused with the juice and peel of lemons.

» **Luxardo** is the original maraschino liqueur.

» **Malibu** is a clear blend of coconut and Caribbean rum.

» **Marie Brizard Liqueurs** offers a complete line of extremely fine liqueurs.

» **Midori** is a green, honeydew melon spirit.

» **Mozart Chocolate Liqueur** is made from praline-nougat and milk chocolate blended with kirsch.

» **Orange Curaçao** is made from the peel of the bittersweet Curaçao orange, which grows on the Dutch island of Curaçao in the West Indies.

» **Ouzo** is an anise-based liqueur from Greece.

» **Patrón Citrónge** is an orange-flavored liqueur from the famous tequila maker.

» **Rumple Minze** is a peppermint schnapps originally from Germany.

» **Sambuca** is made from two main ingredients, witch elderbush (*sambucus nigra,* hence the name of the drink) and licorice, which gives this liqueur its dominant taste. It's related to the licorice-flavored anise and pastis drinks of France, ouzo of Greece, mastika of the Balkans, and raki of Turkey.

» **Sloe Gin** has a confusing name. It's not a gin (although small amounts of gin are used in its making). Sloe comes from *sloeberry,* a small, deep-purple wild plum that grows principally in France.

» **Southern Comfort** is made from a secret recipe that contains bourbon, brandy, bitters, peaches, and herbs.

» **St-Germain Elderflower Liqueur** is made in France from freshly handpicked elderflower blossoms.

» **Tia Maria Coffee Liqueur** is a Jamaican rum liqueur based on Blue Mountain coffee extracts and local spices.

>> **Triple sec** is made principally from imported orange peel, the wild Curaçao orange, and the sweet, aromatic Spanish Valencia. *Triple sec* means triple dry or three distillations.

>> **Tuaca** is an aged brandy flavored with orange and other fruits and botanicals indigenous to the Tuscan region of Italy.

Storing and Serving Suggestions

Store an unopened aperitif, cordial, digestif, or liqueur bottle in a cool, dry area that's always out of direct light. After a bottle is opened, it should have a shelf life of three years.

Lots of cocktails feature cordials and liqueurs, but here are a few of the most popular (find recipes for each of these in Chapter 20):

>> Aperol Spritz

>> Espresso Martini

>> Last Word

>> Negroni

>> Sidecar

>> White Russian

Chapter **16**
Beer

B eer has been brewed for thousands of years, and today drinkers all over the world enjoy thousands of different varieties of beer. The United States has more than 8,000 craft breweries and more opening up each year as beer continues to grow and evolve.

THE GREAT BEER VOYAGE

Beer enjoys the distinction of coming to the Americas on the *Mayflower* and, in fact, seems to have played a part in the Pilgrims' decision to land at Plymouth Rock rather than farther south as intended. A journal (now in the U.S. Library of Congress), written by one of the passengers, states in an entry from 1620 that the *Mayflower* landed at Plymouth because "we could not now take time for further search or consideration, our victuals being much spent, especially our beer. . . ."

The first commercial brewery in America was founded in New Amsterdam (New York City) in 1613. Many patriots owned their own breweries, among them General Israel Putnam and William Penn. Thomas Jefferson was also interested in brewing and made beer at Monticello. George Washington even had his own brewhouse on the grounds of Mount Vernon, and his handwritten recipe for beer — dated 1757 and taken from his diary — is still preserved.

How Beer Is Made

Basically, *beer* is an alcoholic beverage that's fermented and brewed from barley, hops, water, and yeast (along with corn and rice in some recipes).

More specifically, the beer-brewing process begins with pure water, corn grits, and malted barley. Malted barley is the basic ingredient and is often referred to as the "soul of beer." It contributes to the color and characteristic flavor of beer. *Malted* simply means that the barley has been steeped or soaked in water and allowed to *germinate*, or grow.

Brewing beer is a step-by-step process. It starts with corn grits, malt, and hops. *Hops* are responsible for the rich aroma and the delicate bitterness in beer. Sterile air is added next, along with yeast, which converts sugar into alcohol and carbon dioxide. Overall, the total process takes about one to two months.

Brewers can use two different categories of yeast: bottom and top.

>> **Bottom yeast** settles to the bottom of the tank after converting all the sugar, and the resulting beer is a lager.

>> **Top yeast** rises to the top of the tank when it's done with the sugar, and the beer it produces is an ale.

For much more information on beer, check out *Beer For Dummies* by Marty Nachel and Steve Ettlinger (Wiley). If you're interested in actually making your own beer, grab Marty Nachel's *Homebrewing For Dummies* (Wiley).

Types of Beer

You've probably seen some of the following terms on beer labels, or maybe you've heard them in beer commercials:

>> **Ale** is top-fermented beer. It's a little bitter, usually tastes hoppy, and generally has a higher alcohol content than lagers.

>> **Bitter** beer is a strong ale — usually English — with, as the name implies, a bittersweet taste.

>> **Bock** beer is a dark, strong, slightly sweet lager brewed from caramelized malt.

>> **Ice** beer is brewed at colder-than-normal temperatures and then chilled to below freezing, forming crystals. The crystals are filtered out, leaving a smoother-tasting beer with a slightly higher alcohol content.

>> **India Pale Ale or IPA** is a style within the pale ale category. These are typically made with more hops and have a higher alcohol content.

>> **Lager** is a bottom-fermented beer stored at very low (cold) temperatures for a long period of time (several months). The word *lager* is German for "to store."

>> **Lambic** beer is brewed in Belgium. Ingredients such as peaches, raspberries, cherries, and wheat are added during the brewing process.

>> **Light** beer has fewer calories and less alcohol.

>> **Low-calorie** beer has even fewer calories than light beer (and some would say even less flavor). These beers generally have 55 to 65 calories per serving.

>> **Nonalcoholic** beer or **alcohol-free** beer has little to no alcohol. The aim is to allow the drinker to enjoy the taste without the alcohol content.

>> **Malt liquor** is fermented at a higher temperature than other beers, which results in a higher alcohol content.

>> **Pale ale** is brewed using mainly pale malt and ale yeast and is usually amber colored.

>> **Pilsner** is a light, hoppy, dry lager.

>> **Porter** is a malty dark ale which gets its dark color from brown malt. This style of beer traces back to the 18th century.

>> **Sake** is beer brewed and processed from rice. (Though some consider sake a wine.) Sake is served warm or at room temperature.

>> **Stout** is an ale produced from heavily roasted barley. It's darker in color and has a slightly bitter flavor.

>> **Trappist** beer is brewed in Belgium or the Netherlands by Trappist monks. It contains high levels of alcohol and is usually dark in color.

>> **Wheat** beer is made, as you may expect, with wheat. It's usually garnished with a lemon or orange and even sometimes raspberry syrup.

Storing and Serving Beer

In the United States, beer is served cold (40 degrees Fahrenheit). Lower temperatures tend to dull the taste, so consider 40 degrees the lower limit. Store beer away from sunlight, or you get *skunked* beer, which is never pleasant. Most beers now have labels that say when they were brewed or when to remove them from the shelf.

While beer is mostly served on its own, there are some beer cocktails and beer mixes that your guests and customers might request. For example, the Black and Tan is half a pale ale and then topped with a stout, usually Guinness. Also, a common order is a Boilermaker, which is a beer served with a shot on the side. (See Chapter 20 for recipes.)

Here are some of the most popular beer cocktails:

>> BeerMosa

>> Black Velvet

>> Michelada

>> Summer Shandy or Grapefruit Shandy

Chapter **17**

Hard Teas, Seltzers, and Ready-to-Drink Products

While none of these products is necessarily new, over the past three to five years, hard teas and seltzers have been growing rapidly. Almost every beer brand has a hard tea or seltzer nowadays, and the ready-to-drink (RTD) market continues to grow. This chapter dives in to a little more about each drink category and some of the most popular brands.

Hard Teas

Hard teas are brewed with real tea and come from a variety of sources. In terms of production, some of the alcohol comes from malted barley, while others use fermented sugarcane. Hard teas also come in a variety of flavors with lemon the most popular, which makes sense because hard lemonades are also growing in popularity.

There are a variety of hard teas on the market right now; here are some of the most popular:

>> Bud Light Seltzer Iced Tea

>> Fishers Island Spiked Tea

- **»** LIIT Hard Tea Seltzers
- **»** Owl's Brew Boozy Tea
- **»** Truly Hard Seltzer Iced Tea
- **»** Twisted Tea Hard Iced Tea
- **»** White Claw Hard Seltzer Iced Tea
- **»** White Peaks Hard Steeped Tea

Hard Seltzers

Drinkers have been leaning more toward hard seltzers because they're *usually* lower in sugar and calories compared to your typical beer. Like beer, hard seltzers are usually around 5 percent alcohol by volume (ABV) and can go as high as 12 percent. Usually, these products are made from fermented sugarcane.

Most of the popular beer brands on the market today also offer a variety of hard seltzer flavors. Here are some of the most popular:

- **»** Bud Light Seltzer
- **»** Corona Hard Seltzer
- **»** Henry's Hard Sparkling Water
- **»** Michelob Ultra Organic Seltzer
- **»** Topo Chico Hard Seltzer
- **»** Truly Hard Seltzer
- **»** Vizzy Hard Seltzer
- **»** White Claw Hard Seltzer

Ready-to-Drink Beverages

Ready-to-drink products, or RTDs, are drinks that contain alcohol or, in some cases, an actual spirit, that are ready to be opened up and consumed. In other words, they're bottled or canned cocktails. For that reason, a lot of these RTDs are made by the major spirits companies, which is a good way for them to tap into the trend of hard teas and seltzers.

Overall, these RTDs are an easy way to serve drinks, and drinkers are loving them. However, although some of these are delicious, in our opinion, nothing beats the drinks crafted by a bartender!

Here are some of the most popular RTD products:

- **1800 Tequila** offers a variety of bottled ready-to-drink Ultimate Margarita flavors.
- **Bacardi** offers a variety of canned rum cocktails.
- **Crown Royal** offers different flavors, each made with a signature Crown Royal variant.
- **Cutwater Spirits** offers tequila, vodka, gin, whiskey, and rum canned cocktails.
- **High Noon** offers a variety of flavors, each made with vodka, real juice, and sparkling water.
- **Jack Daniel's & Cola** is, you guessed it, the classic Jack & Coke, but in a can!
- **Ketel One Botanical Vodka Spritz** offers grapefruit and rose, cucumber and mint, and peach and orange blossom.
- **On The Rocks** offers a wide variety of premium bottled cocktails.
- **Playamar by Jose Cuervo** offers a few flavors of tequila seltzer made with Jose Cuervo.
- **Skinny Girl** offers a variety of bottled cocktails.
- **Zing Zang** offers a Bloody Mary, Margarita, Mango Margarita, and Whiskey Sour cans all made with real spirits.

Storing and Serving Suggestions

Because these drinks are usually canned or bottled and can be consumed once opened, most if not all should be kept and served cold.

Serving is easy: Just open and enjoy! You may be able to make a few cocktails with these products, like adding a hard seltzer to vodka to make a spritz–like cocktail or adding in a bit of bourbon to a hard tea. Overall, you can play with hard teas and seltzers in cocktails, but, as always, make sure you're not overserving your guests.

Chapter **18**
Wine

Wine, as you probably know, is made from fermented grapes. It most commonly comes in red, white, or rosé (pink or blush) varieties. There are also sparkling, fortified, and dessert wines. Winemaking dates back to roughly 3000 BC, making it one of the oldest fermented drinks in the world!

TIP

People have written whole books on single types of wine, so it's sort of foolish for us to even pretend to give a comprehensive overview in a single chapter. The focus of this book, after all, is cocktail recipes. A great introduction to buying, serving, and drinking wine is *Wine For Dummies* by Ed McCarthy and Mary Ewing-Mulligan (Wiley). It's full of useful and interesting information, and it makes a great companion to this book.

Wines from Around the World

Climate is a big factor in making good wine. To grow wine-worthy grapes, summers can't be too hot and autumns need to be cool. Light rainfall is necessary in the winter and spring, and the rain needs to taper off in the summer and fall. Harsh, cold winters with hail, frost, and heavy winds are bad for growing grapes.

The type of grape determines the type of wine, and only certain types of grapes grow in certain climates. To make matters even more complicated, the soil of a particular region plays a big role in how its grapes turn out. So while the climate in certain regions of California and France may be perfect for, say, chardonnay grapes, the soil in those regions affects the grapes to the point that the resulting wines from each region are different.

Popular wines named after grapes

Many wines receive their names from the grape they're produced from. See the following list of some popular wines named after grapes:

>> **Barbera** (red, full body): Italy

>> **Cabernet Sauvignon** (red, full body): France, United States, Australia, Chile

>> **Chardonnay** (white, dry): France, United States, Argentina, Australia, South Africa, New Zealand, Italy

>> **Chenin Blanc** (white, light, dry or sweet): France, United States, South Africa

>> **Gamay** (red, light body): France, United States

>> **Gewürztraminer** (white, dry or sweet): Germany

>> **Grenache** (red, dry or sweet): France, United States, Spain

>> **Merlot** (red, full body): France, United States, South America

>> **Pinot Noir** (red, light body): France, United States

>> **Rosé** (pink, white, and red; sweet or dry): France, Spain, United States

>> **Riesling** (white, sweet): Germany, United States, France, Austria

>> **Sauvignon Blanc** (white, dry): France, United States, New Zealand, South Africa, Chile

>> **Semillon** (white, dry): France, United States, Australia

>> **Zinfandel** (red and white, dry): United States

French wines by region

Some popular French wines are as follows. They're named after the region of France from which they originate.

>> **Alsace** (white, dry)

>> **Beaujolais** (red, light body) from Burgundy

>> **Bordeaux** (red and white, dry)

>> **Burgundy** (red and white, dry)

>> **Rhône** (red, full body)

>> **Sauterne** (white, sweet) from Bordeaux

German white wines

The following is a list of some German wines that are worth noting (all are white):

>> **Gewürztraminer** (dry or sweet)

>> **Riesling** (sweet)

Italian wines by region

Italy produces all kinds of regional wines:

>> **Amarone** (red, full body) from Veneto

>> **Barbaresco** (red, full body) from Piedmont

>> **Barbera** (red, full body) from Piedmont

>> **Bardolino** (red, light body) from Veneto

>> **Barolo** (red, full body) from Piedmont

>> **Chianti** (red, light body, sweet) from Tuscany

>> **Orvieto** (white, dry) from Umbria

>> **Pinot Grigio** (white, dry or sweet) from Trentino

>> **Soave** (white, dry) from Veneto

>> **Valpolicella** (red, full body, sweet) from Veneto

Australian wine gaining popularity

Australia's wines are growing in popularity. Here are the names of just a few:

>> **Grenache** (red, full body)

>> **Semillon** (white, dry)

>> **Shiraz** (or **Syrah**) (red, full body)

Notable South American wines

There are a lot of great grapes and wines coming from Chile, Argentina, Brazil, and Uruguay! Some South American wines include:

>> **Chardonnay** (white, dry) from Chile, Argentina, and Uruguay

>> **Malbec** (red, full body) from Argentina

>> **Merlot** (red, full body) from Chile

>> **Torrontés** (white, dry) from Argentina

North American wines for sharing

In the United States, California produces about 80 percent of all wine and is currently the fourth-largest wine producer in the world. Most California wine comes from Napa Valley or Sonoma Valley, and those areas produce both red and white wines in varieties too numerous to list. In addition to California, other U.S. states, such as Washington, New York, Pennsylvania, and Oregon, have been making great wines.

While the U.S. makes most styles of wine, here are the most popular produced:

>> **Chardonnay** (white, dry)

>> **Cabernet Sauvignon** (red, full body)

>> **Pinot Noir** (red, light body)

>> **Riesling** (white, sweet)

>> **Rosé** (pink, sweet)

>> **Sauvignon Blanc** (white, dry)

Poppin' Bubbly, and other Types of Wine

While red and white wines still are the most popular types of wine, other prominent wine styles include port, sherry, sparkling, and vermouth. These are not only delicious and craved by your guests, some, like vermouth, are also commonly used in a variety of classic cocktails.

Port

Port is a sweet, fortified wine to which brandy is added. It's named for Porto — a city in northern Portugal.

Although many wines are sold as port throughout the world, authentic port wine is the unique product of Portugal. By law, it must be made only from approved grape varieties native to the Alto Douro district and grown nowhere else in the country.

Fortification with brandy gives port extra strength and, more important, preserves the fresh flavor of grapes that makes port so delicious.

Port comes in three varieties:

» **Ruby:** Dark in color and fairly sweet

» **Tawny:** Lighter in color and drier because it's aged in casks longer

» **Vintage port:** Released only in certain exceptional years; the fullest and sweetest of all ports

The following are some popular brands:

» Fonseca

» Graham's

» Sandeman

» Taylor's

» Warre's

Sherry

When the English discovered the wines of Jerez, Spain, they called them *jerries*, and the word later evolved into *sherry*. *Sherry* is a fortified wine to which grape brandy is added. Sherry is produced all over the world.

Sherry comes in seven styles:

» **Amontillado:** Medium-dry and full-bodied.

» **Cream:** A smooth, sweet wine. Cream sherry is what results when Oloroso is blended with a sweetening wine, such as Moscatel.

>> **Fino:** Light and very dry.

>> **Manzanilla:** Pale, dry, and light-bodied.

>> **Oloroso:** Gold in color with a strong bouquet; hardier than Amontillado.

>> **Palo Cortado:** Dry and rarest of all the varieties.

>> **Pedro Ximénez** or **PX:** Sweetest and darkest of the sherry wines.

The following are popular sherry brands:

>> Tio Pepe Palomino Fino Sherry

>> Williams & Humbert Dry Sack Fino Sherry

>> Hidalgo Pasada Manzanilla

>> Savory & James Sherry

>> Osborne Sibarita Oloroso Sherry

>> Lustau Sherry

Vermouth

Vermouth originated in the 18th century and is infused with a variety of flavors, including cloves, bitter orange peel, nutmeg, gentian, chamomile, and wormwood, which in German is *wermut*, from which vermouth got its name. After it's flavored, the wine is clarified, pasteurized, and fortified to an alcoholic content of about 18 percent — close to that of sherry.

The standard classification of vermouth is white/dry and red/sweet, but exceptions do exist, including a half-sweet variety known as rosé. And though most dry vermouths are considered French and sweet vermouths are considered Italian, both types are produced in France and Italy, as well as throughout the world, including in the United States.

TIP

Vermouth is an ingredient in many cocktails, most famously the Martini and Manhattan, so you should take as much care and time in selecting a good vermouth as you do other liquor to pour at the bar. Choose the brand of vermouth that tastes best to you — crisp and light, not too heavy or burnt.

Check out the following list of popular brands:

>> Carpano

>> Cinzano

>> Dolin

>> Martini & Rossi

>> Noilly Prat

>> Ransom

>> Villa Massa

Sparkling wines

A monk whose name is now familiar — Dom Pérignon — developed the first sparkling wine in the 1600s in the Champagne region of France.

Sparkling wine made in the Champagne region is called, of course, champagne. It's made with a mix of different grapes (including pinot noir, pinot meunier, and chardonnay) through a process called *méthod champenoise,* which is quite costly and time-consuming. Sparkling wines from other places in the world are made in different ways with different grapes. For example, prosecco is an Italian sparkling wine made from glera grapes. But you can find sparkling wines from places such as California that are made using the *méthod champenoise.*

TIP

For much more information on champagne, check out *Champagne For Dummies* by Ed McCarthy (Wiley).

Storing and Serving Suggestions

There's no sense serving good wine if you're not going to do so at the right temperature. Table 18-1 can help.

Like cocktails, wine should be served in proper glassware. (In general, white and red wines are served in different glass shapes to help with the wine aromas.) And there are safe and appropriate ways to open and serve bottles of wine and champagne; see Chapter 2 for tips and instructions.

TABLE 18-1 Wine Serving Temperatures

Wine Type	Temperature Range
Full-bodied red wines	65°–68°F
Light-bodied red wines	60°–65°F
Dry white wines	50°–55°F
Rosé wines	50°–60°F
Sweet red and sweet white wines	42°–46°F
Sparkling wines and Champagnes	42°–46°F

You can find a wine that's appropriate for every occasion and every meal. If you need more direction than what we provide here, check out *Wine For Dummies* by Ed McCarthy and Mary Ewing–Mulligan (Wiley).

TIP

>> Port is a great after-dinner drink. It also goes well with cheese and cigars. An opened bottle of port has a shelf life of four to six months. Store Port in the fridge or at room temperature.

>> Fino and Manzanilla sherries are usually served chilled as an aperitif (before-dinner drink). Amontillado is perfect between meals or with soup and charcuterie boards. Cream sherry can be served at any time, chilled or over ice.

>> Champagne and sparkling wines should be stored in a cool, dark place away from heat, light, vibrations, and severe temperature variations. Sparkling wines are ready for consumption when they're shipped to the market.

TIP

Before serving, chill the wine well, but don't freeze it. Place the bottle in a bucket filled with ice and water for 30 to 40 minutes. You can also chill a bottle in the fridge for several hours, but don't keep it in there for an extended period of time. The excessive cold and the vibration of the motor will cause the flavor to go a little flat.

Serve champagne in tall flute or tulip glasses at a temperature of 42 to 46 degrees Fahrenheit. When serving, pour a small amount into each glass and allow it to settle. Then fill each glass two-thirds full.

» You need to refrigerate a bottle of vermouth after opening. The shelf life of an open bottle, when refrigerated, is approximately one year.

» Wine is also great in cocktails. Most famously, wine is used in Wine Spritzer, White and Red Sangrias, and Mulled Wine — all of which can be found in the recipes in Chapter 20.

Chapter **19**

Low- and No-Alcohol Options

Alcohol-free drinks aren't just for pregnant women or designated drivers, nor should they be. For many people, not drinking alcohol is a lifestyle choice. Regardless of the reason, as a professional or home bartender you should stock drink options that every guest can feel comfortable ordering.

Obviously, no-alcohol drinks like juices and sodas are important to stock for making cocktails. In this chapter, we discuss the growing category of low- and no-alcohol beer, wine, and spirits that offer tasty alternatives.

REMEMBER

Be sure to read each label carefully to confirm whether a spirit contains any alcohol by volume (ABV) even if the name suggests it's a no-alcohol variety.

No-Alcohol Beer

Low- and no-alcohol beer options have been around for years. But you may not know that by law, no-alcohol beer sold in the United States can contain up to 0.5 percent alcohol by volume (ABV). That's less alcohol than most beers, which contain at least

5 percent ABV. However, any alcohol may be too much alcohol for abstaining guests, so stick to one of the following 0 percent ABV varieties:

>> **Budweiser** offers Zero (0.0%).

>> **Coors** offers Edge (0.5%).

>> **Brooklyn Brewery** offers a Special Effects Hoppy Amber (0.5%).

>> **Heineken** offers 0.0% (0.0%).

>> **Miller** offers Sharp's (0.4%).

>> **O'Doul's** offers a Premium (0.4%) and an Amber (0.2%).

>> **Rightside Brewing** offers a Citrus Wheat (0.5%).

>> **St. Pauli** offers a Non-Alcoholic beer from Germany (0.5%).

No-Alcohol Wine

Not all no-alcohol wine is bottled grape juice, although it may seem like it! Actually, some NA wine has less sugar than grape juice and tastes like regular wine.

Like NA beer, NA wine can contain up to 0.5 percent ABV compared to wine with alcohol that has around 12 percent ABV.

The process for making NA wine is similar to your regular wine with alcohol, but the alcohol is carefully removed at the end of the process. Like all wines, it's important to read the label to confirm what's inside. For this scenario, you're looking for wine labels that say "alcohol-removed" or "dealcoholized" so you know you're getting a quality no-alcohol product.

NA wine comes in red, white, rosé, and even sparkling versions. Here are some of the current most popular no-alcohol wine options. (*Note:* All options below are 0.5 percent ABV unless noted otherwise:

>> **Ariel** offers a Cabernet Sauvignon and Chardonnay.

>> **Fre** offers a Sparkling Brut, Sparkling Rosé, Chardonnay, Moscato, Rosé, White Zinfandel, Red Blend, Merlot, and Cabernet Sauvignon.

>> **Lyre's** offers a Classico Grande (0.0%).

>> **St. Regis** offers a Brut, Chardonnay, Secco, Shiraz Rosé, and Cabernet Sauvignon.

No-Alcohol Spirits

No-alcohol spirits are the newest of the bunch, and this is an ever-growing category.

There are many varieties in this space, including products that taste similar to bourbon and tequila but without the alcohol. Most products actually go through the distillation process, and the brands do a great job of making sure each product has a similar taste and flavor profile as its spirited counterpart.

Here are some of the current most popular options, all of which are less than 0.5 percent ABV:

>> **Lyre's** offers an American Malt, Dry London Spirit, Pink London Spirit, Italian Spritz, Italian Orange, Agave Blanco, Dark Cane, Orange Sec, Spiced Cane, Amaretti, and an Apéritif Dry.

>> **Seedlip** offers Grove 42, Spice 94, and Garden 108.

>> **Ritual** makes zero proof tequila, rum, whiskey, and gin alternatives.

Serving Suggestions

Whether you're making a cocktail using just juices and sodas or mixing with one of the NA spirits listed in the previous section, there are a ton of fun and delicious mocktail options for you to make. Some of the most popular NA drinks include a Virgin Piña Colada, Arnold Palmer, and the No-Jito (a spiritless Mojito). Check out Chapter 24 for fun NA drink recipes and serving suggestions.

TIP

We suggest making available at least one of these NA options (beer, wine, or spirit) so everyone is able to find something in your bar to enjoy.

3

Drink Recipes: Creating Classic Cocktails and More

Chapter **20**
Recipes from A to Z

You probably bought this book just for this chapter, which lists the recipes for about a thousand drinks. Some are classic drinks that you've probably heard of; others are new and trendy. Most are quite good; some may not be for everyone.

This cute little icon to the right of a drink name indicates a classic drink. The appropriate glass for each drink is shown to the left of its list of ingredients.

If you're looking for nonalcohol drinks, see Chapter 24. You won't find punches in this chapter, either. They're in Chapter 23.

One final note, just in case, the terms *straight up* and *neat* mean without ice.

REMEMBER

7 & 7

| 1½ oz. Seagram's 7 Whiskey | Combine over ice. |
| 3 oz. 7UP | |

24 Karat Nightmare

| 1 oz. Goldschläger | Combine in a shot glass. |
| 1 oz. Rumple Minze | |

A-Bomb

½ oz. vodka
½ oz. coffee liqueur
½ oz. Irish cream
½ oz. orange liqueur

Shake with ice, strain, and serve in a highball glass.

Absente Frappè

2 oz. Grande Absente
½ oz. anisette
4 oz. soda water or seltzer

Combine ingredients in a tall glass with a mountain of crushed ice.

Absolution

1 oz. Absolut Vodka
5 oz. champagne
Lemon peel for garnish

In a fluted champagne glass, add ingredients. Cut a lemon peel in the form of a ring to represent a halo. The lemon peel can be either wrapped around the top of the glass or floated on top of the champagne.

Created by Jimmy Caulfield at the River Café, New York, NY.

Acapulco Gold

1¼ oz. tequila
⅝ oz. Grand Marnier
1 oz. sweet & sour mix

Blend with ice.

The After Ten

1 oz. Galliano
1 oz. Remy Martin Cognac
3 oz. coffee
Whipped cream

Rim glass with brown sugar. Add Galliano, cognac, and freshly brewed coffee and top with whipped cream.

Alabama Slammer

1 oz. amaretto
1 oz. Sloe Gin
1 oz. Southern Comfort
Splash lemon juice

Shake ingredients and serve in a shot glass.

One of the first popular shots. Cover with napkins or a coaster. You can also serve this one over ice in a highball glass.

The Alamo Splash

1½ oz. Jose Cuervo Gold Tequila
1 oz. orange juice
½ oz. pineapple juice
Splash 7UP

Mix well with cracked ice, strain, and serve right from a glass in a thin, well-aimed stream directly into the recipient's mouth or on the rocks!

Albuquerque Real

1½ oz. tequila
½ oz. triple sec
½ oz. sweet & sour mix
¼ oz. cranberry juice
Splash Grand Marnier

Stir all but Grand Marnier in the glass. Float the Grand Marnier on top.

Algonquin

1½ oz. blended whiskey
1 oz. dry vermouth
1 oz. pineapple juice
3 ice cubes

Combine all ingredients in a shaker and shake. Strain into chilled cocktail glass.

Could be named for the famous round table.

Almond Lemonade

1¼ oz. vodka
¼ oz. amaretto
4 oz. lemonade

Shake with ice and strain into a shot glass.

Summer in Italy.

Amaretto Sour

1 egg white (optional)
1½ oz. amaretto
¾ oz. bourbon
1 oz. lemon juice
¼ oz. simple syrup
Angostura bitters for garnish

If you're adding in egg white, you must dry shake first. Add ingredients into a shaker with ice and shake. Strain into a rocks glass and garnish with a few dashes of angostura bitters.

Ambrosia

1 oz. Applejack
1 oz. brandy
¼ oz. Cointreau
¼ oz. lemon juice
2 oz. champagne

Shake the first four ingredients over ice and strain into a champagne flute. Fill with champagne.

This drink was created at Arnaud's restaurant in New Orleans immediately following the end of Prohibition. The word "ambrosia" comes from the Greek mabrotos, *meaning "immortal."*

Ambush

1 oz. Bushmills Irish Whiskey
1 oz. amaretto
5 oz. coffee
Whipped cream (optional)

Serve hot in mug. Top with whipped cream (if desired).

Americano

1 oz. Martini & Rossi
   Rosso Vermouth
1 oz. Campari
Club soda
Orange twist for garnish

Build with ice in a highball glass. Top with club soda and an orange twist.

A classic from Italy.

Añejo Spicy Margarita

1½ oz. Don Julio Añejo Tequila
¼ oz. Grand Marnier
½ oz. lime juice
¼ oz. simple syrup
1 tsp. chili powder
Lime wedge for garnish

Shake and strain into an ice-filled rocks glass. Garnish with lime wedge and serve.

Angel's Delight

½ oz. grenadine
½ oz. triple sec
½ oz. Sloe Gin
½ oz. heavy cream

Layer this drink in the order listed. Start with grenadine on the bottom and finish with cream on top.

Angostura Costa Del Sol

1½ oz. cream sherry
2 oz. orange juice
2 oz. cream
2 dashes angostura bitters

Shake with ice and serve in a rocks or highball glass.

Anti-Freeze

1½ oz. vodka
½ oz. Midori

Shake with ice, strain, and serve.

Aperol Spritz

2 oz. Aperol
3 oz. prosecco
1 oz. club soda
Orange slice for garnish

Pour into a wine or copa glass and top with soda. Garnish with an orange slice.

Apricot Sour

2 tbsp. lemon juice
½ tsp. superfine sugar
2 oz. apricot brandy
3-4 ice cubes
Lemon twist for garnish

Combine all ingredients in a shaker and shake vigorously. Strain into a chilled cocktail glass. Garnish with lemon twist.

The hot drink of the '60s.

A Tinker Tall

1¼ oz. Irish whiskey
3 oz. ginger ale
3 oz. club soda

Combine ingredients with lots of ice in a tall glass.

Aunt Rose

1¼ oz. Irish whiskey
2 oz. cranberry juice
2 oz. orange juice

Shake. Serve in a tall glass with ice.

Yes, there is an Aunt Rose from Ireland.

Autumn Delight

2 oz. Japanese whisky
4 oz. apple cider
1 tsp. ground cinnamon
Apple slices for garnish

Add all ingredients into a shaker with ice. Shake and strain into highball glass with ice. Garnish with apple slices and serve.

Autumn Harvest

1½ oz. Hudson Maple Rye Whiskey
½ oz. Calvados Apple Brandy
½ oz. fresh lemon juice
¼ oz. port wine
¼ oz. agave
2 dashes angostura bitters
Dash ground cinnamon
Orange peel for garnish

Add all ingredients into a shaker with ice. Shake and strain into rocks glass with ice. Garnish with orange peel and serve.

Created by Marc Filoramo, Hoboken, NJ.

Aviation

2 oz. gin
¼ oz. maraschino liqueur
¼ oz. crème de violette liqueur
½ oz. freshly squeezed
   lemon juice
Lemon peel for garnish

Fill mixing glass with ice. Add ingredients and shake well. Strain into a martini glass. Add lemon peel for garnish.

A Vin Line

1½ oz gin
½ oz. Giffard Rhubarb Liqueur
½ oz. St- Germaine
   Elderflower Liqueur
½ oz. fresh lemon juice
3–4 mint leaves
1 oz. red wine

Combine first four ingredients and mint into a shaker with ice and shake. Strain into a champagne flute and float red wine on top with bar spoon.

Created by Marc Filoramo, Hoboken, NJ.

B & B

1 oz. Bénédictine
1 oz. brandy

Stir and serve in a snifter.

An easy one to remember.

B-52

½ oz. Grand Marnier
½ oz. Kahlúa
½ oz. Baileys Irish Cream

Shake with ice. Strain or serve over ice.

You can also serve this one as a shot.

Bacardi & Cola

1½ oz. Bacardi Light or Dark Rum
Cola
Lemon juice for garnish

Pour rum into tall glass filled with ice. Fill with your favorite cola and garnish with a squeeze of a lemon.

Bacardi Blossom

1¼ oz. Bacardi Light Rum
1 oz. orange juice
½ oz. lemon juice
½ tsp. sugar

Blend with crushed ice and pour.

Sweet as a spring flower.

Bacardi Cocktail

1¼ oz. Bacardi Light Rum
1 oz. lime juice
½ tsp. sugar
½ oz. grenadine

Mix in a shaker with ice and strain into a chilled cocktail glass.

The New York Supreme Court ruled in 1936 that a Bacardi Cocktail is not a Bacardi Cocktail unless it's made with Bacardi Rum. You can also serve this one over ice in a rocks glass.

Bagpiper

1½ oz. scotch
3 oz. coffee
Whipped cream

Stir in an Irish coffee glass and top with whipped cream.

Baileys & Coffee

1½ oz. Baileys Irish Cream
5 oz. coffee

Pour the Irish cream into a cup of steaming coffee.

Easy enough.

Baileys French Dream

1½ oz. Baileys Irish Cream
½ oz. raspberry liqueur
2 oz. half & half
1 cup of ice

Add all ingredients into a blender, blend for 30 seconds, and serve.

Baileys Iced Cappuccino

5 oz. double-strength coffee
½ cup ice
2 oz. Baileys Irish Cream
1 oz. half & half
2 tsp. sugar
Whipped cream and cinnamon
(optional)

Brew a pot of double-strength coffee and set aside to cool. In a blender, combine the other ingredients. Add the cooled coffee. Blend for 10 seconds and pour into a 10 oz. glass filled with ice. Top with a dollop of whipped cream and sprinkle of cinnamon (if desired).

Baileys Mint Kiss

1 oz. Baileys Irish Cream
3 oz. coffee
½ oz. Rumple Minze
½ oz. peppermint schnapps
Whipped cream

Combine ingredients. Top with fresh whipped cream.

Bamboo Cocktail

1½ oz. sherry
¾ oz. dry vermouth
Dash angostura bitters

Stir with ice and strain.

This drink was invented around 1910 by bartender Charlie Mahoney of the Hoffman House in New York, NY.

Banana Daiquiri

1¼ oz. light rum
¼ oz. lemon juice or lime juice
½ tsp. sugar
1 banana
2 cups of ice

Blend with ice and serve.

Peel the banana, of course.

Banana Rum Cream

1½ oz. Puerto Rican dark rum
½ oz. crème de banana
1 oz. light cream

Shake well. Serve straight up or with ice.

The Barbados Cocktail

2 oz. Mount Gay Rum
½ oz. Cointreau
½ oz. sweet & sour mix

Shake with ice and serve.

Barracuda

1¼ oz. dark rum
1 oz. pineapple juice
½ oz. lime juice
¼ tsp. sugar
Champagne

Shake everything but the champagne. Serve in a champagne flute and fill to the top with champagne.

Bat Bite

1¼ oz. Bacardi Silver Rum
4 oz. cranberry juice
Lime or lemon wedge for garnish

Pour ingredients in a glass filled with ice. Squeeze and drop in one lime or lemon wedge. Stir and serve.

Bay Breeze

1½ oz. Tito's Vodka
1½ oz. pineapple juice
3 oz. cranberry juice

Stir. Serve over ice.

Quite refreshing.

Beach Party

1¼ oz. light or dark rum
1 oz. pineapple juice
1 oz. orange juice
1 oz. grenadine
2 cups of ice

Blend with ice.

Keep the sand out of this one.

Beachcomber

1½ oz. white rum
¾ oz. lime juice
¼ oz. triple sec
Dash maraschino liqueur

Shake. Serve straight up or with ice.

Bee's Knees

2 oz. gin
¾ oz. fresh lemon juice
½ oz. honey syrup (1:1
    honey to water)

Add ingredients into a shaker with ice. Shake and strain into chilled coupe glass.

Beers Knees

1½ oz. gin
1 oz. freshly squeezed
    lemon juice
1 oz. honey syrup
3 oz. wheat beer
Lemon wedge for garnish

In a pint glass, add gin, lemon juice, and honey syrup. Fill with ice, shake vigorously, and strain into a chilled Collins glass. Top with wheat beer. Garnish with a lemon wedge.

Bellini

1½ oz. white peach puree
2 oz. chilled Prosecco
Peach slice for garnish

Add white peach puree into a chilled champagne flute. Top with Prosecco and garnish with a peach slice.

Invented at Harry's Bar in Venice, Italy, by Giuseppi Cipriani on the occasion of an exhibition of the work of Venetian painter Bellini.

Bermuda Rose

1 oz. Bombay Gin
¼ oz. apricot-flavored brandy
½ oz. lime juice
Dash grenadine

Shake with ice and strain.

Bermuda Rum Swizzle

1 oz. Gosling's Black Seal Rum
1 oz. Gosling's Gold
   Bermuda Rum
2 oz. orange juice
2 oz. pineapple juice
Dash grenadine
Dash bitters
Orange slice for garnish

Churn vigorously with ice. Strain into a highball glass with ice. Garnish with an orange slice.

Bewitched

1 oz. B&B
1 oz. vodka
1 oz. cream

Stir over ice or shake with ice and pour.

Bitch on Wheels

¼ oz. Martini & Rossi Extra
   Dry Vermouth
1 oz. Bombay Gin
¼ oz. Pernod
¼ oz. white crème de menthe

Shake ingredients with ice and strain into a chilled cocktail glass.

Invented at Stars in San Francisco, CA.

Black Buck

1¼ oz. Bacardi Black Rum
Ginger ale

Pour rum in a tall glass with ice. Fill with ginger ale and garnish with lemon.

Black Currant Martini

1 oz. Godiva Liqueur
1 oz. gin
¼ oz. crème de cassis
⅙ oz. lemon juice
⅙ oz. lime juice
Cherry for garnish

Combine ingredients with ice, shake well, and strain into a cocktail glass. Garnish with a cherry.

Black Ice

1 oz. Black Sambuca
1 oz. vodka
¼ oz. crème de menthe

Shake with ice and strain.

You can also serve this one over ice in a highball glass.

Black Magic

½ oz. vodka
¾ oz. coffee liqueur
Dash lemon juice

Mix the first two ingredients with cracked ice in a shaker. Add a dash of lemon juice.

Black Manhattan

1½ oz. Bushmills Black Bush Irish Whiskey
¼ oz. sweet vermouth
Cherry for garnish

Fill mixing glass with ice. Add Irish whiskey and sweet vermouth. Stir and strain into a chilled cocktail glass filled with ice. Garnish with a cherry.

Black Martini

1½ oz. Absolut Kurant Vodka
Splash Chambord

Stir ingredients and serve straight up or over ice.

Invented at the Continental Cafe in Philadelphia, PA.

Black Orchid

1 oz. vodka
½ oz. Blue Curaçao
1½ oz. cranberry juice

Build over ice in a rocks glass.

A flower very rare and a drink very sweet.

Black Russian

2 oz. vodka
1 oz. Kahlúa

Add vodka and then Kahlúa to a glass filled with cubed ice. Stir briskly. Add cream for a White Russian.

Black Velvet (also known as a Bismarck or Champagne Velvet)

2 oz. Guinness Stout
2 oz. champagne

Layer the champagne over the Guinness in a champagne flute.

Blackthorn #1

1½ oz. Irish whiskey
1½ oz. dry vermouth
3–4 dashes Pernod
3–4 dashes bitters

Shake or blend with ice. Pour into a chilled rocks glass. You can use Sloe Gin in place of Irish whiskey.

Blackthorn #2

1½ oz. Bushmills Irish Whiskey
½ oz. Noilly Prat Dry Vermouth
Dash anisette

Stir with ice. Serve in a cocktail glass.

Blarney Stone Cocktail

2 oz. Irish whiskey
½ tsp. Pernod
½ tsp. triple sec
¼ tsp. grenadine
Dash bitters
Orange peel and a green olive
    for garnish

Shake with ice and strain. Serve with a twist of orange peel and green olive.

Blonde Babe

2 oz. SKYY Infusions Pineapple
1 oz. freshly squeezed lime juice
¾ oz. triple sec
¾ oz. crème de cacao
Lime wedge for garnish

Combine all ingredients in a cocktail shaker with ice. Shake vigorously and strain into a martini glass. Garnish with a lime wedge.

Blood & Sand

¾ oz scotch
¾ oz. sweet vermouth
¾ oz. cherry liqueur
¾ oz. orange juice
Orange peel for garnish

Shake and strain into a chilled cocktail glass. Garnish with orange peel.

Blood Ohranj

3 parts Stoli Ohranj Vodka
1 part blood orange juice
1 part Campari
Splash club soda

Stir ingredients with ice.

Bloody Bull

1¼ oz. vodka
2½ oz. tomato juice
1½ oz. beef bouillon
1–2 tsp. lemon juice
Dash Worcestershire sauce
Dash Tabasco Sauce
Dash pepper

Combine with ice in a shaker. Strain into a coffee glass.

Bloody Caesar

1¼ oz. vodka
2½ oz. Clamato juice
Dash Tabasco Sauce
Dash Worcestershire sauce
Dash pepper and salt
Celery stalk or lime wheel
    for garnish

Pour vodka into a glass with ice and fill with Clamato juice. Add a dash of Tabasco, Worcestershire, pepper, and salt. Garnish with a celery stalk or a lime wheel.

A popular drink in Canada.

Bloody Maria

1½ oz. tequila
2½ oz. tomato juice
Dash Worcestershire sauce
Dash Tabasco Sauce
Dash salt and pepper
Dash lemon juice
Celery heart for garnish

Combine in a tall glass over ice and stir. Garnish with a celery heart.

Bloody Mary ⓨ

2 oz. vodka
4 oz. tomato juice
Dash Worcestershire sauce
Dash Tabasco Sauce
Dash salt and pepper
Dash lemon juice
Celery stalk for garnish

Pour vodka over ice in a glass. Fill with tomato juice. Add a dash or two of Worcestershire sauce, lemon juice, and Tabasco Sauce. Stir and garnish with a celery stalk. For those who enjoy their Bloody Marys extremely spicy, add more Tabasco or even horseradish.

The most famous of the "Hair of the Dog" morning-after cocktails.

Bloody Molly

1½ oz. Jameson Irish Whiskey
3 oz. tomato juice (seasoned to taste) or prepared Bloody Mary mix
Dash lemon juice
Celery heart for garnish

Combine in a tall glass over ice and stir. Garnish with a celery heart.

Bloody Pizza

1 oz. tomato juice
½ oz. Villa Massa Limoncello
¾ oz. vodka
⅓ juice of a lemon
Splash of Tabasco Sauce
Splash of Worcestershire sauce
Pinch of ground pepper
Skewer mozzarella pearls, cherry tomatoes, and basil leaves for garnish

Mix all ingredients, then serve in a martini glass with the skewer garnish.

The Bloomin' Apple

1¼ oz. Jameson Irish Whiskey
2 oz. apple juice
Dash Cointreau
Orange peel for garnish

Combine in a mixing glass with ice and stir. Pour into a highball glass and garnish with a slice of orange peel.

C'MON BABY, LIGHT MY FIRE

Jerry Thomas (nicknamed Professor) created the Blue Blazer in 1849 at the El Dorado Saloon in San Francisco, California. Perfecting his technique, Thomas made this drink famous: He ignited the whiskey and tossed the flaming liquid between two silver tankards, thus mixing the ingredients while illuminating the bar with liquid fire.

Blueberry Mojito

¼ cup fresh blueberries
4 mint leaves, plus more for garnish
½ oz. lime juice
2 tbsp. sugar
2 oz. soda water
1 oz. light rum

Place fresh blueberries and mint leaves in bottom of glass. Add lime juice and sugar. Muddle. Add soda water and light rum. Garnish with mint leaves.

Blue Blazer

2 oz. Scotch whisky
2 tsp. sugar
3 oz. hot water
Cinnamon sticks for garnish

Pour all ingredients into a pan and heat very gently until the sugar has dissolved. Place a teaspoon into a short tumbler and pour drink carefully into the glass (the spoon keeps the glass from cracking). Serve with cinnamon sticks.

Blue Lagoon

1½ oz. vodka
½ oz. Blue Curaçao
3 oz. lemonade
Cherry for garnish

Combine ingredients over ice in a highball glass. Garnish with a cherry.

Created around 1960 at Harry's Bar in Paris, France, by Harry's son, Andy MacElhone.

Bobby Burns

1 oz. scotch	Build in a cocktail glass over ice. Stir
1 oz. sweet vermouth	and serve.
½ oz. Bénédictine	

A great Scotsman.

Boilermaker

2 oz. spirit of your choice	Serve spirit in a shot glass with a
10 oz. beer	glass of beer on the side as a
	chaser.

A beer and a shot, a delicious combo.

Bolero

1½ oz. Rhum Barbancourt	Stir. Serve straight up or with ice.
½ oz. Calvados	
2 tsp. sweet vermouth	
Dash bitters	

You can also serve this drink as a shot.

Bonbini

1 oz. light or dark rum	Stir and serve with ice.
¼ oz. Orange Curaçao	
Dash bitters	

Boogie-Woogie

2 oz. Grey Goose Vodka L'Orange	Mix with ice and garnish with a twist
3 oz. grapefruit juice	of lime.
1 oz. lemon juice	
Dash bitters	

Boston Breeze

1 oz. Coco Lopez Cream	Blend and serve in a margarita
of Coconut	glass.
1¼ oz. Cruzan Rum	
3 oz. cranberry juice	
1 cup ice	

Botanical Spritz

2 oz. Ketel One Botanical Vodka
Soda water

Add in Ketel One Botanical and top with soda water.

Boulevardier

1½ oz. bourbon
1 oz. Campari
1 oz. sweet vermouth
Orange twist for garnish

Shake with ice and strain into a cocktail glass. Garnish with orange twist.

Bourbon Sling

1 tsp. superfine sugar
2 tsp. water
1 oz. lemon juice
2 oz. bourbon
Lemon twist for garnish

In a shaker half-filled with ice cubes, combine the sugar, water, lemon juice, and bourbon. Shake well. Strain into a glass. Top with a lemon twist.

Bourbon Street

1½ oz. bourbon
½ oz. Disaronno Amaretto

Shake with ice and strain into a shot glass.

Brainstorm

1¾ oz. Irish whiskey
¼ oz. dry vermouth
Dash Bénédictine
Orange peel for garnish

Stir all ingredients and strain into a cocktail glass. Decorate with a twist of orange peel.

Bramble

2 oz. gin
1 oz. fresh lemon juice
2 tsp. simple syrup
½ oz. crème de mure
Lemon wheel and blackberry
  for garnish

Add gin, lemon juice, and simple syrup into a shaker with ice. Shake and strain into a rocks glass with crushed ice. Top with crème de mure, and garnish with lemon wheel and a blackberry.

Brandy Alexander

1½ oz. brandy
½ oz. dark crème de cacao
1 oz. cream or ice cream

Shake with ice. Strain and serve.

A sweet and tasty classic.

Brandy Crusta

Sugar
2 oz. Brandy
¼ oz. Orange Curaçao
½ oz. fresh lemon juice
½ oz. simple syrup
1 tsp. maraschino liqueur
1 dash bitters

Rim a coupe glass with sugar and set aside. Add all ingredients into a cocktail shaker with ice. Shake and strain into the rimmed coupe and serve.

Brass Knuckle

1 oz. bourbon
½ oz. triple sec
2 oz. sweetened lemon mix

Shake with ice and serve in a highball glass with ice.

Brave Bull

1½ oz. tequila
½ oz. coffee liqueur

Stir and serve over ice.

You can also serve this one as a shot.

Brazilian Rose

3 oz. guava juice
Splash triple sec
2 oz. Leblon Cachaça
Rose petal for garnish

Pour the guava juice and triple sec into a shaker. Fill the shaker with ice and add Leblon Cachaça. Shake vigorously. Serve in a martini glass. Garnish with a rose petal.

Breakfast Martini

2 oz. gin
¾ oz. Cointreau or triple sec
¾ oz. freshly squeezed
    lemon juice
1 tsp. orange marmalade
Lemon twist for garnish

Mix or shake in cocktail shaker filled with ice cubes. Strain into a cocktail glass and serve. Garnish with a lemon twist.

A breakfast martini is a form of cocktail created by Bartender Salvatore Calabrese.

Bronx

1½ oz. gin
½ oz. dry vermouth
½ oz. sweet vermouth
½ oz. fresh orange juice

Shake with ice and strain.

Bubble Gum

½ oz. melon liqueur
½ oz. vodka
½ oz. crème de banana
½ oz. orange juice
Dash grenadine

Serve in a shot glass.

Buck-a-Roo

1¼ oz. light or dark rum
4 oz. root beer

Pour rum into a Collins glass filled with ice. Fill with root beer.

Bucking Irish

1¼ oz. Irish whiskey
5 oz. ginger ale
Lemon twist for garnish

Combine in an ice-filled Collins glass. Garnish with a lemon twist.

Buff Martini

3 parts vodka
1 part Baileys Irish Cream
1 part Kahlúa
Ground coffee or cinnamon
  for garnish

Stir gently with ice and strain. Add a sprinkle of freshly ground coffee or cinnamon.

Bullshot

1½ oz. vodka
1 tsp. lemon juice
Dash Worcestershire sauce
Dash Tabasco Sauce
4 oz. chilled beef bouillon
Dash salt and pepper
Lemon wedge for garnish

Shake and strain into a highball glass filled with ice. Garnish with a lemon wedge.

One of the "Hair of the Dog" hangover cures, along with the Bloody Mary.

Bungi Jumper

1¼ oz. Irish Mist Liqueur
4 oz. orange juice
½ oz. cream
Splash amaretto

Mix all but the amaretto in a highball glass. Float the amaretto on top. Serve straight up or over ice.

Stretch this one for a while.

Bunratty Peg

1½ oz. Irish whiskey
¾ oz. Irish Mist Liqueur
¼ oz. amaretto or Drambuie

Stir with ice and strain into a chilled cocktail glass.

You can also serve this drink with ice in a rocks glass.

Burnt Orange

1 oz. Ketel One Oranje vodka
½ oz. bourbon
2½ oz. Ruby Red Grapefruit Juice
½ oz. simple syrup

Shake and strain into a rocks glass.

Bushmills Fuzzy Valencia

1½ oz. Bushmills Irish Whiskey
¾ oz. amaretto
3 oz. orange juice

Serve in a tall glass over ice.

Bushranger

1 oz. Dubonnet
1 oz. Puerto Rican white rum
2 dashes bitters

Stir and serve over ice.

Bushwacker

2 oz. Coco Lopez Cream
   of Coconut
2 oz. half & half
1 oz. Kahlúa
½ oz. dark crème de cacao
½ oz. rum
1 cup ice

Blend and serve in a margarita glass.

Butterscotch Bomber

½ oz. vodka
½ oz. Baileys Irish Cream
½ oz. butterscotch schnapps

Shake with ice and serve in a shot glass.

You can also serve this one over ice in a highball glass.

Buttery Finger

¼ oz. Irish cream
¼ oz. 360 Vodka
¼ oz. butterscotch schnapps
¼ oz. coffee liqueur

Combine in a shot glass.

You can also serve this drink over ice in a highball glass.

Cafe Cooler

5 oz. coffee
½ oz. Romana Sambuca
½ oz. half & half
Dash brown sugar

Pour coffee over ice. Add sambuca and half & half. Add brown sugar to taste.

Caffé Europa

1 oz. Galliano
1 oz. Cointreau
3 oz. coffee
Whipped cream

Add Galliano, Cointreau, and freshly brewed coffee and top with whipped cream.

Caipirinha

½ lime, plus a slice for garnish
2 tsp. superfine sugar
2 oz. Leblon Cachaça

Cut the lime into 4 wedges. Muddle the lime and sugar in a shaker. Fill the shaker with ice and add Leblon Cachaça. Shake vigorously. Serve in a rocks glass. Garnish with a lime slice.

Caipírissima

5 freshly cut lime wedges
1½ oz. rum
Splash freshly squeezed lime juice
1 tbsp. refined sugar

Muddle 4 lime wedges in a shaker. Add rum, lime juice, and refined sugar, and shake vigorously with ice. Strain contents into a chilled martini glass and garnish with remaining lime wedge.

If you like Mojitos, give this one a try.

Caipiroska

½ oz. simple syrup
½ lime, cut into wedges
2 oz. vodka
Small spoonful of brown sugar

Pour the simple syrup onto the lime wedges in an old-fashioned glass. Muddle well before adding vodka and filling with crushed ice. Stir all ingredients together well. Top with more crushed ice.

Cajun Martini

2 oz. Absolut Peppar Vodka
¼ oz. dry vermouth
Habanero-stuffed olive for garnish

Serve chilled and straight up. Garnish with a habanero-stuffed olive.

Created at the Continental Cafe in Philadelphia, PA.

Cameron's Kick

¾ oz. Irish whiskey
¾ oz. scotch whisky
Juice of ¼ lemon
2 dashes bitters

Shake well with cracked ice and strain into a cocktail glass.

Camino Reál

1½ oz. reposado tequila
½ oz. banana liqueur
1 oz. orange juice
Dash lime juice
Dash Coco Lopez Coconut Milk
Lime slice for garnish

Shake or blend. Garnish with a lime slice.

Campari & Soda

2 oz. Campari
Club soda
Lemon twist for garnish

Top Campari with club soda in a Collins glass. Add a lemon twist.

Can–Can

1 oz. tequila
½ oz. French vermouth
2 oz. grapefruit juice
1 tsp. sugar
Orange twist for garnish

Shake together over ice and serve with an orange twist.

Candy Apple

1 oz. apple schnapps
1 oz. cinnamon schnapps
1 oz. apple juice

Shake with ice and strain into a shot glass.

Cannonball

1½ oz. Captain Morgan
    Spiced Rum
3 oz. pineapple juice
¼ oz. white crème de menthe

Pour the rum and pineapple juice over ice. Float the crème de menthe on top.

Big noise in a rocks glass.

Canton Sunrise

1½ oz. Domaine de Canton
    Ginger Liqueur
1½ oz. orange juice
Splash grenadine

Combine over ice.

Cape Codder #1

1¼ oz. vodka
3 oz. cranberry Juice
Dash lime juice

Combine in a chilled cocktail glass over ice. Garnish with a lime wedge.

Cape Codder #2

1½ oz. vodka
4 oz. cranberry juice
Club soda
Orange slice for garnish

Combine vodka and cranberry juice over ice in a tall glass. Fill with club soda. Garnish with an orange slice.

Captain & Cola

1½ oz. Captain Morgan
    Spiced Rum
3 oz. cola

Stir in a tall glass with ice.

Captain's Berry Daiquiri

1¼ oz. Captain Morgan
    Spiced Rum
½ cup strawberries or
    raspberries, plus more
    for garnish
1 tsp. lime juice
½ tsp. sugar
½ cup crushed ice

Blend. Garnish with berries.

Captain's Colada

1¼ oz. Captain Morgan
  Spiced Rum
1 oz. Coco Lopez Cream
  of Coconut
3 oz. pineapple juice
  (unsweetened)
½ cup crushed ice
Pineapple spear for garnish

Blend. Garnish with a pineapple spear.

Carajillo

1¾ oz. Licor 43
1 oz. hot espresso coffee

Half fill a glass with ice cubes and pour Licor 43 over the top. Serve alongside the cup of hot espresso and, before drinking, pour the coffee over the liqueur and stir.

On its way to becoming a new classic.

Caramel Apple

½ oz. 99 Apples Schnapps
1 oz. butterscotch schnapps

Shake with ice and strain to serve as a shooter.

Caribbean Joy

1¼ oz. silver rum
1 oz. pineapple juice
¾ oz. lemon juice

Shake and serve over ice.

Carolaretto

1½ oz. Baileys Irish Cream
1½ oz. amaretto

Shake or stir and serve over ice.

Carrot Cake

¾ oz. Goldschläger
¾ oz. Baileys Irish Cream
¾ oz. coffee liqueur

Shake with ice. Pour over rocks or serve straight up.

Cassis Cocktail

1 oz. bourbon
½ oz. dry vermouth
1 tsp. crème de cassis

Shake with cracked ice. Strain into a chilled cocktail glass.

Catalina Margarita

1¼ oz. Jose Cuervo Gold Tequila
1 oz. peach schnapps
1 oz. Blue Curaçao
4 oz. sweet & sour mix
1 cup crushed ice

Blend with crushed ice.

Cavalier

1½ oz. tequila
½ oz. Galliano
1½ oz. orange juice
½ oz. cream
1 cup crushed ice

Blend with crushed ice and strain into a cocktail glass.

CC & Soda

1¾ oz. Canadian Club Whisky
3 oz. club soda

Serve in a Collins glass with ice.

A Canadian favorite.

Celtic Bull

1½ oz. Irish whiskey
2 oz. beef consommé or bouillon
2 oz. tomato juice
1–2 dashes Worcestershire sauce
Dash Tabasco Sauce
Dash freshly ground pepper

Mix all ingredients with cracked ice in a shaker or blender. Pour into a chilled highball glass.

A variation of the Bloody Bull, which is derived from the Bloody Mary.

Celestial Fresh

1½ oz. Ron Inmortal
   Colombian Rum
½ oz. Tawney Port
½ oz. Monin Blackcurrant
½ oz. lime juice
8 leaves spearmint
2 dashes tea bitters

Combine ingredients into a cocktail shaker. Add ice and shake. Pour the cocktail with the same shaken ice, and pour crushed ice on top. Garnish with spearmint and aromatize with tea bitters.

Cele-Tini

2 oz. Ketel One Vodka
½ oz. dry vermouth
1 oz. fresh celery juice

Shake and strain into a chilled martini glass

Inspired by L. Petrella.

Celtic Highball

2 oz. Tullamore Dew
⅛ oz. grenadine
Club soda

Combine first two ingredients in a glass and fill with club soda.

Cement Mixer

¾ shot Irish cream
¼ shot lime juice

Pour ingredients directly into the glass. Let the drink stand for 5 seconds and it will coagulate.

This drink will stick to your ribs.

Chai Time

1 oz. Baileys Irish Cream
½ oz. vanilla vodka
6 oz. hot chai tea
Grated cinnamon for garnish

Add all ingredients into coffee or tea mug and stir. Garnish with grated cinnamon and serve.

Chambord Kamikaze

1 oz. vodka
½ oz. Chambord
¼ oz. triple sec
¼ oz. lime juice

Shake with ice and strain into a shot glass.

Tastes sort of like a Purple Hooter.

Champagne Cocktail ⓨ

1 cube sugar
Dash bitters
3 oz. champagne, chilled
Lemon twist for garnish

Place sugar cube on bar spoon and dash with bitters. Drop cube into a chilled champagne flute and add in champagne. Garnish with a lemon twist.

Champerelle

½ oz. Cointreau
½ oz. anisette
½ oz. Green Chartreuse
½ oz. cognac

Layer this drink in the order listed. Start with Cointreau on the bottom and finish with cognac on top.

Champs Élysées

½ oz. grenadine
½ oz. brown crème de cacao
½ oz. Orange Curaçao
½ oz. green crème de menthe
½ oz. cognac

Layer this drink in the order listed. Start with grenadine on the bottom and finish with cognac on top.

Chamu

½ oz. Chambord
1 oz. Malibu Rum
½ oz. vodka
3 oz. pineapple juice

Combine ingredients in a tall glass with ice. Fill with pineapple juice.

Charlotte

2 oz. Barrell Seagrass
½ oz. giffard china china bigallet
½ oz. Lagavulin 8
¼ oz. apricot liquor

Add all ingreidents into a mixing glass with ice

Created by Marc Figueiras, Jersey City, NJ

Cherried Cream Rum

1½ oz. rum
½ oz. cherry brandy
½ oz. light cream

Shake with ice and strain.

Cherry Pop

2 oz. juice from Ole Smoky
    Moonshine Cherries, plus the
    cherries for garnish
2 oz. cola

Combine both ingredients in a
Mason or other glass jar and stir.
Garnish with Ole Smoky Moonshine
Cherries.

Chicago Style

¾ oz. light rum
¼ oz. triple sec
¼ oz. anisette
¼ oz. lemon or lime juice

Blend with ice.

The windy one.

Chi-Chi

1 oz. Coco Lopez Cream
    of Coconut
2 oz. pineapple juice
1½ oz. vodka
1 cup ice

Blend until smooth.

Move over rum; vodka is in this one.

The Chimayo Cocktail

1¼ oz. silver tequila
¼ oz. crème de cassis
1 oz. fresh apple cider or
    apple juice
¼ oz. lemon juice
Apple wedge for garnish

Fill a glass with ice. Pour the
ingredients over ice and stir.
Garnish with an apple wedge.

China Beach

¾ oz. ginger liqueur
1 oz. cranberry juice
Splash vodka

Shake with ice and serve over ice.

Chinatown

1 part Domaine de Canton
    Delicate Ginger Liqueur
1 part Bacardi 151 Rum

Shake with ice and strain into a shot
glass.

Chip Shot

¾ oz. Irish cream
¾ oz. crème de menthe
1½ oz. coffee

Combine in a glass and stir.

Perfect after golf or cookies.

Chocolate Covered Cherry

1½ oz. chocolate vodka
½ oz. cherry soda

Chill chocolate vodka and pour in a shot glass. Top with cherry soda.

Chocolate Martini Cocktail

Cocoa powder to rim glass
2 oz. Bacardi O
1 oz. light crème de cacao
Splash Disaronno Amaretto
Chocolate candy kiss

Rim a martini glass with cocoa powder. In a shaker with ice, combine the Bacardi O, crème de cacao, and amaretto. Strain into the martini glass. Drop in the chocolate candy kiss.

Chocolate Martini #1

1 oz. Absolut Vodka
½ oz. Godiva Chocolate Liqueur
Lemon twist for garnish

Shake over ice; strain into a chilled cocktail glass with a lemon twist garnish.

For your sweet tooth.

Chocolate Martini #2

1½ oz. vodka
Dash white crème de cacao
Orange peel for garnish

Pour vodka and crème de cacao over ice. Shake or stir well. Strain and serve in a chocolate-rimmed cocktail glass straight up or over ice. Garnish with an orange peel.

To rim the glass, first rub a piece of orange around the top of the glass and then gently place the glass upside down in a plate of unsweetened chocolate powder.

Cilver Citron

1¼ oz. Absolut Citron Vodka
2 oz. chilled champagne

Combine in a champagne glass.

Citron Cooler

1¼ oz. Absolut Citron Vodka
½ oz. fresh lime juice
Tonic water
Lime wedge for garnish

Pour vodka and lime juice over ice in a tall glass. Fill with tonic. Garnish with a lime wedge.

Citron Kamikazi

¾ oz. Absolut Citron Vodka
¾ oz. triple sec
¾ oz. lime juice

Pour vodka, triple sec, and lime juice over ice in a glass. Shake well and strain into a glass. Serve straight up or over ice. Garnish with a lime wedge.

Can also be made into shots.

Citroska

2 oz. citrus vodka
¼ oz. simple syrup
3 oz. lemon-lime soda
Sprig of mint for garnish

Add simple syrup to a highball glass. Fill with ice, add vodka, and fill with soda. Garnish with a mint sprig.

Clam Voyage

1 oz. Bacardi Light or Dark Rum
¼ oz. apple-flavored brandy
1 oz. orange juice
Dash orange bitters

Blend with ice and serve in a margarita glass.

Clover Club

1½ oz. Martin Miller's Gin
½ oz. dry vermouth
¾ oz. lemon juice
½ oz. simple syrup
Whole raspberries for garnish

Combine ingredients, including raspberries, in a shaker with ice; shake until chilled then strain. Remove the ice from the shaker and add the drink back into the tin and shake a second time without the ice. Strain into a cocktail glass. Garnish with raspberries.

Co-Charge

1½ oz. vodka
½ oz. cognac
½ oz. cherry brandy

Mix all ingredients with cracked ice in a shaker or blender and pour into a chilled cocktail glass.

Coco Caribbean

2 oz. Ciroc Coconut Vodka
4 oz. pineapple juice

Combine in a tall glass with ice.

Coco Loco (Crazy Coconut)

1½ oz. tequila
3 oz. pineapple juice
2 oz. Coco Lopez Cream
   of Coconut
Pineapple spear for garnish

Blend. Garnish with a pineapple spear.

Coco Margarita

1¼ oz. Blanco Tequila
1 oz. sweet & sour mix
1½ oz. pineapple juice
½ oz. fresh lime juice
½ oz. Coco Lopez Cream
   of Coconut
Fresh pineapple wedge
   for garnish

Shake or blend ingredients. Garnish with fresh pineapple wedge.

Cocomotion

4 oz. Coco Lopez Cream
   of Coconut
2 oz. lime juice
1½ oz. Puerto Rican dark rum
1½ cups ice

Blend and serve in a margarita glass.

Coconut Almond Margarita

1¼ oz. blanco tequila
2½ oz. sweet & sour mix
½ oz. Coco Lopez Cream
  of Coconut
¼ oz. amaretto
½ oz. fresh lime juice
Lime wedge for garnish

Shake and serve over ice. Garnish with a wedge of lime.

You can also blend the ingredients with ice.

Coconut & Strawberry Lemonade

3 strawberries, plus a slice
  for garnish
1½ oz. CÎROC Coconut Vodka
1 oz. lemon juice
¾ oz. honey syrup
  (1:1 honey to water)
Soda water
Lemon twist for garnish

Muddle the 3 strawberries. Add remaining ingredients and shake with ice. Strain into a Collins glass and top with soda water. Garnish with a slice of strawberry on the rim and a lemon twist.

Coconut Batida

2 oz. cachaça
2 oz. Coco Lopez Cream
  of Coconut
2 oz. condensed milk
½ oz. simple syrup
Toasted coconut for garnish

Blend all ingredients in a blender until smooth. Serve in a Collins glass. Garnish with toasted coconut.

Coconut Bellini

2 oz. Coco Lopez Cream
  of Coconut
3 oz. champagne
2 oz. peach puree
½ oz. peach schnapps
1 cup ice

Blend until smooth.

This famous Bellini is made with Coco Lopez.

Coffee Cream Cooler

1¼ oz. light or dark rum
Cold coffee
Cream

Pour rum into a tall glass half filled with ice. Fill with cold coffee and cream to desired proportions.

Cointreau Santa Fe Margarita

1½ oz. Jose Cuervo Gold Tequila
¾ oz. Cointreau
2 oz. sweet & sour mix
2 oz. cranberry juice

Blend ingredients and serve in a margarita glass.

Cointreau Strawberry Margarita

1¼ oz. Jose Cuervo Gold Tequila
¾ oz. Cointreau
2 oz. sweet & sour mix
3 oz. frozen strawberries

Blend ingredients and serve in a margarita glass.

Colorado Bulldog

1 oz. vodka
1½ oz. coffee liqueur
4 oz. cream
Splash cola

Pour first three ingredients over ice. Add a splash of cola. Stir briefly.

There is another name for this drink. You've heard it but won't see it in print.

Colosseum Cooler

1 oz. Romana Sambuca
3 oz. cranberry juice
Club soda

Combine sambuca and cranberry juice in a tall glass. Fill with soda and garnish with a lime wedge.

Commando Fix

2 oz. Irish whiskey
¼ oz. triple sec
½ oz. lime juice
1–2 dashes raspberry liqueur

Fill a glass with ice. Add Irish whiskey, triple sec, and lime juice. Stir slowly. Dot the surface of the drink with raspberry liqueur.

Commodore

1 part bourbon
1 part crème de cacao
1 part lemon juice
1 dash grenadine

Shake with ice and serve over ice.

Conchita

1¼ oz. tequila
½ oz. lemon juice
6 oz. grapefruit juice

Combine first two ingredients in a chilled highball glass. Fill with grapefruit juice and stir.

Continental

1 oz. light rum
¼ oz. green crème de menthe
¾ oz. lime juice
¼ tsp. sugar (optional)

Blend with ice.

Cool Citron

1 oz. Absolut Citron Vodka
½ oz. white crème de menthe

Shake and serve over ice.

Copper Illusion Martini

1 oz. gin
½ oz. Grand Marnier
½ oz. Campari
Orange slice for garnish

Stir ingredients and garnish with an orange slice.

Invented at the Gallery Lounge at the Sheraton in Seattle, WA.

Cork Comfort

1½ oz. Irish whiskey
¾ oz. sweet vermouth
¼ oz. Southern Comfort
3–4 dashes bitters

Shake with ice or blend. Pour into a chilled rocks glass.

Corkscrew

¾ oz. light rum
¼ oz. brandy
¼ oz. port wine
½ oz. lemon or lime juice

Stir. Serve over ice.

Corpse Reviver #1

1 oz. Calvados
1 oz. cognac
½ oz. sweet vermouth

Add all ingredients into a shaker with ice. Shake and strain into a chilled martini glass and serve.

Corpse Reviver #2

¼ oz. Absinthe
¾ oz. London Dry Gin
¾ oz. Lillet Blanc
¾ oz. orange liqueur
¾ oz. lemon juice

Rinse a chilled martini glass with Absinthe and discard. Add in gin, Lillet Blanc, orange liqueur, and lemon juice to a cocktail shaker with ice. Shake and strain into rinsed glass and serve.

Cosmo Kaze

2 oz. vodka
½ oz. triple sec
Dash lime juice
Splash cranberry juice

Combine ingredients and pour over ice.

A red, nonshot variation of the Kamikaze.

Cosmopolitan

2 oz. citron vodka
¾ oz. Cointreau
¾ oz. lime juice
½ oz. cranberry juice

Shake with ice and strain.

There are many variations of the Martini. This one works.

Cowboy

2 oz. Jim Beam Bourbon
4 oz. milk

In an ice-filled shaker, shake the bourbon with milk. Strain into a Collins glass.

A great way to add calcium to your diet.

Cran Razz

2 oz. tequila
2 oz. cranberry juice
1 oz. raspberry liqueur

In a shaker, mix all ingredients. Serve over ice.

Cranberry Martini

1 oz. Mozart Chocolate Liqueur
1 oz. Absolut Vodka
1 oz. cranberry juice
Lime twist for garnish

Combine with ice and shake well. Garnish with a lime twist.

Cranberry Sauce Martini

1 oz. Stoli Ohranj Vodka
¼ oz. cranberry juice
Sweetened cranberries
   for garnish

Shake with ice and strain or serve over ice. Garnish with cranberries that have been soaked in simple syrup.

Cranpeppar

1¼ oz. Absolut Peppar Vodka
Cranberry juice

Pour vodka over ice in a tall glass. Fill with cranberry juice.

Crantini

2 oz. Bacardi Limón Rum
Touch Martini & Rossi Extra
   Dry Vermouth
Splash cranberry juice
Cranberries and lemon twist
   for garnish

Shake and serve straight up. Garnish with cranberries and a lemon twist.

Invented at Mr. Babbington's in New York, NY.

Creamy Oranges

1 oz. Galliano
1 oz. half & half or heavy cream
1 oz. orange juice

Combine over ice.

Creamy Orange Treat

1½ oz. Stoli Ohranj Vodka
½ oz. Irish cream

Combine over ice.

Creamy Orange–Vanilla Smoothie

½ oz. vanilla vodka
1 oz. orange vodka
1½ medium scoops
    vanilla ice cream
Orange peel for garnish

Blend ingredients. Pour over ice.
Garnish with orange peel.

Creature from the Black Lagoon

1 oz. Jägermeister
1 oz. Romana Black

Shake with ice and strain into a
shot glass.

Back to the water.

Creole

1¾ oz. white rum
2 splashes lemon juice
3½ oz. beef bouillon
Dash pepper
Dash salt
Dash Tabasco Sauce
Dash Worcestershire sauce

Combine over ice.

Crest of the Wave

1¼ oz. gin
1½ oz. grapefruit juice
1½ oz. cranberry juice

Combine in a tall glass over ice.

Cricket

¾ oz. rum
¼ oz. white crème de cacao
¼ oz. green crème de menthe
1 oz. cream

Blend ingredients with ice.

Crimson Cranberry

1½ oz. Jameson Black Barrel
½ oz. cinnamon syrup
½ oz. lemon juice
1 oz. club soda
1 oz. cranberry juice
1 dash bitters
Fresh cranberries for garnish

Add all ingredients except club soda into a shaker with ice. Shake and strain into rocks glass with ice. Garnish with fresh cranberries.

Cripple Creek

½ oz. tequila
½ oz. bourbon
1 oz. orange juice
½ oz. Galliano

Shake the first three ingredients and strain into a glass. Float the Galliano on top.

Crocodile Bite

1¼ oz. Irish whiskey
2 oz. orange juice
1 oz. Grand Marnier
7Up
Orange or lemon slice for garnish

Combine first 3 ingredients in a tall glass with ice. Top with 7UP. Garnish with a slice of orange or lemon and serve.

Are there crocodiles in Ireland?

Cuba Libre

1 oz. Bacardi Rum
3 oz. cola
Juice of ¼ lime

Add rum and lime to a glass filled with ice. Fill with cola and garnish with a lime wedge.

Rum & Coke with a lime.

Cucumber Martini

2 slices of cucumber, plus more for garnish
¼ oz. simple syrup
2 oz. Ketel One Botanical Cucumber and Mint Vodka
½ oz. lime juice
½ oz. prosecco

Muddle cucumber with simple syrup in a cocktail shaker. Add in vodka, lime juice, and ice and shake. Strain into a martini glass and top with prosecco. Garnish with cucumber slices and serve.

Created by A. Vieira, Hoboken, NJ.

Cuervo Alexander

1 oz. Jose Cuervo Gold Tequila
1 oz. coffee liqueur
1 oz. wild cherry brandy
2 scoops vanilla ice cream

Blend until smooth.

A little kick to the Brandy Alexander.

Cutthroat

1¼ oz. cranberry vodka
Orange juice

Add vodka to a tall glass with ice. Fill with orange juice.

Sort of a cranberry screwdriver.

Czar

1 oz. vodka
1 oz. cranberry vodka
1 oz. pineapple juice
1 oz. cranberry juice

Shake all ingredients with ice. Strain into a rocks glass.

Daiquiri

2 oz. light rum
1 oz. fresh lime juice
¾ oz. simple syrup

Mix in shaker with ice and strain into a chilled cocktail glass.

The original Daiquiri was made with Bacardi Rum in 1896. You can add bananas, orange juice, peaches, and any other fruit that you enjoy. You can also serve this one in a highball glass over ice.

Dancing Leprechaun

1½ oz. Irish whiskey
1½ oz. lemon juice
Club soda
Ginger ale
Lemon twist for garnish

Combine the whiskey and the lemon juice. Shake with ice. Strain and add ice. Fill the glass with equal parts club soda and ginger ale. Stir gently. Touch it up with a twist of lemon.

Danish Viking

1¾ oz. Ron Zacapa 23 Rum
½ oz. sweet vermouth
1 dash chocolate bitters
1 dash angostura bitters
Orange twist for garnish

Combine all ingredients into a shaker with ice. Shake and strain into a chilled coupe glass. Garnish with an orange twist.

Created by R. Just, Miami, FL.

Dark 'N' Stormy

1½ oz. Gosling's Black Seal Rum
4 oz. ginger beer
Lime or lemon wedge for garnish (optional)

Pour the rum over ice and top with ginger beer. Garnish with lime or lemon wedge (if desired).

Bermuda's national drink.

Dean Martini

2 oz. Ketel One Vodka, chilled
Olive
1 Lucky (cigarette)
1 book of matches

Pour the vodka into a cocktail glass and garnish with an olive. Place the cigarette and matches on the side.

Invented at the Continental Cafe in Philadelphia, PA.

Dempsey Rum Runner

1 shot Hendrick's Gin
1 tsp./pkt. sugar
Dash bitters
3 oz. pineapple juice

Shake well and serve.

Devil Wears Nada

1½ oz. vodka
¼ oz. Aperol
¾ oz. honey simple syrup
½ oz. fresh lime juice
½ oz. sauvignon blanc
Cucumber ribbons for garnish

Add all ingredients into a shaker with ice. Shake and strain into rocks glass with ice. Garnish with cucumber and serve.

Created by Mike Fikaris from New York, NY.

Dewey Martini

1½ oz. Absolut Vodka
Dash extra dry vermouth
Dash orange bitters

Shake and strain into a cocktail glass or serve over ice.

Dingle Dram

1½ oz. Irish whiskey
½ oz. Irish Mist Liqueur
Coffee soda
Cash crème de cacao
Whipped cream

Pour Irish whiskey and Irish Mist into a chilled highball glass along with several ice cubes. Fill with coffee soda. Stir gently. Add a float of crème de cacao. Top with dollop of whipped cream.

Dirty Harry

1 oz. Grand Marnier
1 oz. Tia Maria Coffee Liqueur

Shake with ice and strain.

Do you feel lucky? This will make your day.

Dirty Shirley

2 oz. vodka
1 oz. grenadine
8 oz. lemon-lime soda
Maraschino cherry for garnish

Combine in a tall glass with ice and stir. Garnish with a maraschino cherry.

Dixie Dew

1½ oz. bourbon
½ oz. white crème de menthe
½ tsp. Cointreau or triple sec

In a mixing glass half filled with ice cubes, combine all the ingredients. Stir well. Strain into a cocktail glass.

Dixie Stinger

3 oz. bourbon
½ oz. white crème de menthe
½ tsp. Southern Comfort

In a shaker half filled with ice cubes, combine all the ingredients. Shake well. Strain into a cocktail glass.

Dizzy Lizzy

1½ oz. bourbon
1½ oz. sherry
Dash lemon juice
Club soda

Combine first three ingredients in a tall glass with ice. Fill with club soda.

Double Gold

½ oz. Jose Cuervo Gold Tequila
½ oz. Goldschläger

Shake with ice and strain into a shot glass.

Dragon Palmer

2 oz. Bacardi Dragonberry Rum
1½ oz. lemonade
1½ oz. ice tea
Lemon wedge for garnish

Pour ingredients over ice in a tall glass and garnish with a lemon wedge.

Dream Shake

1 oz. Baileys Irish Cream
1 oz. coffee liqueur

Shake with ice and strain into a shot glass.

Duck Pin

1 oz. Chambord
1 oz. Southern Comfort
½ oz. pineapple juice

Shake with ice and strain into a shot glass.

Eclipse

1½ oz. Bushmills Black Bush
  Irish Whiskey
Seltzer water
Orange slice for garnish

Fill a highball glass with ice. Add Irish whiskey. Fill with seltzer water and stir. Garnish with an orange slice.

Eggnog

2 eggs, separated
¼ cup sugar, divided
1½ cups whole milk
½ cup heavy cream
½ cup bourbon or brandy
Grated nutmeg for garnish

In a bowl, mix yolks with ⅛ cup sugar until fluffy. Do the same with the egg whites in another bowl. In the bowl with the egg yolks, stir in milk, heavy cream, and bourbon or brandy. Then fold in the beaten egg whites. Do one more stir and pour into rocks glasses and top with grated nutmeg for garnish.

El Diablo

1½ oz. reposado tequila
½ oz. crème de cassis
½ oz. lime juice
3 oz. ginger beer
Lime wedge for garnish

Add first three ingredients into a cocktail shaker with ice. Shake and strain into a highball glass with ice. Top with ginger beer and garnish with lime wedge and serve.

Electric Lemonade

1¼ oz. vodka
½ oz. Blue Curaçao
2 oz. sweet & sour mix
Splash 7UP
Lemon slice for garnish

Blend. Pour over ice in a tall glass and garnish with a lemon slice.

Electric Peach

1 oz. vodka
¼ oz. peach schnapps
½ oz. cranberry juice cocktail
¼ oz. orange juice
Lemon slice for garnish

Blend. Pour over ice in a tall glass and garnish with a lemon slice.

Elegant Martini (Gin)

1¾ oz. gin
½ oz. dry vermouth
¼ oz. Grand Marnier, plus a dash to finish

Stir the first three ingredients with ice. Strain or serve on ice. Float Grand Marnier on top.

Elegant Martini (Vodka)

1½ oz. vodka
Dash extra dry vermouth
¼ oz. Grand Marnier, plus a dash to finish

Stir the first three ingredients with ice. Serve on ice or straight up. Float Grand Marnier on top.

Embassy Cocktail

¾ oz. rum
¾ oz. Jamaican rum
¾ triple sec
½ oz. lime juice
Dash bitters

Shake and strain into a martini glass.

Emerald Isle

¾ shot Irish whiskey
¾ shot green crème de menthe
2 scoops vanilla ice cream
Soda water

Blend the first three ingredients and then add soda water. Stir after adding soda water.

It's green.

Emerald Martini

2 oz. Bacardi Limón Rum
Splash Martini & Rossi Extra Dry Vermouth
Splash Midori

Stir with ice. Serve on ice or straight up.

Invented at the Heart and Soul in San Francisco, CA.

Erie Tour

1 oz. Irish Mist Liqueur
1 oz. Irish cream
1 oz. Irish whiskey

Combine over ice.

Espresso Martini

2 oz. vodka
½ oz. coffee liqueur
1 oz. espresso
½ oz. simple syrup
Coffee beans for garnish

Add all ingredients into a shaker with ice. Shake and strain into a chilled martini glass. Garnish with coffee beans.

More versions of this cocktail can be found in Chapter 22.

Espresso Oaxaca

1½ oz. San Cosme Mezcal
½ oz. red vermouth
1 oz. espresso
½ oz. honey

Fill all ingredients in a shaker filled with ice and shake firmly. Serve in a rocks glass filled with ice.

Extra Nutty Irishman

1 oz. Irish Mist Liqueur
1 oz. Frangelico
1 oz. Irish cream
Whipped cream

Shake. Serve in a goblet-type glass. Top with whipped cream.

Eye Drop

1 oz. Rumple Minze
1 oz. Stoli Vodka
1 oz. ouzo

Shake with ice and strain into a shot glass.

The Fascinator

1½ oz. gin
½ oz. Cointreau
¼ oz. Campari
¾ oz. freshly squeezed lime juice

Combine all ingredients in a shaker with ice. Shake and strain into chilled glass.

Fascinator Martini

1½ oz. vodka
Dash Martini & Rossi Extra
  Dry Vermouth
Dash Pernod
Mint sprig for garnish

Stir and serve straight up or over ice. Garnish with a mint sprig.

You can also serve this one over ice in a highball glass.

The Fashionista

¾ oz. pomegranate juice
3 oz. Moët Impérial Champagne
A pink rose petal for garnish

Pour the pomegranate juice into a flute glass. Fill with Moët Impérial. Stir gently with a long spoon. Place a pink rose petal over the drink.

Fifth Avenue

1 oz. dark crème de cacao
1 oz. apricot brandy
1 oz. cream

Layer this drink in the order listed. Start with crème de cacao on the bottom and finish with cream on top.

Fifty-Fifty Martini

1½ oz. gin
1½ oz. dry vermouth
Lemon twist for garnish

Stir ingredients over ice in a shaker and strain into a chilled martini glass. Garnish with a lemon twist.

'57 T-Bird with Honolulu License Plates

1 part orange liqueur
1 part dark rum
1 part Sloe Gin
1 part orange juice

Shake with ice and strain into a shot glass.

Get a designated driver.

'57 T-Bird with Texas License Plates

1 oz. Cointreau
½ oz. dark rum
½ oz. Sloe Gin
½ oz. grapefruit juice

Shake with ice and strain into a shot glass.

Fire

| | 1¼ oz. Fireball Cinnamon Whisky
¼ oz. cinnamon schnapps | Combine over ice. |

A hot one.

Firebird

| | 1½ oz. Fireball Cinnamon Whisky
4 oz. cranberry juice | Combine over ice. |

Fire Fly

| | 1¼ oz. Tito's Vodka
2 oz. grapefruit juice
Dash grenadine | Combine vodka and grapefruit juice in a tall glass over ice. Add grenadine. |

The First Lady

| | 2 oz. rye whiskey
1 oz. triple sec
Splash orange juice
Orange wheel for garnish | Combine rye whiskey, triple sec, and orange juice in a shaker. Shake well and strain. Serve up in a martini glass and garnish with an orange wheel. |

Fizz

| | 1½ oz. rum
¼ oz. lemon juice
¼ oz. grenadine
4 oz. club soda | Pour rum and lemon juice into a highball glass filled with ice. Add grenadine and fill with club soda. |

Flaming Fireball

| | 2 oz. cinnamon schnapps
Dash Tabasco Sauce | Combine in a shot glass. |

Flamingo

| | 1½ oz. rum
Dash grenadine
1 oz. pineapple juice
Juice of ¼ lime | Shake and serve over ice. |

Flirting with the Sandpiper

1½ oz. light rum
½ oz. cherry brandy
3 oz. orange juice
2 dashes orange bitters

Stir well. Serve over ice.

Foggy Day Martini

1½ oz. dry gin
¼ oz. Pernod
Twist of lemon peel for garnish

Shake and pour over ice or serve straight up. Garnish with a lemon peel twist.

Fool's Gold

1 oz. vodka
1 oz. Galliano

Shake with ice and strain into a shot glass.

43 Amigos

1½ oz. tequila
½ oz. Licor 43
½ oz. triple sec
½ oz. lime juice
Lime wedge for garnish

Shake. Strain into a chilled martini glass. Garnish with a lime wedge.

43 Caipirinha

3 lime wedges
3 orange slices
1½ oz. cachaça
1 oz. Licor 43

Muddle lime and orange in a mixing glass. Add cachaça and Licor 43. Shake well and pour into a rocks glass.

Four Leaf Clover

1¼ oz. Bushmills Irish Whiskey
2 oz. orange juice
2 oz. sweet & sour mix
Splash green crème de menthe

Shake first three ingredients and top with crème de menthe. Serve over ice or straight up.

Don't overlook this one.

Fourth of July

⅓ shot grenadine
⅓ shot vodka
⅓ shot Blue Curaçao

Layer this drink in the order listed. Start with grenadine on the bottom and finish with Blue Curaçao on top.

Freddy Finkle

1¾ oz. tequila
3 oz. orange juice
¼ oz. Galliano

Stir tequila and orange juice in a rocks glass. Top with Galliano.

Yes, there was this guy named Freddy.

French Colada

1½ oz. rum
¾ oz. cognac
1 scoop crushed ice
¾ oz. sweet cream
¾ oz. Coco Lopez Cream
  of Coconut
1½ oz. pineapple juice
Splash crème de cassis

Blend with ice.

French Connection

½ oz. cognac
½ oz. Grand Marnier

Serve straight up in a brandy snifter or shake with ice and strain.

You can also serve this drink as a shot.

French Cosmo

2 oz. Grey Goose Vodka L'Orange
½ oz. triple sec
½ oz. peach schnapps
Orange peel for garnish

Shake with ice. Garnish with an orange peel.

French Kiss

1½ oz. Noilly Prat
    Rouge Vermouth
1½ oz. Noilly Prat Dry Vermouth
Twist of lemon peel for garnish

Combine over ice. Add a twist of lemon peel for garnish.

French Kiss Martini

2 oz. orange vodka
¼ oz. Lillet Blanc

Stir gently with ice. Serve straight up or over ice.

French 75

1½ oz. cognac
½ oz. lemon juice
½ oz. simple syrup
Champagne
Lemon twist for garnish

Combine everything but champagne. Shake and pour in a champagne glass. Fill with champagne. Garnish with a lemon twist.

This is the classic recipe. The modern version coming up next includes gin.

French 75 (Modern)

1½ oz. gin
½ oz. lemon juice
½ oz. simple syrup
Champagne
Lemon twist for garnish

Combine everything but champagne. Shake and pour in a champagne glass. Fill with champagne. Garnish with a lemon twist.

French Martini

1½ oz. vodka
½ oz. raspberry liqueur
½ oz. pineapple juice
Lemon peel or raspberry skewer
    for garnish

Combine ingredients into a shaker with ice and shake. Strain into a chilled martini glass. Garnish with lemon twist or raspberry skewer.

French Tickler

1 part Goldschläger
1 part Grand Marnier

Shake with ice and strain into a shot glass.

Frosé

1 bottle of rosé
½ cup sugar
2½ oz. fresh lemon juice
8 oz. strawberries
4 cups of ice
Peach schnapps (optional)

Cut strawberries into chunks. Into a large blender, add in all ingredients with ice. Blend and divide among 6 chilled martini glasses. Add in a floater of peach schnapps (if desired).

This recipe serves 6.

Frozen Daiquiri

2 oz. white rum
¾ oz. simple syrup
1½ oz. fresh lime juice
Lime wheel for garnish

Add all ingredients into a blender with ice and blend. Garnish with a lime wheel.

Frozen Irish Coffee

2 oz. Irish whiskey
1 oz. Baileys Irish Cream
1 oz. Kahlúa
1 shot espresso
1 scoop vanilla ice cream
Coffee grounds for garnish

Add all ingredients into a blender with ice and blend. Garnish with coffee grounds.

Frozen Margarita

2 oz. tequila
¾ oz. orange liqueur
1 oz. fresh lime juice
Lime wheel for garnish

Add all ingredients into a blender with ice and blend. Pour into a salt-rimmed glass and garnish with a lime wheel.

THE ORIGINS OF THE FRENCH 75

FABLES AND LORE

If you request this drink, you may receive a mix of gin and champagne. In the French trenches of World War I, gin was scarce, but cognac and champagne were not. American soldiers soon discovered that a combination of the two produced an effect similar to getting zapped by an artillery piece known as French 75. Hence why we included both recipes!

Frozen Negroni

2 oz. gin
¾ oz. Aperol
¾ oz. sweet vermouth
1 pinch salt
3 dashes grapefruit bitters

Add all ingredients into a blender with ice and blend.

Frozen Smash

8 oz. bourbon
7 oz. simple syrup
6 oz. lemon juice
6 oz. lime
3 oz. water
2 cups of ice
Lemon wheel and mint for garnish

Add all liquid ingredients into a blender with ice. Pour into 4 rocks glasses and garnish with lemon wheel and mint.

This recipe serves 4.

Frisco Cocktail

1¼ oz. rye whiskey
¾ oz. Bénédictine
Twist of lemon peel for garnish

Stir with cracked ice and strain. Serve with a twist of lemon peel.

Fru-Fru

¾ oz. banana liqueur
1 oz. peach schnapps
Dash lime juice
1 oz. pineapple juice

Shake with ice and strain into a glass.

Fudgy Concoction

1 oz. vodka
¼ oz. crème de cacao
¼ oz. chocolate syrup

Shake and serve over ice.

Full Moon

½ oz. Ole Smoky
 Blackberry Moonshine
½ oz. Ole Smoky White Lightnin'
½ oz. Ole Smoky Apple
 Pie Moonshine
½ oz. Ole Smoky
 Moonshine Peaches
1½ oz. sweet & sour mix

Combine all ingredients in a tall glass and stir to mix well.

Fuzzy Navel

1¼ oz. DeKuyper Peach Schnapps
3 oz. orange juice

Pour schnapps over ice in a rocks glass. Fill with orange juice and stir well.

This famous drink was cocreated by Ray Foley working with National Distillers, which became Jim Beam, now Beam Suntory.

THE ORIGIN OF THE FUZZY NAVEL

FABLES AND LORE

In 1985, at a private bar on Park Avenue in New York City, two lovers of the drink, Jack Doyle, who worked for the DeKuyper company, and Ray Foley, a bartender from New Jersey, were trying to create a cocktail for a brand new product, DeKuyper Peachtree Schnapps. Jack was mixing it with orange juice and Ray was cutting an orange for garnish when Jack made the remark that he could still smell the fuzz of the DeKuyper Peachtree Schnapps through the orange juice. Ray looked at the orange, saw the word "navel" printed on the skin, and they had their name: the Fuzzy Navel.

Fuzzy Rita

1½ oz. tequila
½ oz. peach liqueur
½ oz. Cointreau
1½ oz. lime juice

Combine over ice in a tall glass.

Margarita's cousin.

G & C

1 oz. Galliano
1 oz. cognac

Shake with ice and strain into a shot glass.

Gaelic Flip

2 oz. Irish whiskey
⅓ oz. simple syrup
1 oz. sweet vermouth
1 tsp. allspice liqueur
1 egg
Nutmeg for garnish

Add all ingredients into a shaker without ice and hard dry shake. Add in ice and shake again. Strain into a chilled coupe glass and garnish with nutmeg.

Galliano Hot Shot

1 oz. Galliano
1 oz. hot coffee
Dash whipped cream

Combine in a shot glass.

Hot and sweet.

Gentle Bull

1½ oz. tequila
1 oz. heavy cream
¾ oz. coffee liqueur
1 scoop crushed ice
Whipped cream and a cherry
for garnish

Shake. Top with whipped cream and a cherry.

George Bell

Crushed ice
1½ oz. Irish whiskey
1 strip lemon peel
3–4 oz. ginger ale

Fill a tall glass with crushed ice to the ¾ level. Add Irish whiskey. Twist lemon peel over the drink to release its oil and then drop it in. Top with ginger ale.

Ghost Colada

2.5 oz. Ghost Tequila
  (spicy tequila)
2 oz. pineapple juice
2 oz. Coco Lopez Cream
  of Coconut
1 oz. fresh lime juice
1 oz. simple syrup
Diced pineapples for garnish

In a cocktail shaker, add ice and all liquid ingredients and shake. Strain into chilled glass and garnish with diced pineapples.

Gibson

2 oz. dry gin
½ oz. dry vermouth
Cocktail onion

Stir with ice. Add the cocktail onion. Serve straight up or on ice.

Gimlet

2 oz. Gin
½ oz. fresh lime juice
½ oz. simple syrup
Lime wheel for garnish

Mix gin and lime juice in a glass with ice. Strain and serve in a cocktail glass. Garnish with a lime wheel.

Gin & Tonic

2 oz. gin
Tonic
Lime wedge for garnish

In a glass filled with ice, add gin and fill with tonic. Add a lime wedge.

WHERE'D THE GIBSON COME FROM?

The true origin of the Gibson isn't clearly defined. Some say this drink was named after New York artist Charles Dana Gibson by his bartender, Charles Connolly of the Players Club in New York. Others credit a business man from San Francisco named D.K. Gibson at the Bohemian Club. And finally, another story credits Billie Gibson, a fight promoter.

Gin Cocktail

1 oz. gin
2 oz. Dubonnet
Lemon twist for garnish

Stir over ice. Add a lemon twist.

Also known as the Dubonnet Cocktail.

Gin Fizz

2 oz. gin
1 oz. lemon juice
¾ oz. simple syrup
1 egg white
Club soda

Shake all ingredients except club soda in a cocktail shaker without ice. Then, add ice and shake again. Strain into a Collins glass with ice. Top with club soda.

Gin-Gin Mule

2 mint sprigs
1 oz. simple syrup
¾ oz. fresh lime juice
1¾ oz. Tanqueray Gin
1 oz. ginger beer

In a shaker, muddle 1 mint sprig with simple syrup and lime juice. Add in gin and ice and shake. Strain into a Collins glass with ice and add in ginger beer. Garnish with the remaining mint sprig and serve.

Created by Audrey Saunders.

Gin Rickey

2 oz. gin
½ oz. lime juice
Club soda
Lime wheel for garnish

In a tall glass filled with ice, add gin and lime juice. Fill with club soda and stir. Garnish with a lime wheel.

Gin Spritz

½ oz. grapefruit juice
1 oz. gin
2 oz. Aperol
Carbonated water or club soda

Squeeze grapefruit into highball glass and add ice. Add gin and Aperol and top up with carbonated water or club soda.

Glenbeigh Fizz

1½ oz. Irish whiskey
1 oz. medium sherry
½ oz. crème de noyaux
½ oz. lemon juice
Club soda

Pour all ingredients except club soda in a chilled highball glass with several ice cubes and stir. Fill with club soda.

Glorious Awakening

1½ oz. Ron Inmortal Colombian Rum
1½ oz. pineapple extract
1 oz. espresso
1½ oz. coffee liqueur
Dash angostura bitters
Coffee bean for garnish

Combine ingredients into a cocktail shaker. Add ice cubes and shake for 10 seconds. Strain into a chilled glass. Garnish with a coffee bean.

Godfather

1½ oz. scotch
½ oz. amaretto

Combine in a rocks glass over ice.

A drink you can't refuse.

Godmother

1 oz. vodka
¼ oz. amaretto

Combine in a rocks glass over ice.

A woman you can't refuse.

Gold Furnace

2 oz. Goldschläger
2 dashes Tabasco Sauce

Combine in a shot glass.

Gold Rush

2 oz. Goldschläger
1 oz. Cuervo Gold Tequila

Shake with ice and strain into a shot glass.

Golden Boy

1½ oz. bourbon
½ oz. rum
2 oz. orange juice
1 tsp. lemon juice
1 tsp. simple syrup
1 scoop crushed ice
Dash grenadine

Mix all ingredients, except the grenadine, in a shaker. Strain mixture into a chilled glass. Top with a dash of grenadine.

Golden Cadillac

¼ oz. Galliano
1 oz. white crème de cacao
1 oz. cream

Mix in a blender with a little ice at a low speed for a short time. Strain into a champagne glass. You can substitute a scoop of vanilla ice cream for cream.

Golden Dream

1 oz. Galliano
¼ oz. triple sec
½ oz. orange juice
½ oz. cream

Shake with cracked ice. Strain into a cocktail glass.

You can also serve this one over ice in a highball glass.

Golden Girl Martini

1¾ oz. dry gin
¾ oz. dry sherry
1 dash angostura bitters

Stir gently with ice. Serve straight up or over ice.

Golden Martini

2½ oz. Seagram's Extra Dry Gin
¼ oz. French vermouth
Lemon peel twist for garnish

Stir gently with ice. Serve straight up or over ice. Garnish with a lemon peel twist.

Good and Plenty

1 oz. anisette
1 oz. blackberry brandy

Shake with ice and strain into a shot glass.

Gotham

1½ oz. vodka
1½ oz. rosa vermouth
¼ oz. amaro
2 dashes orange bitters
Lemon peel twist for garnish

Add ingredients into a mixing glass with ice and stir. Strain into a chilled martini glass and garnish with a lemon twist.

The Grackle

1½ oz. Tito's Vodka
½ oz. Bitter Herbal Liqueur
2 oz. fresh blood orange juice

Shake and strain into a rocks glass with ice.

Grafton Street Sour

1½ oz. Irish whiskey
½ oz. triple sec
1 oz. lime juice
¼ oz. raspberry liqueur

Mix all ingredients except the raspberry liqueur with cracked ice in a shaker or blender and strain into a chilled cocktail glass. Top with raspberry liqueur.

You can also serve this one on ice.

Grand Am

1 oz. Grand Marnier
1 oz. Disaronno Amaretto

Shake with ice and strain into a shot glass.

Grand Orange

1½ oz. orange vodka
Dash extra dry vermouth
Splash Grand Marnier
Orange peel slice for garnish

Stir gently with ice; serve straight up or over ice. Garnish with a slice of orange peel.

Grand Royale

1½ oz. Grand Marnier
6 oz. pineapple juice

Pour Grand Marnier into a tall glass with ice. Add pineapple juice and serve.

Granny Goose

2 oz. Grey Goose Vodka
¼ oz. Grand Marnier
Orange twist for garnish

Shake with ice and strain into a chilled martini glass. Serve straight up or on the rocks. Add an orange twist for garnish.

Grape Crush

1 oz. vodka
1 oz. black raspberry liqueur
2 oz. sweet & sour mix
1 oz. 7UP
Orange slice or cherry for garnish

Serve over ice in a Collins glass. Garnish with an orange slice or cherry.

Grape Punch

1¼ oz. light rum
Grape juice
Lime or lemon juice

Pour rum into a tall glass filled with ice. Fill with grape juice and add a squeeze of lime or lemon.

Grasshopper

½ oz. green crème de menthe
½ oz. white crème de cacao
2 oz. cream

Combine in a blender with ice and blend until smooth. Strain into a coupe glass.

A grasshopper walks into a bar. Bartender says, "We have a drink named after you." The grasshopper replies, "You have a drink named Bruce?"

Great Dane

1 oz. Aquavit
½ oz. cherry brandy
½ oz. orange bitters
1 dash cranberry juice

Shake and strain into a chilled cocktail glass.

Great White

1¼ oz. Irish whiskey
2 oz. apple juice
1 oz. White Curaçao
Mint sprig for garnish

Combine over ice in a tall glass and garnish with a mint sprig.

Coco's delight!!

Green Chili

1 part peach schnapps
1 part Midori
Dash Tabasco Sauce

Shake with ice and strain into a shot glass.

Green Devil

1 oz. gin
½ oz. crème de menthe
½ oz. lime juice

Shake with ice and strain into a shot glass.

Green Hornet

½ oz. vodka
¼ oz. Midori
½ oz. sweet & sour mix

Shake with ice; serve straight up or over ice.

Green Lizard

1 oz. Green Chartreuse
1 oz. Bacardi 151 Rum
¼ oz. Rose's Lime Juice

Layer this drink by pouring Chartreuse first, then the rum, and then the lime juice.

Green Sneaker

1 oz. vodka
½ oz. Midori
½ oz. triple sec
2 oz. orange juice

Stir with ice, strain, and serve straight up.

Green Tea Highball

2 oz. Japanese whisky
2 oz. green tea
Club soda

In a highball glass with ice, add in Japanese whisky and green tea. Stir and top with club soda, then serve.

Greg's Revival

¾ oz. London Dry Gin
¾ oz. Lillet Blanc
¾ oz. pomegranate liqueur
¾ oz. lemon juice
Absinthe

Rinse a chilled martini glass with Absinthe and discard. Add in gin, Lillet Blanc, pomegranate liqueur, and lemon juice to a cocktail shaker with ice. Shake and strain into rinsed glass and serve.

Inspired by Ryan Foley.

Gremlin

½ oz. vodka
¾ oz. Blue Curaçao
¾ oz. rum
½ oz. orange juice

Shake with ice, strain, and serve straight up.

Greyhound

1½ oz. vodka
Grapefruit juice
Lime wheel for garnish

Pour vodka over crushed ice in a tall glass. Fill with grapefruit juice. Garnish with lime wheel.

Some people will order this drink by saying, "Can I have a vodka and grapefruit juice?"

Grit Cocktail

2½ oz. Irish whiskey
¼ oz. red vermouth

Shake and then strain.

Gunga Din Martini

3 parts dry gin
1 part dry vermouth
Juice of ¼ orange
Pineapple slice for garnish

Shake with ice. Garnish with a
pineapple slice.

Gypsy Martini

1½ oz. vodka or gin
Dash Martini & Rossi Extra
    Dry Vermouth
Cherry for garnish

Shake with ice; serve straight up or
on ice. Garnish with a cherry.

Hank Panky

1½ oz. gin
1½ oz. sweet vermouth
2 dashes Fernet – Branca
Orange twist for garnish

Add all ingredients in a mixing glass
with ice and stir. Strain into a chilled
cocktail glass. Garnish with an
orange twist.

Harbor Breeze

1¼ oz. lemon-flavored rum
½ oz. fresh kiwi puree
2 oz. pear nectar
Kiwi wheel and lemon twist
    for garnish

Add ingredients in a shaker. Shake
with ice and strain into a martini
glass. Garnish with a kiwi wheel and
a lemon twist.

Harbor Life

1 oz. Chambord
1 oz. Puerto Rican rum
1 oz. orange juice

Shake with ice and strain into a shot
glass.

Harbor Lights

1 oz. Galliano
1 oz. Remy Martin Cognac

Shake with ice and strain into a shot
glass.

Hard Citrus Tea

1 oz. citrus vodka
Top with hard iced tea or hard
    iced tea seltzer

In a highball glass, add in citrus vodka and stop with your favorite hard iced tea flavor. Stir and serve.

Hard Hat

1¼ oz. rum
1¼ oz. fresh lime juice
1 tsp. sugar
¼ oz. grenadine
Club soda

In a shaker with ice, combine all but the club soda. Stir and strain into a glass with ice. Fill with club soda.

Hard Seltzer Cocktail

1 oz. vodka
Top with hard seltzer

In a highball glass, add in vodka and top with your favorite hard seltzer flavor. Stir and garnish with fresh fruit.

Hard Seltzer Collins

2 oz. gin
½ oz. simple syrup
½ oz. lemon juice
Top with hard lemon seltzer

In a highball glass, add in first three ingredients and stir. Top with hard lemon seltzer and serve.

Hard Seltzer Rickey

1½ oz. bourbon
½ oz. simple syrup
1 oz. lemon juice
Top with hard lime seltzer

In a highball glass, add in first three ingredients and stir. Top with hard lime seltzer and serve.

Hard Seltzer Spritz

2 oz. Aperol
3 oz. prosecco
Top with hard grapefruit seltzer

In a wine glass, add in first two ingredients and stir. Top with hard grapefruit seltzer and serve.

Harry's Martini

1¾ oz. dry gin
¾ oz. sweet vermouth
¼ oz. Pernod
Mint sprig for garnish

Stir gently with ice; serve straight up or on ice. Garnish with mint sprig.

Harvard Cocktail

1½ oz. brandy
¾ oz. sweet vermouth
2 tsp. fresh lemon juice
1 tsp. grenadine
Dash bitters

Shake ingredients and serve over ice in a rocks glass.

Harvey Wallbanger

1 oz. vodka
3 oz. Orange juice
¼ oz. Galliano

In a tall glass with ice, add vodka and fill the glass ¾ full with orange juice. Float the Galliano on top.

Havana Sidecar

1½ oz. rum
¾ oz. lemon juice
¾ oz. triple sec

Mix with ice and serve on ice.

Hawaiian

1 part gin
1 part orange juice
Dash Orange Curaçao

Shake with ice. Serve on ice.

Hawaiian Highball

2½ oz. Irish whiskey
2 tsp. pineapple juice
1 tsp. lemon juice
Club soda

Combine the whiskey with the juices. Add ice and fill with soda. Stir gently.

Hawaiian Night

1 oz. light rum
Pineapple juice
¼ oz. cherry-flavored brandy

Pour rum into a tall glass half-filled with ice. Fill with pineapple juice and float cherry-flavored brandy on top.

Hawaiian Pipeline

1½ oz. pineapple vodka, chilled
2 oz. orange juice
1 oz. cranberry juice

Shake. Serve over ice in a tall glass.

Hazelnut Martini

2 oz. Absolut Vodka
Splash Frangelico
Orange slice for garnish

Stir with ice and serve straight up. Garnish with an orange slice.

Invented at the Martini Bar at the Chianti Restaurant in Houston, TX.

Headlock

¼ oz. brandy
¼ oz. amaretto
¼ oz. Irish whiskey
¼ oz. Irish cream

Layer this drink by pouring the brandy first, then the amaretto, and so on.

Heart-Shaped Box

Absinthe
2 oz. Bulleit Rye
¼ oz. maraschino liqueur
¼ oz. simple syrup
2 dashes Peychaud's Bitters
2 dashes angostura bitters
Lemon peel for garnish

Rinse rocks glass with Absinthe and discard. Combine ingredients into a shaker with ice and shake. Strain into Absinthe-rinsed glass with ice. Garnish with lemon peel and serve.

Created by G. Sutton at Lombardi Hospitality Group.

Heartthrob

1¼ oz. cranberry vodka
¼ oz. peach schnapps
¼ oz. grapefruit juice

Shake. Serve in a tall glass with ice.

Heat Wave

1 oz. dark rum
½ oz. peach schnapps
Pineapple juice
Splash grenadine

Add rum and schnapps to a highball glass with ice. Fill with pineapple juice. Add a splash of grenadine.

Hemingway Daiquiri

2 oz. white rum
¾ oz. lime juice
½ oz. maraschino liqueur
½ oz. fresh grapefruit juice
Lime wheel for garnish

Shake and strain into a chilled coupe glass. Garnish with lime wheel.

Hendrick's Floradora

1½ oz. Hendrick's Gin
½ oz. lime juice
½ oz. raspberry syrup
½ oz. spicy ginger beer
Raspberries and lime wheel for garnish

Assemble ingredients and shake well. Serve over ice in a Collins glass. Garnish with two raspberries and a lime wheel.

Hennessy Martini

1½ oz. Hennessy V.S. Cognac
Dash lemon juice

Shake with ice and strain or serve straight up.

Invented at Harry Denton's in San Francisco, CA.

Hibiscus Cooler

1½ oz. Don Julio
    Reposado Tequila
1 oz. fresh lemon juice
¾ oz. hibiscus raspberry syrup

Add all ingredients into a shaker with ice and shake. Strain into a rocks glass.

Created by V. Leon, Miami, FL.

Highball ⓨ

1½ oz. American whiskey
3 oz. ginger ale

Combine and stir.

Hole in One

1¾ oz. scotch whisky
¾ oz. dry vermouth
¼ oz. lemon juice
1 dash orange bitters

Place ingredients into a mixing glass
with ice and stir. Strain into a chilled
coupe glass and serve.

Hollywood

1 oz. vodka
1 oz. black raspberry liqueur
Cranberry juice

Combine ingredients in a tall glass
with ice. Fill with cranberry juice.

Hollywood Stunt Double

1 oz. vodka
1 oz. Chambord
1 oz. pineapple juice

Shake with ice and strain into a shot
glass.

Home Run

1 oz. bourbon
1 oz. light rum
1 oz. brandy
2 tsp. lemon juice

Shake with ice and serve over ice.

Take a swig at this one.

The Honeymooner

2 oz. mead
½ oz. amaretto
½ oz. cream
Cinnamon for garnish

Shake ingredients and pour over
ice. Garnish with cinnamon.

Honey Nut Cocktail

1½ oz. Irish whiskey
1½ oz. Frangelico
1½ oz. half & half

Shake ingredients and serve over ice in a rocks glass.

Honolulu Hurricane Martini

2 oz. dry gin
¼ oz. French vermouth
¼ oz. Italian vermouth
⅛ oz. pineapple juice

Shake with ice and strain.

Horny Bull

1¼ oz. tequila
Orange juice

Add tequila to a chilled highball glass filled with ice. Fill with orange juice.

Horse's Neck

2 oz. bourbon or rye whiskey
4 oz. ginger ale
Lemon peel for garnish

Add bourbon or rye into a Collins glass with ice. Top with ginger ale. Garnish with lemon peel.

Hot Bomb

¾ oz. tequila
¼ oz. cinnamon schnapps

Shake with ice; strain into a shot glass.

Hot in Cork

2½ oz. Irish whiskey
2 oz. boiling water
Lemon slice and cloves for garnish

Combine in the glass and garnish with a slice of lemon and some cloves.

Hot Irish Coffee

¾ oz. Bushmills Irish Whiskey
1 oz. peppermint schnapps
Hot coffee
Whipped cream

Combine first two ingredients in the glass. Fill with coffee and stir well. Top with whipped cream.

Optional: Sprinkle with candy mint shavings.

Hot Irishman

½ slice fresh lemon
4 cloves
2 tsp. sugar (brown if available)
Pinch cinnamon
3 oz. boiling water
1½ oz. Irish whiskey

Stud the lemon slice with cloves. Put lemon, sugar, and cinnamon into a warm glass. Add boiling water and Irish whiskey. Stir well and serve.

Hot Irish Monk

2 oz. Irish whiskey
1 oz. Frangelico
4 oz. hot chocolate
Whipped cream
Toasted hazelnuts

Stir thoroughly and then add a thick cap of whipped cream; sprinkle with chopped, toasted hazelnuts.

Hot Pants

¼ oz. Absolut Peppar Vodka
1 oz. peach schnapps

Combine over ice.

Bottoms up.

Hot Port

1½ oz. Irish whiskey
2 oz. red or tawny port
2 oz. water

Pour ingredients into a saucepan. Heat to boiling point but do not boil. Pour into a mug. Add a cinnamon stick and an orange slice.

Hot Toddy 🍸

1½ oz. whiskey
3 oz. hot water
¼ oz. lemon juice
1 teaspoon honey or sugar
Cinnamon stick

Pour into mug and stir. Garnish with cinnamon stick.

Usually with whiskey but can also be made with rum or scotch.

Hula-Hoop

1½ oz. vodka
2 oz. pineapple juice
½ oz. orange juice

Combine over ice.

Hurricane

2 oz. dark rum
2 oz. light rum
1 oz. lime juice
1 oz. orange juice
½ oz. passion fruit juice
½ oz. simple syrup
Splash grenadine

Combine in a shaker with ice and shake. Strain into a hurricane or Collins glass with ice.

Iceberg Martini

2 oz. gin
¼ oz. white crème de menthe
Mint leaves for garnish

Stir with ice and strain. Garnish with mint.

Created at the Martini Bar at Chianti Restaurant in Houston, TX.

Imperial

1¼ oz. bourbon
1¼ oz. orange liqueur
Splash simple syrup
1 scoop crushed ice
Splash club soda

Mix together all the ingredients except the club soda in a shaker. Strain the mixture into a rocks glass over ice. Top off the glass with club soda.

Incredible Hulk

1 oz. Hpnotiq
1 oz. cognac

Layer over ice and then stir for transformation.

Inoculation Shot

1 oz. Jose Cuervo Gold Tequila
¼ oz. Blue Curaçao

Shake with ice and strain into a shot glass.

International Coffee

½ oz. Irish cream
½ oz. Chambord
5 oz. coffee

Pour Irish cream and Chambord into a cup of hot coffee.

One of many international coffees.

Irish Betty

6 oz. hot milk
1 tsp. sugar
1½ oz. Irish whiskey

Pour the milk into a mug. Add the sugar and whiskey. Stir well.

Irish Buck

1½ oz. Jameson Irish Whiskey
Lemon peel
Ginger ale

Pour whiskey into chilled highball glass with cracked ice. Twist a lemon peel over the drink and drop it in. Fill with ginger ale.

Irish-Canadian Sangaree

2 tsp. Irish whiskey
1¼ oz. Canadian whisky
1 tsp. orange juice
1 tsp. lemon juice
Nutmeg for garnish

Combine and stir well. Add ice and dust with nutmeg.

Irish Candy

1½ oz. Baileys Irish Cream
½ oz. chocolate raspberry liqueur
½ oz. white crème de cacao

Build over ice. Stir and serve.

Irish Car Bomb

1 oz. Irish whiskey
½ oz. Baileys Irish Cream
½ glass Guinness Stout

Add Irish whiskey into a shot glass and pour the Baileys slowly over, causing it to layer. Serve side by side with the Guinness.

Also called Irish Slammer, Irish Drop Shot, or Dublin Drop. Guest should drop shot into the pint and drink.

Irish Celebration

1¼ oz. Bushmills Irish Whiskey
¼ oz. green crème de menthe
Splash champagne

Shake the first two ingredients well with ice and strain. Top with champagne.

Irish Charlie

1 oz. Irish cream
1 oz. white crème de menthe

Shake with ice and strain into a shot glass.

You can also layer the Irish cream over the crème de menthe.

Irish Coffee

1¼ oz. Irish whiskey
Hot coffee
Cream
Sugar

Pour Irish whiskey in a warm glass or mug. Fill with coffee. Stir in cream and sugar to taste.

Irish Collins

2 oz. Irish whiskey
1 tsp. powdered sugar
Juice of a small lemon
Club soda

Combine the first three ingredients in a tall glass filled with ice. Fill with club soda and stir.

A variation on the Tom Collins and Whiskey Collins.

Irish Cooler

2 oz. Irish whiskey
6 oz. club soda
Lemon peel for garnish

Pour whiskey into a highball glass over ice cubes. Top with soda and stir. Garnish with a lemon peel spiral.

Irish Cowboy

1 oz. Baileys Irish Cream
1½ oz. bourbon

Shake or stir over ice.

Irish Dream

½ oz. Irish cream
½ oz. hazelnut liqueur
½ oz. dark crème de cacao
1 scoop vanilla ice cream

Combine ingredients in a blender with ice. Blend thoroughly. Pour into a Collins or parfait glass. Serve with a straw.

Irish Eyes

1 oz. Irish whiskey
¼ oz. green crème de menthe
2 oz. heavy cream
Maraschino cherry for garnish

Shake well with crushed ice. Strain into a chilled cocktail glass. Garnish with maraschino cherry.

This will make you smile.

Irish Fix

2 oz. Irish whiskey
½ oz. Irish Mist Liqueur
1 oz. pineapple juice
½ oz. lemon juice
½ tsp. simple syrup

Fill glass with ice. Combine ingredients and stir.

Irish Flag

⅓ shot green crème de menthe
⅓ shot Irish cream
⅓ shot Grand Marnier

Layer this drink in the order listed. Start with crème de menthe on the bottom and finish with Grand Marnier on top.

Irish Goodbye

¾ oz. Midori
¾ oz. Baileys Irish Cream, chilled

Layer this drink by pouring the Midori first and then adding the Irish cream.

Irish Kiss

¾ oz. Irish whiskey
½ oz. peach schnapps
4 oz. ginger ale
2 oz. orange juice
Lime wheel for garnish

Combine ingredients in an ice cube–filled Collins glass. Garnish with a lime wheel.

Irish Knight

2 oz. Bushmills Irish Whiskey
2 dashes Noilly Prat
   Dry Vermouth
2 dashes Bénédictine
Orange peel for garnish

Combine in a rocks glass with ice. Add a twist of orange peel.

Irish Mule

2 oz. Irish whiskey
½ oz. fresh lime juice
4 oz. ginger beer

Pour all ingredients over ice in a glass. Stir.

Irish Rainbow

1½ oz. Irish whiskey
3–4 dashes Pernod
3–4 dashes Orange Curaçao
3–4 dashes maraschino liqueur
3–4 dashes bitters

Mix all ingredients with cracked ice in a shaker or blender. Pour into a chilled rocks glass. Twist an orange peel over the drink and drop it in.

Irish Rickey

1½ oz. Tullamore Dew
1 cube ice
Juice of ½ lime
Carbonated water
Lime wedge for garnish

Combine first three ingredients in a highball glass. Fill with carbonated water and stir. Add a lime wedge.

Irish Rose

1½ oz. Jameson Irish Whiskey
½ oz. Plymouth Sloe Gin
⅓ oz. St- Germain
    Elderflower Liqueur
3 drops rose water
3 lime squeezes
Ginger ale
Rose petal for garnish (optional)

Add all ingredients except the ginger ale into a mixing glass. Shake and strain over fresh ice in a highball glass. Top with ginger ale. Garnish with a lime squeeze and rose petal (if desired).

Irish Shillelagh

1½ oz. Irish whiskey
½ oz. Sloe Gin
½ oz. light rum
1 oz. lemon juice
1 tsp. simple syrup
2 peach slices, diced
Raspberries and cherry
    for garnish

Mix all ingredients with cracked ice in a shaker or blender. Pour into a chilled rocks glass. Garnish with raspberries and a cherry.

Irish Sling

1 lump sugar
1 oz. Tullamore Dew
1 oz. gin

Crush sugar with ice in a glass. Add Tullamore Dew and gin. Stir.

Irish Sour

1½ oz. Irish whiskey
1 tsp. sugar
Juice of ½ lemon
Maraschino cherry and orange
  slice for garnish

Shake vigorously with ice until frothy. Stir into sour glass. Add a maraschino cherry and an orange slice.

Iron Cross

1 part apricot brandy
1 part Rumple Minze

Layer brandy over Rumple Minze in a shot glass.

Isla Grande Iced Tea

1½ oz. dark rum
3 oz. pineapple juice
Unsweetened brewed iced tea

Combine the first two ingredients in a tall glass with ice. Fill with iced tea.

Island Tea

1½ oz. vodka
1 oz. grenadine
1 tsp. lemon juice
Mint sprig for garnish

Combine with ice and shake. Strain over ice in a rocks glass and garnish with a mint sprig.

Italian Colada

¼ oz. Coco Lopez Cream
  of Coconut
1½ oz. Puerto Rican white rum
¼ oz. amaretto
¾ oz. sweet cream
2 oz. pineapple juice

Blend with crushed ice.

Italian Stallion

1½ oz. Dewar's White
  Label Scotch
2 oz. Galliano

Stir ingredients in an ice-filled rocks glass. Serve on the rocks.

Jackie's Juice

2 oz. Riazul Extra Añejo Tequila
4 oz. Coco Lopez Coconut Water
Squeeze of lime juice

Toss over crushed ice in a rocks glass with a lime squeeze.

J.D.'s Hideout

2 oz. Irish whiskey
¾ oz. lemon juice
¼ oz. honey syrup

Add all ingredients into shaker and strain into a highball glass filled with ice.

Inspired by J.D. Fallon.

J.J.'s Shamrock

1 oz. Irish whiskey
½ oz. white crème de cacao
½ oz. green crème de menthe
1 oz. milk

Mix in a shaker or blender with cracked ice and serve in a chilled glass.

Jack & Coke

1¾ oz. Jack Daniel's Whiskey
3 oz. cola

Combine over ice and stir.

Jack of Spades

1 oz. lemon juice
1 egg white
2 oz. Tanqueray no. TEN Gin
¾ oz. blackberry syrup

Add lemon juice and egg white into a shaker and dry shake vigorously. Then, add in the gin, blackberry syrup (1:1 blackberries and water), and ice and shake. Double strain into a coupe glass and serve.

Inspired by J. Muskett III.

Jack Rose

2 oz. Laird's Applejack
1 oz. lemon juice
½ oz. grenadine
Lemon twist for garnish

Shake and strain. Garnish with lemon twist

Jackson Martini

1½ oz. Absolut Vodka
Dash Dubonnet
Dash bitters

Stir with ice. Serve with ice or strain.

Jade

1½ oz. white rum
¾ oz. lime juice
1 bar spoon sugar
Dash triple sec
Dash green crème de menthe

Shake with ice. Serve over ice.

Jäger Bomb

1½ oz. Jägermeister
½ can Red Bull

Serve in a glass with ice.

Drop a shot glass of Jäger into a pint glass with Red Bull, and then drink the whole thing.

Jalisco Old Fashioned

2 oz. reposado tequila
1 tsp. agave nectar
2 dashes angostura
    orange bitters
Orange peel for garnish

Add all ingredients into a glass and stir. Garnish with orange peel.

Jamaican Dust

1 oz. Mount Gay Rum
½ oz. coffee liqueur
½ oz. pineapple juice

Shake with ice and strain into a shot glass.

James Bond Martini #1

3 oz. Gordon's Gin
1 oz. vodka
½ oz. Lillet Blanc
Lemon peel for garnish

Shake ingredients with ice until very cold. Pour into a chilled glass. Then add a large, thin slice of lemon peel.

From the 1967 movie Casino Royale.

James Bond Martini #2

½ oz. Martini & Rossi Extra
    Dry Vermouth
1½ oz. vodka
1½ oz. gin
½ oz. Lillet Blanc
Lemon twist for garnish

Stir with ice and strain. Garnish with a lemon twist.

Jamie's Highland Special

½ oz. green crème de menthe
½ oz. Galliano
½ oz. blackberry liqueur
½ oz. Kirschwasser

Layer this drink in the order listed. Start with crème de menthe on the bottom and finish with Kirschwasser on top.

Japanese Highball

2 oz. Japanese whisky
4 oz. soda water

Combine ingredients in a highball glass with ice. Stir and serve.

Japanese Old Fashioned

1½ oz. Japanese whisky
¼ oz. simple syrup
3–4 dashes angostura bitters
Orange peel for garnish

Add all ingredients into a glass and stir. Garnish with orange peel

Also can sub in green tea simple syrup!

Japanese Sidecar

2 oz. sake
1 oz. apricot liqueur
½ oz. simple syrup
¼ oz. fresh lemon juice

Combine all ingredients in a shaker and shake vigorously. Strain into a chilled cocktail glass.

Japanese Sour

1 egg white
2 oz. Japanese whisky
¼ oz. lemon juice
¼ oz. yuzu or lime juice
¼ oz. honey
2 dashes angostura bitters

Add in egg white to the shaker and dry shake vigorously. Then, add in all liquid ingredients with ice and shake vigorously again. Shake and double strain into a chilled glass. Garnish with a few light dashes of angostura bitters.

Jelly Bean

1 oz. anisette
1 oz. blackberry-flavored brandy

Combine in a rocks glass over ice.

You can also strain this one into a shot glass.

Jellyfish

1 oz. Irish cream
1 oz. white crème de cacao
1 oz. amaretto
1 oz. grenadine

Pour first three ingredients directly into the glass. Pour grenadine in the center of the glass.

Jersey Devil

1½ oz. Laird's Applejack
½ oz. Cointreau
½ tsp. sugar
½ oz. Rose's Lime Juice
½ oz. cranberry juice

Shake ingredients and serve over ice.

John Daily

2 oz. vodka
2 oz. lemonade
2 oz. iced tea
Lemon wedge for garnish

Add all ingredients into a highball glass with ice. Stir and serve. Garnish with lemon wedge.

John Collins

1 oz. lemon juice
½ oz. simple syrup
2 oz. bourbon or whiskey
4 oz. club soda
Lemon wheel and maraschino cherry for garnish

Pour lemon juice, simple syrup, and whiskey in a highball glass filled with ice. Fill the glass with club soda and stir. Garnish with a skewer of a lemon wheel and maraschino cherry.

This is Tom's brother.

Johnnie on the Spot

1½ oz. Johnnie Walker Green Label
½ oz. apple syrup
3 oz. chai tea

Add all ingredients into a coffee or tea mug and stir.

Jolly Rancher #1

¾ oz. peach schnapps
¾ oz. apple schnapps
2½ oz. cranberry juice

Combine in a tall glass with ice.

Jolly Rancher #2

¾ oz. Midori
¾ oz. peach schnapps
¾ oz. cranberry juice

Shake with ice and strain into a shot glass.

Journalist Martini

1½ oz. dry gin
¼ oz. sweet vermouth
¼ oz. dry vermouth
1 dash bitters
1 dash lemon juice
1 dash Orange Curaçao

Stir with ice. Serve over ice or strain.

Juicy Fruit

1 oz. Absolut Vodka
½ oz. peach schnapps
½ oz. Midori
½ oz. pineapple juice

Shake with ice and strain into a shot glass.

Jumping Gerry

1¼ oz. rum
4 oz. pineapple juice
½ oz. lime juice
Dash bitters

Shake with ice and serve over ice.

Inspired by G. Scales

Jungle Bird

1½ oz. rum
¾ oz. Campari
1½ oz. pineapple juice
½ oz. lime juice
½ oz. demerara syrup
Pineapple wedge for garnish

Shake and strain into a rocks glass with ice. Garnish with pineapple wedge and serve.

Kahlúa & Cream

2 oz. Kahlúa
1 oz. cream/milk

Combine in a rocks glass and stir.

The Kahlúa Colada

1 oz. Coco Lopez Cream
   of Coconut
2 oz. pineapple juice
1 oz. Kahlúa
½ oz. rum
1 cup ice

Blend with ice and serve in a
margarita glass.

Kahlúa Iced Cappuccino

1½ oz. Kahlúa
1 oz. Irish cream
4 oz. cold coffee
Dash cinnamon

Pour Kahlúa and Irish cream into
coffee and sprinkle with cinnamon.

Kath's Clockout

1 oz. Kahlúa
1 oz. dark rum
2 scoops vanilla or
   chocolate ice cream
1 cup of ice

Blend with ice.

Inspired by K.B. Fallon

Kamikaze

1 oz. vodka
½ oz. Cointreau
¼ oz. Rose's Lime Juice

Shake with ice and strain into a shot
glass.

Kentucky Cocktail

2 oz. bourbon
2½ oz. pineapple juice

Shake with ice and serve over ice or
strain.

Kentucky Colonel

1½ oz. Jim Beam Bourbon
½ oz. Bénédictine
Lemon twist for garnish

Shake with ice. Strain into chilled cocktail glass. Add a lemon twist.

Kentucky Martini

1½ oz. Maker's Mark Bourbon
½ oz. amaretto
2 oz. Orange Slice Soda

Stir with ice; strain.

Invented at the Martini Bar at the Chianti Restaurant in Houston, TX. A Kentucky Martini from a bar in Texas — only in America.

Kerry Cooler

2 oz. Irish whiskey
1½ oz. sherry
1¼ tbsp. crème de almond
1¼ tbsp. lemon juice
Club soda
Lemon slice for garnish

Combine (except the soda) with ice and shake well. Strain into a glass with ice and add soda. Top with a lemon slice.

Key Largo

2 oz. Mount Gay Rum
½ oz. Coco Lopez Cream
    of Coconut
1 scoop orange sherbet
Orange slice for garnish

Blend ingredients slowly. Garnish with an orange slice.

Key Lime Pie

2 oz. Licor 43
1 oz. vodka
Splash lime juice

Shake over ice and strain.

Kilkenny Waterfall

6 fresh blueberries, plus more
    for garnish
½ oz. simple syrup
1½ oz. Irish whiskey
2 oz. apple juice
½ oz. pineapple juice
1 dash cherry bitters

In a Boston shaker, add blueberries and simple syrup; muddle hard. Fill the shaker with ice and add all other ingredients. Shake well and double strain into a tall glass filled with ice. Garnish with blueberries on a cocktail pick.

Killer Colada

2 oz. coconut rum
3 tbsp. Coco Lopez Coconut Milk
3 tbsp. pineapple (crushed)
2 cups crushed ice
Pineapple wedge for garnish

Blend at high speed. Serve with a pineapple wedge.

King Alphonse

1 oz. dark crème de cacao
1 oz. cream

Layer the cream on top of the crème de cacao.

King George Cocktail

1¼ oz. Crown Royal
    Canadian Whisky
½ oz. lemon juice
1½ oz. pineapple juice
½ oz. simple syrup
1 oz. club soda
Orange wheel and cherry
    for garnish

Shake the whisky, juices, and simple syrup and top with club soda. Strain into a highball glass and garnish with half an orange wheel skewered with a cherry.

Kir or Kir Royale

3 oz. champagne
Splash crème de cassis

Fill the glass with champagne and add a splash of crème de cassis.

Kissed by a Rose

1 oz. Tanqueray no. TEN Gin
1 oz. Aperol
1 oz. lingonberry-infused
    Lillet Rosè
Rose petal for garnish

To make the infusion, combine equal parts Lillet and lingonberry jam, muddle lingonberries, and let sit for three days. Strain through chinois. Then, combine all ingredients into a mixing glass with ice and stir. Double strain into a rocks glass, serve over a large ice cube, and garnish with a rose petal.

Created by R. Kling, Washington, D.C.

Kiss Me Katie

1 oz. Irish cream
½ oz. crème de cacao
½ oz. raspberry liqueur

Shake with ice and strain into a shot glass.

Kiwi Caipirinha

2 oz. cachaça
½ lime
½ kiwi
1 tbsp. refined sugar
¼ oz. sweet lemonade

In a shaker, muddle lime, kiwi, sugar, and sweet lemonade. Add in cachaça and ice and shake. Strain into an ice-filled rocks glass and serve.

Created by A. Vieira, Hoboken, NJ.

Kiwi Cooler

½ kiwi, plus more for garnish
2 oz. tequila
½ oz. lime juice
½ oz. agave nectar
1 oz. cucumber juice

Muddle kiwi in a shaker. Add all other ingredients and fill with cubed ice. Shake and then strain into a Collins glass over cubed ice. Garnish with kiwi discs.

Koala Hug

1¼ oz. Jameson Irish Whiskey
2 oz. lemon juice
1 oz. Cointreau
Dash Pernod
Orange slice for garnish

Shake with ice. Serve in a tall glass with ice cubes. Garnish with an orange slice and straws.

Kokonut Breeze

2 parts coconut vodka
1 part Coco Lopez Coconut Water
1 part pineapple juice
½ part simple syrup
Lemon wedge for garnish

Build ingredients in a highball glass and stir. Add ice and garnish with a lemon wedge.

Krazy Kangaroo

1¼ oz. Jameson Irish Whiskey
Dash Pernod
2 oz. orange juice
Orange rind for garnish

Pour into a mixing glass with ice. Stir and strain into a glass or serve over ice. Garnish with orange rind.

Kretchma

1 oz. vodka
1 oz. crème de cacao
½ oz. lemon juice
½ tsp. grenadine

Mix all ingredients with cracked ice in a shaker or blender. Strain into a chilled glass.

La Bomba

1¼ oz. tequila
¾ oz. Cointreau
1½ oz. pineapple juice
1½ oz. orange juice
2 dashes grenadine
Lime wheel for garnish

Shake all ingredients except grenadine. Pour into glass and add grenadine. Garnish with a lime wheel.

Lady Day

1 egg white (optional)
1 oz. Tanqueray Gin
1 oz. fresh passion fruit puree
1 oz. Campari
½ oz. honey
Angostura bitters

If using egg white, hard shake dry. Then, in the same shaker, add all other ingredients with ice and shake. Double strain into a coupe glass and garnish with drops of angostura bitters.

Created by W. Codman, Boston, MA.

Lady Hamilton

2 oz. dark rum
⅛ oz. fresh lime juice
1 oz. passion fruit juice
1 oz. orange juice
1 oz. ginger ale
Maraschino cherry and pineapple slice for garnish

Combine ingredients in a tall glass. Garnish with a maraschino cherry and a pineapple slice.

Lady Nora

1½ oz. mezcal
1 oz. rosé
½ oz. lime juice
4 oz. grapefruit soda

Rim a rocks glass with salt and set aside. Combine first three ingredients into a cocktail shaker with ice and shake. Strain into rimmed glass and top with grapefruit soda.

La Jollarita

1½ oz. tequila
½ oz. Cointreau
½ oz. Chambord

Shake, strain, and serve.

Last Word

¾ oz. gin
¾ oz. Green Chartreuse
¾ oz. maraschino liqueur
¾ oz. fresh lime juice

Shake and strain into a chilled martini glass.

Latin Lover

1 oz. tequila
½ oz. amaretto

Combine in a rocks glass over ice.

You can also serve this one as a shot (without the ice).

Lemon Chiffon

1½ oz. vodka
¼ oz. triple sec
1 oz. sweet & sour mix
Lemon wedge

Shake ingredients with ice and serve over ice. Squeeze and drop in a fresh lemon wedge.

Lemon Ice

¼ oz. lemon
2 tsp. sugar
2 oz. vanilla vodka
Top with ginger ale

Muddle fresh lemon with sugar and place in a Collins glass. Add ice and vanilla vodka. Fill with ginger ale.

Lemongrad

1½ oz. citrus vodka
3–4 oz. cranberry juice

Serve over ice.

Lemontini

Cointreau
2 oz. citrus vodka
½ oz. dry vermouth

Line a cocktail glass with Cointreau and pour out excess. Combine vodka and vermouth over ice in a mixing glass. Strain into the cocktail glass.

Leprechaun

1½ oz. Irish whiskey
3 oz. tonic water
3–4 ice cubes
Lemon peel for garnish

Put whiskey and tonic water in a rocks glass. Add ice cubes and stir gently. Drop in a slice of lemon peel.

Leprechaun's Libation

3½ oz. cracked ice
½ oz. green crème de menthe
½ oz. Bushmills Irish Whiskey

Fill blender with cracked ice. Add crème de menthe and Bushmills Irish Whiskey. Blend. Pour into a goblet or large wine glass.

Courtesy of Beach Grill in Westminster, CO.

Liar's Martini

1½ oz. dry gin
½ oz. Martini & Rossi Extra
  Dry Vermouth
¼ oz. Orange Curaçao
¼ oz. sweet vermouth

Stir gently with ice and strain.

Who lies after a couple of chilled Martinis?

Licorice Stick

1 oz. vodka
1 oz. anisette
½ oz. triple sec

Shake with ice and strain into a shot glass.

Lillet Spritzer

2 oz. Lillet Blanc
¼ oz. triple sec
Brut champagne
Orange slice for garnish

Build cocktail over ice, top with champagne, and garnish with an orange slice.

You can substitute club soda for the champagne.

Li'l Orphan Annie

1½ oz. Irish whiskey
1 oz. Baileys Irish Cream
1 tbsp. chocolate syrup
1 tsp. shaved chocolate

Combine all ingredients except the shaved chocolate in a shaker and shake vigorously. Strain into a glass. Garnish with shaved chocolate.

Limp Deuces

1 oz. cinnamon schnapps
1 oz. Rumple Minze

Layer schnapps over Rumple Minze.

Loca Pasión (Crazy Passion)

1½ oz. tequila
2 oz. pomegranate juice
2 oz. chilled champagne
Splash grenadine
1 fresh strawberry

Pour tequila, pomegranate juice, and champagne into a glass flute. Top with grenadine and a whole strawberry.

Long Island Iced Tea

½ oz. vodka
½ oz. rum
½ oz. gin
½ oz. triple sec
½ oz. tequila
½ oz. sour mix
Cola

Shake the first six ingredients over ice and strain into a glass. Top with cola.

There are many variations on this popular drink.

WHAT TWISTED GENIUS CREATED LONG ISLAND ICED TEA?

This drink does hail from Long Island, specifically the Oak Beach Inn in Hampton Bays. Spirits writer John Mariani credits bartender Robert (Rosebud) Butt as the inventor, whose original recipe called for an ounce each of clear liquors (vodka, gin, tequila, light rum), a half ounce of triple sec, some lemon juice, and a splash of cola.

This drink comes in many forms and is still popular with young drinkers, though not with those who have to get up early the next day.

Long Island Sweet Tea

½ oz. Seagram's Sweet Tea Vodka
½ oz. gin
½ oz. dark rum
½ oz. añejo tequila
½ oz. triple sec
1 oz. sweet & sour mix
3 oz. cola

Combine ingredients in a tall glass with ice.

Lost Lake

2 oz. aged Jamaican rum
¾ oz. passion fruit syrup
¾ oz. fresh lime juice
½ oz. pineapple juice
¼ oz. maraschino liqueur
¼ oz. Campari

Shake and strain into a tall glass with pebble or crushed ice.

Named for the Lost Lake Bar in Chicago.

Lovers' Margarita

1 oz. Agavero
1 oz. reposado tequila
Splash fresh lime juice
Lime wedge for garnish

Pour over ice. Garnish with a lime wedge. Salt the rim beforehand if you prefer.

Double the recipe and serve with two straws per couple.

Low Tide Martini

3 oz. vodka
½ oz. dry vermouth
1 tsp. clam juice
Smoked clam for garnish

Shake ingredients with ice and strain into a chilled martini glass. Garnish with a smoked clam.

Loyal Martini

2 oz. Ketel One Vodka
3 drops balsamic vinegar

Stir gently with ice; strain.

From the Bar d'O in New York, NY.

Lucky Lady

¾ oz. light rum
¼ oz. anisette
¼ oz. white crème de cacao
¾ oz. cream

Blend with crushed ice and serve in a margarita glass.

Madras

1¼ oz. vodka
2 oz. orange juice
2 oz. cranberry juice

Pour vodka over ice in a tall glass. Fill halfway with orange juice and top it off with cranberry juice.

The Mage

1 oz. gin
¼ oz. St-Germain Elderflower Liqueur
½ oz. fresh lemon juice
½ oz. simple syrup
¼ tsp. butterfly pea powder
4 oz. sparkling water

Add all ingredients except sparkling water into a cocktail shaker with ice. Shake and strain into a highball with ice. Top with sparkling water and serve.

Inspired by J. D'Alessandro.

Magical Mojito

8–10 mint leaves
2 oz. Bacardi Limon Rum
¾ oz. fresh lime juice
2 dashes bitters
1 fist-size ball pink cotton candy
1 sprig fresh mint for garnish

In a mixing glass, gently muddle the mint leaves. Add rum, lime juice, and bitters with ice and shake vigorously. Place cotton candy atop a chilled cocktail glass and carefully strain the drink over the cotton candy, allowing it to melt into the drink. Garnish with a sprig of fresh mint.

Mai Tai

1½ oz. white rum
¾ oz. dark rum
½ oz. Orange Curaçao
½ oz. fresh lime juice
½ oz. orgeat syrup
Mint, cherry, and pineapple
    for garnish

Shake and strain. Garnish with mint, cherry, and pineapple.

Some also add in simple syrup, but we like this recipe.

Maiden's Prayer

2 oz. dry gin
½ oz. Cointreau
½ oz. orange juice
½ oz. lemon juice

Shake with ice and strain into a glass.

FABLES AND LORE

MAI TAI: OUT OF THIS WORLD

Vic Bergeron invented the Mai Tai in 1944 at his Polynesian-style Oakland bar. He didn't want fruit juices detracting from the two ounces of J. Wray Nephew Jamaican rum he poured as the base for his creation. He merely added a half ounce of French orgeat (an almond-flavored syrup), a half ounce of Orange Curaçao, a quarter ounce of rock candy syrup, and the juice of one lime. Customer Carrie Wright of Tahiti, the first to taste the concoction, responded, "Mai tai . . . roe ae!" (Tahitian for "Out of this world . . . the best!")

The Mai Tai became famous, and conflicting stories about its origins aggravated Bergeron so much that he elicited a sworn statement from Mrs. Wright in 1970, testifying to his authorship of the cocktail.

Main Squeeze #1

1½ oz. crème de strawberry
   liqueur
2 oz. cranberry juice
2 oz. orange juice
Club soda

Combine first three ingredients in a
tall glass and top with club soda.

Main Squeeze #2

1½ parts Stoli Ohranj Vodka
¼ part triple sec
1 part freshly squeezed
   orange juice
Club soda
Orange slice

Build vodka, triple sec, and orange
juice over ice in a tall glass and stir.
Fill with club soda to the top and
garnish with an orange slice.

Malibu Bay Breeze

1½ oz. Malibu Rum
2 oz. cranberry juice
2 oz. pineapple juice

Combine over ice.

Malibu Cove

½ oz. Malibu Rum
½ oz. Myers's Dark Rum
½ oz. white rum
2 oz. pineapple juice
2 oz. sweet & sour mix

Shake all ingredients with ice and
serve over ice.

Malibu Rain

1 oz. vodka
1½ oz. pineapple juice
½ oz. Malibu Rum
Splash orange juice

Shake with ice and serve over ice.

Mamie Taylor

2 oz. blended scotch
¾ oz. fresh lime juice
Ginger beer

Add in blended scotch and fresh
lime juice into a rocks glass with ice.
Stir and fill with ginger beer.

Manhattan

2 oz. rye whiskey
1 oz. sweet vermouth
2 dashes angostura bitters
Cherry for garnish

Add all ingredients in a mixing glass and stir. Strain into a chilled coupe glass. Garnish with a cherry.

Mango Margarita

2 oz. tequila
1½ oz. mango juice
¾ oz. lime juice
½ oz. agave syrup

Add all ingredients into a cocktail shaker with ice and shake. Strain into a rimmed rocks glass filled with ice and serve.

Maple Old Fashioned

2 oz. bourbon
½ oz. maple simple syrup
2 dashes bitters
Orange peel for garnish

Create your own maple simple syrup by combining 1 cup maple syrup and 1 cup water into a pot and bring to a boil. In a rocks glass, add in maple simple syrup, bourbon, and bitters and stir. Garnish with orange peel.

Margarita

1 oz. tequila
1 oz. Cointreau or triple sec
1 oz. sweet & sour mix or
    lime juice
1 cup of crushed ice
Lime wheel for garnish

Blend with crushed ice. Serve in a salt-rimmed glass. Garnish with a lime wheel.

MANHATTAN

FABLES AND LORE

The Manhattan recipe was created around 1874 at the Manhattan Club, New York, for Lady Randolph Churchill, Winston's mother. She was attending a banquet in honor of the lawyer and politician Samuel J. Tilden.

Margarita Madres

1¼ oz. Jose Cuervo Gold Tequila
½ oz. Cointreau
½ oz. sweet & sour mix
1½ oz. orange juice
1½ oz. cranberry juice
Lime wedge for garnish

Blend with crushed ice. Garnish with a lime wedge.

Martini

2 oz. gin
1 oz. dry vermouth
Lemon twist or green olive for garnish

Add ingredients into a mixing glass with ice and stir. Strain into a martini glass. Garnish with a lemon twist or a green olive.

Martini Bellini

2 oz. vodka or gin
¼ oz. peach schnapps

Shake or stir vodka or gin and schnapps over ice. Strain and serve in a cocktail glass straight up or over ice.

From the Gallery Lounge Sheraton in Seattle, WA.

Martini Picante

2 oz. Absolut Peppar Vodka
Jalapeño
Olive

Stir with ice and strain. Add a jalapeño and an olive.

From the Gallery Lounge Sheraton in Seattle, WA.

Martinez

2 oz. gin
1½ oz. sweet vermouth
¼ oz. Luxardo
    Maraschino Liqueur
2 dashes angostura bitters

Add ingredients into a mixing glass with ice. Stir and strain into a chilled coupe glass.

Matcha Highball

2 oz. Japanese whisky
½ oz. fresh lemon juice
½ oz. honey syrup
¼ tsp. matcha green tea powder
Club soda
Lemon wheel for garnish

Add all ingredients except club soda into a shaker with ice. Shake and strain into highball glass with ice. Top with club soda and garnish with lemon wheel and serve.

Mary Pickford

1½ oz. white rum
1½ oz. pineapple juice
1 splash grenadine

Shake with crushed ice. Serve over ice or strain.

Named after the actress.

Melon Ball

¾ oz. Midori
1 oz. vodka
4 oz. orange juice

Combine in a glass and stir.

Menil

3 raspberries
1½ oz. Yellow Rose
    Outlaw Bourbon
¾ oz. lemon juice
¾ oz. simple syrup
3 dashes Peychaud's Bitters
Sparkling rosé

Muddle raspberries in a cocktail shaker. Add ice and remaining ingredients. Double strain into a flute and top with sparkling rosé.

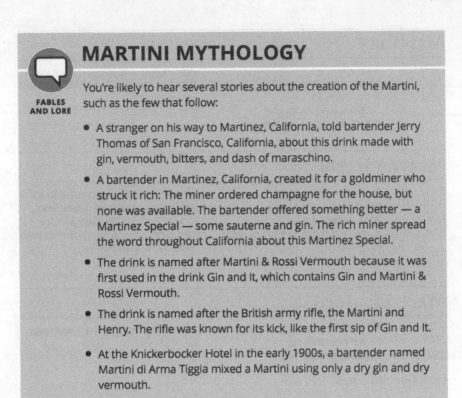

MARTINI MYTHOLOGY

FABLES AND LORE

You're likely to hear several stories about the creation of the Martini, such as the few that follow:

- A stranger on his way to Martinez, California, told bartender Jerry Thomas of San Francisco, California, about this drink made with gin, vermouth, bitters, and dash of maraschino.

- A bartender in Martinez, California, created it for a goldminer who struck it rich: The miner ordered champagne for the house, but none was available. The bartender offered something better — a Martinez Special — some sauterne and gin. The rich miner spread the word throughout California about this Martinez Special.

- The drink is named after Martini & Rossi Vermouth because it was first used in the drink Gin and It, which contains Gin and Martini & Rossi Vermouth.

- The drink is named after the British army rifle, the Martini and Henry. The rifle was known for its kick, like the first sip of Gin and It.

- At the Knickerbocker Hotel in the early 1900s, a bartender named Martini di Arma Tiggia mixed a Martini using only a dry gin and dry vermouth.

Metropolitan

1 oz. sweet vermouth
1½–2 oz. brandy
½ tsp. simple syrup
2 dashes bitters
4–5 ice cubes

Combine all ingredients except one or two ice cubes in a shaker and shake vigorously. Put one or two ice cubes in a chilled cocktail glass. Strain the drink into the glass.

Mexican Banana

1½ oz. Sauza Tequila
¾ oz. crème de banana

Pour ingredients into a rocks glass filled with ice.

Mexican Berry

1 oz. Chambord
1 oz. Jose Cuervo Tequila

Shake with ice and strain into a shot glass.

Mexican Candy

1 oz. Ghost Tequila (spicy tequila)
½ oz. watermelon pucker
¼ oz. lime juice
Tajin

Add all ingredients into a shaker with ice. Shake and strain into a tajin-rimmed glass with ice.

Mexican Hot Tea

1½ oz. tequila
Hot water
½ tsp. sugar
1 pat butter
Cinnamon stick and nutmeg

Pour tequila into a rocks glass and fill with hot water. Add sugar and stir in butter. Garnish with a cinnamon stick and a sprinkle of nutmeg.

Mexico Rose

½ oz. Dano's Dangerous Tequila
1 oz. lime Juice
½ oz. grenadine (or crème de cassis)

Combine in a rocks glass filled with ice.

Mezcal Express

2 oz. San Cosme Mezcal
2 oz. pineapple juice
½ oz. lemon juice
Tajin
Pineapple wedge for garnish

Add all the ingredients in a mixing glass and stir with a spoon. Pour into a tall glass and add Tajin. Garnish with pineapple wedge.

Mezcal Margarita

2 oz. mezcal
¾ oz. lime juice
½ oz. agave syrup

Add all ingredients into a cocktail shaker with ice and shake. Strain into a rimmed rocks glass filled with ice and serve.

Mezcal Mule

2 oz. mezcal
½ oz. agave nectar
¾ oz. lime juice
4 oz. ginger beer
Lime wedge for garnish

Stir with ice. Garnish with a lime wedge.

Should be served in a bronze cup or mug.

Mezcal Negroni

1 oz. mezcal
1 oz. Campari
1 oz. sweet vermouth
Orange wheel for garnish

Stir with ice. Garnish with an orange wheel.

Miami Shades

1 oz. orange vodka
¼ oz. peach schnapps
2 oz. grapefruit juice

Combine over ice.

Miami Special

1 oz. Bacardi Light Rum
¼ oz. white crème de menthe
¾ oz. lemon or lime juice

Blend with ice.

Miami Vice

½ Strawberry Daiquiri
½ Piña Colada
Pineapple wedge for garnish

Pour the Strawberry Daiquiri into the bottom of the glass and top with Piña Colada. Garnish with pineapple wedge and serve.

See recipes for both Strawberry Daiquiri and Piña Colada later in this section.

Mickey Finn Martini

1½ oz. Absolut Vodka
Dash extra dry vermouth
Splash white crème de menthe
Mint leaf for garnish

Stir with ice and strain. Garnish with mint leaf.

Midnight Orchid

1½ oz. cranberry vodka
¼ oz. Chambord
2 oz. pineapple juice
½ oz. half & half

Shake. Serve over crushed ice or blend with ice.

Milanese Gin & Tonic

1 oz. Tanqueray no. TEN Gin
1 oz. Campari
Tonic water

Combine in a highball glass with ice, stir, and top with tonic water.

Milk & Honey

1 oz. Irish Mist Liqueur
1 oz. Irish cream

Combine in a rocks glass on ice.

Mimosa

3 oz. champagne
2 oz. orange Juice

Combine in a champagne flute and stir.

A classic brunch drink.

Mind Eraser

1½ oz. vodka
1½ oz. Kahlúa
Splash of club soda

Shake the vodka and Kahlúa with ice and strain into a shot glass. Top with club soda.

Mint Cooler

1 oz. gin
¼ oz. peppermint schnapps
Club soda

In a tall glass with ice, combine the first two ingredients. Fill the glass with club soda.

Mint Julep

5 mint leaves, plus more
  for garnish
¼ oz. simple syrup
2 oz. Maker's Mark Bourbon

In a glass, mash four mint leaves with simple syrup. Fill the cup with crushed ice. Add bourbon and garnish with a mint leaf.

A favorite at the Kentucky Derby. Don't forget that it's served in a silver or gold cup.

THE MIMOSA: A FRENCH CREATION

The Mimosa was created around 1925 at the Ritz Hotel Bar in Paris, France. It took its name from the mimosa flowering plant, whose color it resembles.

Mintini or Gin Stinger

2 oz. gin
¼ oz. white crème de menthe

Stir gently with ice and strain.

Mocha Melt

1 oz. Jose Cuervo Gold Tequila
5 oz. freshly brewed strong, hot coffee
1 pkg. hot cocoa mix (single-serving envelope)
½ oz. coffee brandy
Whipped cream

Combine ingredients in a glass and stir. Top with whipped cream.

Mocha Mint

¾ oz. coffee-flavored brandy
¾ oz. white crème de menthe
¾ oz. white crème de cacao

Combine ingredients in a glass and stir. Strain into a cocktail glass.

Mockingbird

1¼ oz. tequila
2 tsp. white crème de menthe
1 oz. fresh lime juice

Combine in a shaker and shake vigorously. Strain into a chilled cocktail glass with ice.

Mojito 🍸

¾ oz. simple syrup
½ lime, cut into wedges, plus
    more for garnish
8–10 mint leaves
2 oz. rum
¼ oz. club soda
Mint sprig for garnish

Combine simple syrup, lime, and mint leaves, and muddle ingredients to extract the juice of the limes. Fill glass halfway with crushed ice. Add rum and stir to combine. Top with more crushed ice and club soda. Garnish with a lime wedge and a sprig of fresh mint.

Mojito (Bee)

12 mint leaves
Juice of ½ lime
1 tsp. honey
2 oz. rum
1 oz. club soda
Mint sprig or lime wheel
    for garnish

Place mint leaves and crushed ice in a glass. Muddle well with a pestle. Add lime juice, honey, and rum. Stir well. Top off with club soda. Stir. Garnish with mint sprig or a lime wheel.

Monkey Gland

2 oz. Dry gin
1½ oz. fresh orange juice
1 tsp. grenadine
1 tsp. simple syrup
1 tsp. absinthe

Shake all ingredients in a shaker with ice. Strain into a chilled cocktail glass.

Monsoon

¼ oz. vodka
¼ oz. coffee liqueur
¼ oz. amaretto
¼ oz. Irish cream
¼ oz. hazelnut liqueur

Shake with ice; serve over ice.

Montego Margarita

1½ oz. rum
½ oz. triple sec
1 oz. lemon or lime juice
1 scoop crushed ice

Blend with crushed ice and serve.

Moonraker

1½ oz. Jose Cuervo
Especial Tequila
4 oz. pineapple juice
½ oz. Blue Curaçao

Pour the tequila and pineapple juice into a glass almost filled with ice cubes. Stir well. Drop the Curaçao into the center of the drink.

Morning Glory Fizz

2 oz. vodka
½ oz. white crème de cacao
1 oz. light cream
4 oz. club soda
Freshly grated nutmeg

Pour the vodka, crème de cacao, and cream into a shaker two-thirds full of ice cubes. Shake well. Strain into an ice-filled Collins glass. Add club soda; stir well. Sprinkle with nutmeg.

Moscow Chill

1½ oz. vodka
4 oz. Dr Pepper
Lime wedge for garnish

Pour vodka over shaved ice in a champagne glass. Fill with Dr Pepper. Garnish with a lime wedge.

Moscow Mule

1½ oz. Smirnoff Vodka
½ oz. lime juice
4 oz. ginger beer
Lime wedge for garnish

Stir with ice. Garnish with a lime wedge.

Should be served in a bronze cup or mug.

Mr. President

2 oz. rye whiskey
1 oz. ginger liqueur
Splash champagne

Combine rye whiskey and ginger liqueur in a shaker. Shake well and strain. Serve in a martini glass and float the champagne on top.

Ms. Tea

1¼ oz. Tito's Vodka
3 oz. iced tea

Mix with ice; serve over ice.

Mudslide

¼ oz. coffee liqueur
1 oz. vodka
¼ oz. Irish cream
Cola

Combine first three ingredients in a glass with ice and fill with cola.

My BFF

2 oz. Branca (Fernet)
2 oz. Fresca
Orange slice for garnish

Serve in a tall glass with ice and garnish with an orange slice.

Myers's Heatwave

¾ oz. Myers's Dark Rum
½ oz. peach schnapps
6 oz. pineapple juice
1 splash grenadine

Pour rum and schnapps over ice. Fill with pineapple juice and add a splash of grenadine.

Myers's Sharkbite

1¼ oz. Myers's Dark Rum
Orange juice
Splash grenadine

Add rum to a tall glass with ice. Fill with orange juice. Add a splash of grenadine.

Naked and Famous

¾ oz. Mezcal
¾ oz. Aperol
¾ oz. yellow chartreuse
¾ oz. lime juice

Add all ingredients into a cocktail shaker with ice. Shake and strain into a chilled coupe glass.

Nation Cocktail

1½ oz. tequila
1½ oz. pineapple juice
1½ oz. orange juice
¼ oz. Blue Curaçao

Combine first three ingredients over ice. Float Blue Curaçao.

You can also serve this one without ice.

Negroni ⟨Y⟩

1 oz. gin
1 oz. dry vermouth
1 oz. Campari
Orange peel for garnish

Combine in a rocks glass over ice. Garnish with an orange peel.

Nellie Jane

½ oz. Grand Marnier
1 oz. vanilla vodka
1 oz. orange vodka
½ oz. Marie Brizard Parfait Amour
Splash fresh lime juice
Orange peel for garnish

Combine ingredients in an ice-filled glass. Stir and strain. Garnish with an orange peel.

Nervous Breakdown

1½ oz. vodka
½ oz. Chambord
Splash cranberry juice
Soda

Combine the first three ingredients in a tall glass. Fill with soda.

Neva

1½ oz. vodka
½ oz. tomato juice
½ oz. orange juice

In a shaker, mix all ingredients. Pour over ice into a stemmed glass.

New Life

1 lump sugar
3 dashes bitters
1½ oz. tequila
Lemon twist for garnish

Muddle sugar and bitters in a rocks glass and fill with crushed ice. Add tequila. Garnish with a lemon twist.

New York Sour

Egg white (optional)
1½ oz. bourbon or rye whiskey
¾ oz. lemon juice
¾ oz. simple syrup
½ oz. red wine

If you're adding in egg white, you *must* dry shake first. Add ingredients into a shaker with ice and shake. Strain into a rocks glass and top with a float of red wine.

A twist on the classic sour recipe dating back to the 1870–1880s.

1951 Martini

Splash Cointreau
2 oz. Gordon's Gin
Anchovy-stuffed olive

Rinse glass with Cointreau. Add the gin and olive.

The return to another classic with a rinse.

Nut House

1½ oz. cranberry vodka
¼ oz. amaretto

Combine over ice.

Nuts & Berries

½ oz. vodka
½ oz. hazelnut liqueur
½ oz. coffee liqueur
¼ oz. cream

Combine with ice and shake. Strain and serve straight up in a rocks glass.

Nutty Professor

1 oz. Irish cream
1 oz. hazelnut liqueur
½ oz. Grand Marnier

Combine over ice.

You can also serve this one straight up in a shot glass.

O'Brian's Song

1 oz. Bushmills Irish Whiskey
½ oz. peach schnapps
1 oz. orange juice
1 oz. sweet & sour mix
Orange slice and cherry
    for garnish

Combine in a Collins glass with ice and stir well. Garnish with an orange slice and a cherry.

O'Casey's Terrier

1 oz. Baileys Irish Cream
1½ oz. J&B Scotch

Stir well over ice.

O'Conor's Toast

1½ oz. Bushmills Irish Whiskey
¼ oz. white crème de menthe

Shake. Serve straight up or over ice.

O'Fallon's Kiss

1½ oz. Irish whiskey
1 oz. peach schnapps
2 oz. orange juice
5 oz. ginger ale
Lime wedge for garnish

Combine over ice in a highball glass and garnish with a lime wedge.

O.J. Malachy

1½ oz. Irish whiskey
3 oz. orange juice

Combine in a tall glass over ice.

Oatmeal Cookie #1

½ oz. butterscotch schnapps
½ oz. Goldschläger
½ oz. Baileys Irish Cream

Layer with schnapps on the bottom, then the Goldschläger, and then the Irish cream.

Oatmeal Cookie #2

¾ oz. Baileys Irish Cream
¾ oz. butterscotch schnapps
½ oz. Jägermeister
¼ oz. cinnamon schnapps

Shake with ice and serve over ice.

You can also strain this one into a shot glass.

Oaxaca Old Fashioned

½ oz. reposado tequila
1½ oz. mezcal
1 tsp. agave nectar
2 dashes angostura bitters
Orange peel for garnish

Add all ingredients into a glass and stir. Garnish with orange peel.

The mezcal adds a little smoke to this version!

Oil Slick

1 oz. Rumple Minze
1 oz. bourbon

Shake with ice and strain into a shot glass.

Old Cuban

4 mint leaves
1 oz. simple syrup
¾ oz. fresh lime juice
1½ oz. aged rum
2 dashes angostura bitters
Champagne

In a cocktail shaker, muddle mint with simple syrup and fresh lime juice. Add in aged rum and bitters with ice and shake. Double strain into cocktail glass and top with champagne.

Old Fashioned (classic)

Cherry and orange slice
¼ tsp. superfine sugar
Splash club soda
1½ oz. American or Canadian Whisk(e)y
2 dashes angostura bitters

Muddle the cherry (without stem), orange slice, sugar, and a splash of club soda. Add the remaining ingredients and stir.

You can also use scotch, brandy, or just about any other spirit in this drink. See the "Oaxaca Old Fashioned" recipe for tequila and mezcal version.

Old Fashioned (modern)

2 oz. bourbon or rye whiskey
¼ oz. simple syrup
2-3 dashes angostura bitters
Orange peel or maraschino cherry for garnish

Add all ingredients into a glass and stir. Garnish with an orange peel or maraschino cherry.

Old Pal

1½ oz. rye whiskey
1 oz. Campari
1 oz. dry vermouth

Shake with ice and strain into a cocktail glass. Garnish with lemon twist.

Old San Juan

Lime wedge
1½ oz. gold rum
½ oz. cranberry juice
1 oz. fresh lime juice

Rim a chilled martini glass with the lime wedge. Combine other ingredients in cocktail shaker with ice. Shake well and strain into the glass. Squeeze lime wedge into the drink and drop it in.

Opening Cocktail

½ oz. Canadian Club Whisky
½ oz. sweet vermouth
½ oz. grenadine

Mix all ingredients in a shaker with crushed ice. Strain the mixture into a chilled cocktail glass.

Orange Blossom

1¼ oz. vodka
3 oz. orange juice
1 tsp. superfine sugar

Stir with ice in a tall glass.

Orange Crush

1½ oz. orange or regular vodka
1¾ oz. triple sec
2 oz. fresh squeezed orange juice

Shake with ice. Strain or serve over crushed ice.

Maryland's drink.

Orange Margarita

1½ oz. tequila
½ oz. triple sec
3 oz. orange juice
½ oz. sweet & sour mix
Strawberries for garnish

Blend. Garnish with strawberries.

Orange Treat

1½ oz. Bacardi O Rum
1½ oz. cream
2½ oz. orange juice

Combine ingredients in a shot glass or mix over ice in a rocks glass.

Orgasm #1

1 oz. Irish cream
1 oz. amaretto
½ oz. Kahlúa

Shake with ice and strain into a shot glass.

Orgasm #2

½ oz. Disaronno Amaretto
½ oz. Kahlúa
½ oz. Baileys Irish Cream
½ oz. cream

Shake with ice and strain into a shot glass.

Outrigger

1 oz. vodka
½ oz. peach schnapps
1 dash lime juice
2 oz. pineapple juice

Combine with ice in a shaker and shake. Strain over ice into a rocks glass.

P.G.'s Tea

1½ oz. rum
¼ oz. orange liqueur
¼ oz. lemon juice
Top with iced tea

Shake with ice and serve in a rocks glass. Top with iced tea.

Inspired by P. Getzow.

Paddy Cocktail

1½ oz. Irish whiskey
¾ oz. sweet vermouth
3–4 dashes bitters

Mix all ingredients with cracked ice in a shaker or blender. Serve in a chilled glass.

Paddy's Wagon

1½ oz. Irish whiskey
1½ oz. sweet vermouth
1–2 dashes bitters
1–2 dashes Southern Comfort

Combine all ingredients in a shaker and shake. Serve straight up or over ice in a chilled glass.

Painkiller

2 oz. Pusser's Rum
1 oz. pineapple juice
1 oz. fresh squeezed orange juice
1 oz. Coco Lopez Cream
    of Coconut
1 cup of ice
Nutmeg and pineapple wedge
    for garnish

Hard shake or blend all ingredients until smooth and pour into a chilled rocks glass. Garnish with freshly ground nutmeg and a pineapple wedge.

Paloma

2 oz. tequila
½ oz. fresh lime juice
Grapefruit soda
Lime wedge for garnish

Add tequila and fresh lime juice into a tall glass with ice. Top with grapefruit soda, stir, garnish with lime wedge, and serve.

Papa Negroni

1½ oz. Don Papa Rum
¾ oz. sweet vermouth
1 oz. Aperol
Sprig of rosemary and grapefruit
    wedge for garnish

In a mixing glass filled with ice, add all ingredients and stir gently. Garnish with rosemary sprig and grapefruit wedge.

Paper Plane

¾ oz. Bourbon
¾ oz. Aperol
¾ oz. Amaro Nonino
    Quintessentia
¾ oz. lemon juice

Add all ingredients into a cocktail shaker with ice. Shake and strain into a chilled coupe glass.

Parisian Pousse-Café

1 oz. Orange Curaçao
1 oz. Kirschwasser
½ oz. Green Chartreuse

Layer this drink in the order listed. Start with Curaçao on the bottom and finish with Chartreuse on top.

Park Avenue Princess

½ lemon
1½ oz. vodka
3 oz. 7UP
¼ oz. fresh lemon juice
¼ oz. red wine

Squeeze and drop half a lemon into a cocktail shaker. Add vodka, 7UP, and lemon juice with ice and stir. Strain into a tall Collins glass with fresh ice, and float red wine over the top of the drink.

Patio Punch

1 oz. Cruzan Citrus Rum
1 oz. Cruzan Pineapple Rum
Splash raspberry liqueur

Mix with ice. Top with orange juice.

Patrón Grapefruit

1 oz. Patrón Silver Tequila
¼ oz. Patrón Citrónge
    Orange Liqueur
2 oz. fresh grapefruit juice
Splash club soda
Grapefruit peel and lime slice
    for garnish

Pour Patrón Silver and Patrón Citrónge over ice. Add grapefruit juice. Top off with splash of club soda. Garnish with grapefruit peel and a lime slice.

Patrón Pineapple

1 oz. Patrón Silver Tequila
¼ oz. Patrón Citrónge
    Orange Liqueur
2 oz. fresh pineapple juice
Squeeze of lime juice
Pineapple wedge and lime slice
    for garnish

Pour Patrón Silver and Patrón
Citrónge over ice. Add pineapple
juice. Finish with a squeeze of lime.
Garnish with pineapple wedge and
a lime slice.

Patrón Pomegranate

1 oz. Patrón Silver Tequila
¼ oz. Patrón Citrónge
    Orange Liqueur
2 oz. fresh pomegranate juice
Squeeze of lemon juice
Orange twist for garnish

Pour Patrón Silver and Citrónge
over ice. Add pomegranate juice.
Finish with a squeeze of lemon.
Garnish with an orange twist.

Patty's Pride

1¼ oz. Irish whiskey
¼ oz. peppermint schnapps

Combine in a shot glass.

You can also serve this one with club soda in a highball glass.

Peach Banana Daiquiri

1½ oz. rum
½ medium banana, diced
1 oz. fresh lime juice
¼ cup sliced peaches (fresh, fro-
    zen, or canned)
1 cup of crushed ice

Blend with crushed ice.

Peach Fizz

2 oz. Crown Royal Peach Whisky
½ oz. orange juice
4 oz. champagne
Mint sprig for garnish

Combine in a champagne glass and
garnish with a mint sprig.

Peach Margarita

1½ oz. Jose Cuervo Gold Tequila
1 oz. triple sec
1 oz. lime juice
½ cup peaches
1 cup of ice
Peach slices for garnish

Blend. Garnish with peach slices.

Peach Melba

½ oz. Captain Morgan
Spiced Rum
¾ oz. raspberry liqueur
2 oz. peach cocktail mix
1 oz. heavy cream
2 peach halves
1 cup of crushed ice
Raspberry syrup

Blend with crushed ice. Top with raspberry syrup.

Peach Picnic

2 oz. Ketel One Botanical Peach &
Orange Blossom
½ oz. peach simple syrup
3 oz. Earl Grey tea

Add all ingredients into a cocktail shaker with ice and shake. Strain into a rocks glass and serve.

Peach Prayer

1½ oz. DeKuyper
Peachtree Schnapps
½ oz. Cointreau
¾ oz. champagne
Splash Sunkist Orange Juice

Combine ingredients over ice.

Peaches & Cream

3 oz. Coco Lopez Cream
of Coconut
2 oz. pineapple juice
1 oz. coffee liqueur
½ oz. rum
1 cup of crushed ice

Blend with crushed ice.

Peachy Irishman

1½ oz. Irish whiskey
1 ripe peach (peeled, pitted, and sliced)
½ cup fresh lime juice
1 oz. apricot brandy
1 tbsp. superfine sugar
Dash vanilla extract
1 cup of crushed ice

Blend with crushed ice.

Pear Vanilla

2 oz. Crown Royal Vanilla Whisky
½ oz. simple syrup
½ oz. fresh lemon juice
Pear slice for garnish

Combine in a tall glass over ice and garnish with a pear slice.

Pearl Necklace

1½ oz. Midori
½ oz. coconut rum
4 oz. orange juice

Combine in a tall glass over ice.

Pecan Pie Martini

2 oz. Catoctin Creek Roundstone Rye Whiskey
1 oz. dark crème de cocoa
1 oz. Frangelico
½ oz. Irish cream

Shake all ingredients with ice. Strain. Serve up in a martini glass.

Pegu Club

2 oz. gin
¾ oz. Orange Curaçao
½ oz. fresh lime juice
1 dash bitters
1 dash orange bitters

Add all ingredients into cocktail shaker with ice. Shake and strain into a chilled cocktail glass.

Penicillin

2 oz. blended scotch
¾ oz. fresh lemon juice
¾ oz. honey-ginger syrup
¼ oz. Islay Single Malt Scotch

Add first three ingredients into a shaker with ice. Shake and strain into a rocks glass with a large cube. With a bar spoon, float the Islay Single Malt Scotch and serve.

A modern classic invented by Sam Ross.

Penichillin

2 oz. blended scotch
¾ oz. fresh lemon juice
¾ oz. honey-ginger syrup
¼ cup of ice
¼ oz. Peated Scotch Whisky

Add first three ingredients into a blender with ice. Blend and strain into a chilled rocks glass. With a bar spoon, float the Peated Scotch and serve.

A fun frozen version of the Penicillin cocktail made at Diamond Reef in Brooklyn, NY.

Peppar Manhattan

1½ oz. Absolut Peppar Vodka
½ oz. sweet vermouth
Cherry for garnish

Mix vodka and sweet vermouth in a cocktail shaker over ice and stir. Strain into a stemmed glass. Add a cherry for garnish.

Peppar the Salty Dog

1¼ oz. Absolut Peppar Vodka
Grapefruit juice

Salt the rim of a rocks glass. Fill with ice. Pour in vodka and fill with grapefruit juice.

Peppermint Kiss

1 oz. Mozart Chocolate Liqueur
1 oz. peppermint schnapps
1 sprig mint

Add chocolate liqueur and peppermint schnapps to an ice-filled rocks glass and stir. Garnish with mint sprig.

Peppermint Patti

¾ oz. peppermint schnapps
½ oz. green crème de menthe

Combine over ice in a rocks glass.

Peppertini

1½ oz. Absolut Peppar Vodka
½ oz. dry vermouth
Green olive for garnish

Mix vodka and dry vermouth in a cocktail shaker over ice. Stir and pour into a rocks glass. Add a green olive for garnish.

Perfect Storm (Rum Mule)

2 oz. rum
Splash fresh lime juice
2 dashes bitters
3 oz. ginger beer

Serve over ice in a rocks glass.

Phoebe Snow

1¼ oz. brandy
1 oz. Dubonnet
¾ oz. Pernod

Shake in a cocktail mixer with ice. Strain into a chilled martini glass.

Pickle Back

1¼ oz. Jameson Irish Whiskey
1 oz. chilled pickle juice

Pour the Jameson (room temperature) in one shot glass and the pickle juice in another. Shoot the Jameson and chase with the pickle juice.

Pickle Tickle

1 oz. tequila
1 oz. pickle juice

Pour the tequila in one shot glass and the pickle juice in another. Shoot the tequila and chase with the pickle juice.

Pimm's Cup

2 oz. Pimm's No. 1
½ oz. lemon juice
Top with ginger ale
Cucumber slice, mint sprig, strawberry, and lemon wheel for garnish

Add Pimm's No. 1 and lemon juice into a highball glass with ice. Top with ginger ale and stir. Garnish with cucumber slice, mint sprig, strawberry, and lemon wheel.

Piña Colada 🍸

2 oz. light or dark rum
1½ oz. pineapple juice
1½ oz. Coco Lopez Cream
   of Coconut
½ oz. fresh lime juice
Pineapple wedge or pineapple
   leaf for garnish

Mix in a shaker and serve over ice,
or blend with crushed ice. Garnish
with pineapple wedge and/or
pineapple leaf.

Piñata

1½ oz. tequila
5 oz. pineapple juice
Pineapple wedge for garnish

Combine in a Collins glass. Garnish
with pineapple wedge.

Piña Verde

1½ oz. Green Chartreuse
1½ oz. pineapple juice
½ oz. fresh lime juice
¾ oz. Coco Lopez Cream
   of Coconut
Mint sprig for garnish

Add ingredients into a shaker with
ice and shake. Strain into a rocks
glass with pebble ice. Garnish with
mint sprig.

Pineapple Bomb

½ oz. Malibu Rum
½ oz. black rum
½ oz. pineapple juice

Shake with ice and strain into a shot
glass.

Pineapple Pie

1¼ oz. pineapple vodka
¼ oz. white crème de cacao
Whipped cream

Shake with ice. Strain into a rocks
glass and add a dollop of whipped
cream.

Pineapple Princess

2 oz. Don Julio Blanco Tequila
1 oz. pineapple juice
½ oz. lime juice
Top with soda water

Add first three ingredients into a tall
glass with ice and stir. Top with
soda water and serve.

Inspired by C. Fallon Foley.

Pineapple Twist

1½ oz. rum
6 oz. pineapple juice
Splash lemon juice

Shake and pour into a tall glass over ice.

Pineapple Upside-Down Cake

1 oz. vanilla vodka
½ oz. butterscotch schnapps
¾ oz. pineapple juice
Splash grenadine

Combine the vanilla vodka, butterscotch schnapps, and pineapple juice in a shaker. Shake and strain into a shot glass. Carefully pour the grenadine down the inside of the glass.

Pink Cadillac with Hawaiian Plates

1¼ oz. tequila
2 oz. pineapple juice
2 oz. cranberry juice
½ oz. sweet & sour mix
Lime wedge for garnish

Combine in a rocks glass. Garnish with a lime wedge.

Pink Gin (a.k.a. Gin & Bitters)

Dash angostura bitters
2 oz. gin

Rinse a chilled glass with bitters. Add gin.

FABLES AND LORE

THE ORIGINS OF PINK GIN

In 1824, Dr. Johann G. B. Siegert created angostura bitters as a remedy for stomach complaints suffered by the Venezuelan army. He named this concoction after the town on the Orinoco River where he had worked.

The British Navy added this product to its medicine chest but soon discovered that it added a whole new dimension to Plymouth gin, and thus Pink Gin came to be.

Pink Lady

1¼ oz. Tanqueray Gin
2 tsp. grenadine
3 oz. half & half

Shake with ice and strain into a cocktail glass or serve over ice.

Pink Lemonade

1¼ oz. vodka
½ tsp. sugar
1¼ oz. sweet & sour mix
1 oz. cranberry juice
Club soda
Juice of ½ lime

Combine vodka, sugar, sweet & sour mix, and cranberry juice in a tall glass. Stir to dissolve sugar. Add ice and top with club soda. Add a squeeze of lime.

Pink Mustang

1 oz. cranberry vodka
1 oz. Rumple Minze

Serve on ice.

Pink Panther #1

1½ oz. tequila
½ oz. grenadine
2 oz. cream or half & half
1 cup of crushed ice

Blend with crushed ice and strain into a chilled glass.

Pink Panther #2

1¼ oz. light rum
¾ oz. lemon juice
¾ oz. cream
½ oz. grenadine

Blend with crushed ice and strain.

Pink Snowball

¾ oz. amaretto
¾ oz. Malibu Rum
¾ oz. grenadine
Whipped cream
Cherry for garnish

Combine the first three ingredients with one good squirt of whipped cream in a shaker with ice. Shake vigorously and strain over ice in a rocks glass. Garnish with a cherry and more whipped cream.

Pink Squirrel

1 oz. crème de almond
1 oz. crème de cacao
4 oz. cream

Shake all ingredients over cracked ice. Strain.

Pirate's Punch

1¾ oz. Rhum Barbancourt
¼ oz. sweet vermouth
Dash bitters

Shake with ice and serve over ice.

Pisco Punch

2 oz. Pisco
2 oz. pineapple juice
1 oz. freshly squeezed lime juice
1 oz. simple syrup
Pineapple square for garnish

Shake with ice. Pour into a Collins glass. Garnish with a square of pineapple.

Pisco Sour

2 oz. Pisco
1 oz. fresh lime juice
½ oz. simple syrup
1 egg white
Bitters

Add Pisco, lime, simple syrup, and egg white into a shaker without ice and hard shake dry. Add ice and shake again. Strain into a chilled rocks glass and garnish with a few drops of bitters.

Planter's Punch

2 oz. rum
1 oz. simple syrup
2 oz. orange juice
Dash grenadine
Splash Myers's Dark Rum

Shake or blend all ingredients except the dark rum and pour into a glass. Top with dark rum.

The Player

¼ oz. fresh lime juice
¼ oz. ginger liqueur
3 oz. Moët Impérial Champagne
Lime peel for garnish

Pour the fresh lime juice and ginger liqueur into a champagne flute. Fill with Moët Impérial. Stir gently with a long spoon. Add lime peel garnish.

PLANTER'S PUNCH

In 1879, Fred L. Myers founded the Myers's Rum distillery in Jamaica and celebrated by creating what he named a Planter's Punch. This concoction became the house specialty at Kelly's Bar in Sugar Wharf, Jamaica, and its popularity spread soon after.

Pomtree Cocktail

2 oz. DeKuyper
   Peachtree Schnapps
2½ oz. POM Wonderful
   Pomegranate Juice

Shake with ice. Strain and serve in a martini glass or pour over the rocks in a rocks glass. Stir.

Created by Ray Foley.

Pop-in-Champagne

4 oz. champagne
1 frozen popsicle

Take your favorite frozen popsicle flavor and add it into a glass of champagne.

Porn Star Martini

1½ oz. vanilla vodka
½ oz. passion fruit liqueur
1 oz. passion fruit puree
½ oz. lime juice
½ oz. vanilla simple syrup
Top with sparkling wine

Add in all ingredients except sparkling wine into a shaker with ice. Shake and strain into a chilled martini glass. Top with sparkling wine and serve.

Pousse-Café #1

¼ oz. grenadine
¼ oz. Yellow Chartreuse
¼ oz. white crème de menthe
¼ oz. Sloe Gin
¼ oz. Green Chartreuse
¼ oz. brandy

Layer this drink in the order listed. Start with grenadine on the bottom and finish with brandy on top.

Pousse-Café #2

½ oz. Bénédictine
½ oz. white crème de cacao
½ oz. Remy Martin Cognac

Layer this drink by pouring the Bénédictine first, then the crème de cacao, and then cognac.

Pousse-Café Standish

½ oz. grenadine
½ oz. white crème de menthe
½ oz. Galliano
½ oz. Kummel Liqueur
½ oz. brandy

Layer this drink in the order listed. Start with grenadine on the bottom and finish with brandy on top.

Power Martini

1½ oz. orange vodka
½ oz. lemon juice
3 oz. orange juice
1 oz. raspberry syrup
Orange peel for garnish

Pour ingredients into a mixing glass, add ice, and shake well. Strain into a chilled glass and garnish with an orange peel.

Prairie Fire

1½ oz. tequila
2 or 3 drops Tabasco Sauce

Combine in a shot glass.

Presbyterian

2–3 oz. bourbon or
   American whiskey
¼ cup of ice
Ginger ale
Club soda

Pour the bourbon into a chilled highball glass. Add ice and top off the glass with equal parts of ginger ale and soda.

Presidente

1½ oz. white rum
6–8 ice cubes
¼ oz. dry vermouth
¾ oz. sweet vermouth
Splash grenadine

Mix with ice and serve.

Princess Mary

2 oz. dry gin
½ oz. crème de cacao
½ oz. fresh cream

Shake with ice and serve in a
margarita glass.

Pulco

2 oz. tequila
½ oz. Cointreau
1½ oz. lime juice

Combine over ice.

Pumpkin Flip

2 oz. pumpkin ale
1 oz. bourbon
½ oz. amaretto
½ oz. agave nectar
1 tsp. pumpkin butter
1 egg
Nutmeg for garnish

Add all ingredients into a shaker
without ice and dry shake
vigorously. Add in ice and shake
again. Strain into a chilled coupe
glass and garnish with nutmeg.

Purple Goose Martini

3 oz. Grey Goose Vodka
1 oz. Chambord

Add ingredients into a mixing glass
with ice and stir. Strain into a
martini glass and serve.

Purple Haze

1 oz. Chambord
1 oz. vodka
½ oz. cranberry juice or sweet &
    sour mix

Combine in a shot glass.

Purple Haze Martini Cocktail

2 oz. Bacardi O Rum
2 oz. lemonade
½ oz. grenadine
½ oz. Blue Curaçao
Orange slice for garnish

Shake with ice. Strain into a martini
glass. Garnish with orange slice.

Purple Hooter

½ oz. vodka
½ oz. black raspberry liqueur
½ oz. cranberry juice
Splash club soda

Shake and strain vodka, black raspberry liqueur, and cranberry juice. Top with a splash of club soda.

Purple Orchid

1 oz. white crème de cacao
1 oz. blackberry brandy
½ oz. cream

Combine in a shot glass.

Purple Passion

1¼ oz. vodka
2 oz. grapefruit juice
2 oz. grape juice
Sugar

Combine ingredients and stir. Chill and add sugar to taste. Serve in a Collins glass.

Queen Elizabeth Martini

1½ oz. Absolut Vodka
Dash extra dry vermouth
Splash Bénédictine

Stir gently with ice and strain.

R & B

1¼ oz. Captain Morgan Original
    Spiced Rum
2 oz. orange juice
2 oz. pineapple juice
Splash grenadine

Pour ingredients over ice.

Racer's Edge

1½ oz. light rum
Grapefruit juice
¼ oz. green crème de menthe

Pour rum into a glass half-filled with ice. Fill with grapefruit juice and float crème de menthe.

Raffles Bar Sling

¾ oz. gin
2 dashes bitters
½ tsp. lime juice
¼ oz. cherry-flavored brandy
Ginger beer
¼ oz. Bénédictine
Mint leaf for garnish

Combine gin, bitters, lime juice, and cherry-flavored brandy with ice in a highball glass. Stir in ginger beer. Float Bénédictine on top. Garnish with mint leaf.

Raging Orange Bull

1½ oz. orange vodka
4 oz. Red Bull Energy Drink

Pour ingredients over ice in a rocks glass.

Rainbow Pousse–Café

½ oz. dark crème de cacao
½ oz. crème de violette
½ oz. Yellow Chartreuse
½ oz. maraschino liqueur
½ oz. Bénédictine
½ oz. Green Chartreuse
½ oz. cognac

Layer this drink in the order listed. Start with crème de cacao on the bottom and finish with cognac on top.

Ramos Fizz

1½ oz. gin
¾ oz. simple syrup
3–4 drops orange-flower water
½ oz. fresh lime juice
½ oz. fresh lemon juice
1 egg white
½ oz. heavy cream
Club soda
2 drops vanilla extract (optional)

Mix ingredients in the order given. Add crushed ice. Shake for a long time, until the mixture acquires body. Strain into a tall glass and top with chilled club soda. Add two drops of vanilla extract on top (if desired).

This drink requires a lot of shaking.

Rasmopolitan

1¼ oz. raspberry vodka
½ oz. Cointreau
1 oz. cranberry juice
Fresh raspberries or lime peel for garnish

Mix in a shaker half-filled with ice. Pour into a chilled martini glass. Garnish with fresh raspberries or a lime peel.

Raspberry Martini

1 oz. Godiva Liqueur
1 oz. Absolut Vodka
½ oz. Chambord or raspberry
liqueur

Combine with ice and shake well.
Serve in a glass whose rim has been
dipped in powdered sugar.

A very sweet, sweet drink.

Raspberry Truffle

1½ oz. raspberry vodka
½ oz. white crème de cacao
½ oz. Chambord
½ oz. half & half

Mix in a shaker half-filled with ice.
Pour into a martini glass rimmed
with cocoa.

Razpiroska

6 raspberries, plus more
for garnish
1 oz. simple syrup or
agave nectar
2 oz. raspberry vodka
Splash club soda

Muddle raspberries with simple
syrup or agave nectar in the bottom
of a rocks glass. Add vodka, fill with
ice, top with club soda, and stir.
Garnish with fresh raspberries.

Razz-Ma-Tazz

1½ oz. vodka
½ oz. Chambord
1½ oz. club soda

Combine and serve over ice in a tall
glass, chilled.

Razzputin

1½ oz. raspberry vodka
3 oz. cranberry juice
2 oz. grapefruit juice
Lime slice

Mix all ingredients, except lime slice,
with cracked ice in a shaker or
blender and serve in a chilled glass.
Garnish with lime slice.

It's raspberry at its jazziest.

Real Gold

1 oz. vodka
1 oz. Goldschläger

Combine in a shot glass.

Red Berry Repartee

2 oz. Cîroc Red Berry Vodka
4 oz. lemon-lime soda
Dash grenadine

Combine in a tall glass with ice.

Red Devil

2 oz. Irish whiskey
1½ oz. clam juice
1½ oz. tomato juice
1 tsp. lime juice
Few drops Worcestershire sauce
Pinch pepper

Combine with ice and shake gently.
Strain straight up.

Redheaded Slut

½ oz. Jägermeister
½ oz. peach schnapps
½ oz. cranberry juice

Shake over ice and strain into a shot
glass.

A relative of the Surfer on Acid.

Red Hook

2 oz. rye whiskey
½ oz. Punt e Mes Italian
Vermouth
¼ oz. maraschino liqueur

Stir with ice and strain into a chilled
cocktail glass.

Red Hot Mama

1¼ oz. rum
4 oz. cranberry juice
2 oz. club soda

Combine ingredients over ice in a
tall glass.

For a less tart version, substitute 7UP for club soda.

Red Lion

1½ oz. Grand Marnier
1 tbsp. Tanqueray Gin
2 tsp. orange juice
2 tsp. lemon juice

Combine in a shaker with ice. Shake
and strain into a martini glass.

Red Over Heels

2 oz. vodka
1 oz. honey-ginger syrup
¾ oz. fresh lemon juice
Lemon peel twirl for garnish

To make honey-ginger syrup, combine ½ oz. of water with ½ oz. of honey and 3-4 slices of ginger. Combine all ingredients in a cocktail shaker with ice. Shake vigorously and strain into a chilled martini glass. Lay a lemon peel twirl across the rim of the glass with cocktail pick.

Red Rouge

1 oz. Captain Morgan Spiced Rum
½ oz. blackberry brandy
2 oz. pineapple juice
½ oz. lemon juice

Stir with ice and serve over ice.

Red Snapper

2 oz. gin
4 oz. tomato juice
½ oz. lemon juice
Dash Worcestershire sauce
Dash tabasco sauce
Pinch of salt and pepper
Pinch of celery salt
Celery stalk and lime wedge
    for garnish

Combine ingredients with ice in a shaker and shake well. Strain into a highball glass with ice. Garnish with celery stalk and lime wedge.

The Blood Mary's Cousin.

Red Tide Martini

2 oz. vodka
1 oz. sweet vermouth
Dash crème de cassis
Dash maraschino liqueur

Shake ingredients with ice and strain into a chilled martini glass.

Ring of Kerry

1½ oz. Irish whiskey
1 oz. Baileys Irish Cream
½ oz. Kahlúa or crème de cacao
1 tsp. shaved chocolate

Mix all ingredients except shaved chocolate with cracked ice in a shaker or blender. Strain into a chilled glass. Sprinkle with shaved chocolate.

Rob Roy ⓨ

2 oz. scotch
¾ oz. sweet vermouth
2 dashes angostura bitters
Brandied cherry for garnish

Stir over ice and strain. Garnish with a brandied cherry.

You can also serve over ice.

Rocket Fuel

1 oz. Rumple Minze
1 oz. Overproof Rum

Combine in a shot glass.

Root Beer

½ oz. Kahlúa
½ oz. Galliano
½ oz. cola
½ oz. beer

Combine in a shot glass.

Rosalind Russell Martini

2½ oz. Absolut Vodka
Dash aquavit

Stir gently with ice and strain.

Named after actress Rosalind Russell. You can also serve this drink over ice.

Rose Quartz

1½ oz. Don Julio Blanco Tequila
1 dash rose water
6 oz. sparkling water
Strawberries and raspberries
    for garnish

Add tequila and rose water into a highball glass with ice. Add sparkling water and stir. Garnish with strawberries and raspberries and serve.

Route 27

1 oz. Double Cross Vodka
1 oz. sherry
½ oz. simple syrup
½ oz. lemon juice
Splash of soda
5 blackberries

Combine all ingredients except blackberries. Shake with ice and pour into a highball glass full of crushed ice. Top with splash of soda and muddled blackberries.

Royal Cape

1¾ oz. Crown Royal
   Canadian Whisky
1 oz. cranberry juice
½ oz. lime juice

Combine over ice.

Royal Stretch

1½ oz. Crown Royal
3 oz. sparkling water or club soda
Splash cherry juice or grenadine
Mint leaf for garnish

Serve over ice in a tall glass with a mint leaf garnish.

Created by Ray Foley.

Ruby Slippers

1 oz. cranberry vodka
1 oz. Goldschläger

Shake and pour over ice.

Rue Morgue

¼ oz. peated scotch
2 oz. Blended scotch
¾ oz. ruby port
½ oz. Bénédictine
¼ oz. high quality crème de cacao

Combine all ingredients in a mixing glass with ice and stir. Rinse the inside of a coupe class with peated scotch and discard. Pour the stirred cocktail into the coupe and serve.

Created by J. Henderson in Boston, MA.

Ruddy McDowell

1½ oz. Irish whiskey
2 oz. tomato juice
1 dash Tabasco Sauce
6–8 ice cubes
Dash freshly ground pepper

Combine all ingredients in a shaker and shake vigorously. Strain into a glass with ice.

Rum & Coke

2 oz. rum
4 oz. cola
Lime wedge for garnish

Stir ingredients with ice. Garnish with a lime wedge.

Rum Flip

2 oz. dark rum
½ oz. heavy cream
1 tsp. granulated sugar
1 egg
Nutmeg for garnish

Add all ingredients into a shaker without ice and hard dry shake. Add in ice and shake again. Strain into a chilled coupe glass and garnish with nutmeg.

Rum Madras

1½ oz. rum
2 oz. cranberry juice
2 oz. orange juice

Shake with ice and strain into a tall glass.

A rum version of the classic Madras.

Rum Old Fashioned

2 oz. dark rum
¼ oz. demerara syrup
2 dashes bitters
2 dashes orange bitters
Orange peel for garnish

Add all ingredients into a glass and stir. Garnish with orange peel.

Rum Sangria

1 oz. light rum
½ oz. gold rum
½ oz. triple sec
1 oz. orange juice
½ oz. pineapple juice
½ oz. grape juice
½ oz. passion fruit juice
½ oz. guava juice
½ oz. cranberry juice
Splash grenadine
Lemon twist for garnish

Combine all ingredients in a Collins glass. Garnish with a lemon twist.

Rum Yum

1 oz. Baileys Irish Cream
1 oz. Malibu Rum
1 oz. cream or milk
1 cup of ice

Blend with ice and serve.

This drink also looks nice in a margarita glass.

Runaway Bride

2 oz. coffee liqueur
½ oz. raspberry-flavored vodka
½ oz. heavy cream, milk,
    or ice cream

Shake with ice. Serve straight up in
a chilled martini glass or over ice.

Created by Ray Foley.

Russian Spring Punch

1½ oz. vodka
¼ oz. Giffard Crème
    de Framboise
¼ oz. Giffard Noir de
    Bourgogne Cassis
¾ oz. lemon juice
¼ oz. simple syrup
1½ oz. Brut Champagne

Add all ingredients except
champagne into a shaker with ice.
Strain into a Collins glass with ice
and top with champagne.

Rusty Nail (a.k.a. Nail Drive)

1½ oz. scotch
¾ oz. Drambuie

Combine in a rocks glass, add ice,
and stir.

Sake-tini

1½ oz. vodka
Dash sake

Gently stir with ice and strain.

Salt Lick

1¼ oz. vodka
2 oz. bitter lemon soda
2 oz. grapefruit juice

Pour ingredients over ice in a salt-
rimmed wine glass.

Salted Caramel

2 parts salted caramel vodka
2 parts soda water
Lime wedge for garnish

Build in an ice-filled highball glass
and stir. Garnish with a lime wedge.

Salty Dog

1½ oz. gin or vodka
3 oz. grapefruit juice

Mix with ice and pour into a salt-rimmed glass.

Santa Fe Maggie

1¼ oz. Jose Cuervo
Gold Tequila
½ oz. triple sec
2 oz. sweet & sour mix
2 oz. cranberry juice
Lime wedge for garnish

Combine ingredients over ice and garnish with a lime wedge.

Savoy Hotel

½ oz. white crème de cacao
½ oz. Bénédictine
½ oz. brandy

Layer this drink in the order listed. Start with crème de cacao on the bottom and finish with brandy on top.

Sazerac Cocktail (Classic)

1 tsp. Absinthe
1 sugar cube
3 dashes Peychaud's Bitters
1½ oz. rye whiskey
Lemon peel for garnish

Rinse chilled rocks glass with Absinthe and discard excess. In a mixing glass, add in sugar cube and bitters, and muddle. Then, add in rest of ingredients into mixing glass with ice and stir. Strain into Absinthe-rinsed glass. Garnish with lemon peel and serve.

Sazerac Cocktail (Modern)

1 tsp. Absinthe
1 sugar cube
3 dashes orange bitters
2 dashes bitters
1¼ oz. rye whiskey
1¼ oz. cognac
½ tsp. water
Lemon peel for garnish

Rise chilled rocks glass with Absinthe and discard excess. In a mixing glass, add in sugar cube and bitters and muddle. Then, add in rest of ingredients into mixing glass with ice and stir. Strain into Absinthe-rinsed glass. Garnish with lemon peel and serve.

Scarlett O'Hara

1½ oz. Southern Comfort
3 oz. cranberry juice

Combine with ice and stir.

Schnappy Shillelagh

2 oz. Irish cream
1 oz. peppermint schnapps

Stir well over ice.

Scofflaw

2 oz. bourbon or rye whiskey
1 oz. dry vermouth
¼ oz. fresh lemon juice
1 dash grenadine
1–2 dashes orange bitters

Shake and strain into a chilled
coupe glass.

Scooby Snack

¾ oz. Malibu Rum
¾ oz. Midori Melon Liqueur
1½ oz. pineapple juice
Splash milk

Combine ingredients in a shaker
with ice. Shake and strain over ice in
a rocks glass or serve as a shot.

Scorpion

1½ oz. vodka
¼ oz. blackberry brandy
⅛ oz. grenadine

Combine in a shot glass.

Scorpion Bowl

6 oz. light rum
1 oz. brandy
6 oz. orange juice
4 oz. lemon juice
1½ orgeat syrup

Combine all ingredients into the
bowl and add in shaved or pebble
ice and serve.

*Serves 2-3. If your bowl has a spot for it, place a high-proof rum shot in the center part
and light the rum for effect. With caution, of course!*

Scorpion Cocktail

1½ oz. rum
1 oz. brandy
2 oz. orange juice
1 oz. lemon juice
½ oz. orgeat syrup

Blend and add into a chilled rocks glass with shaved or pebble ice.

Trader Vic's cocktail from 1972.

Scorpion's Sting

1¾ oz. Absolut Peppar Vodka
¼ oz. white crème de menthe

Combine in a glass over ice.

Scotch & Soda

1½ oz. scotch
3 oz. club soda

Stir with ice and serve.

Play with different simple syrups to add into this classic.

Scotch Irish

1 oz. Baileys Irish Cream
1 oz. J&B Scotch

Shake or stir over ice.

Scotch Sour

Egg white (optional)
½ oz. scotch
¾ oz. lemon juice
¾ oz. simple syrup
1 tsp. sugar
Bitters

If you're adding in egg white, you must dry shake first. Add ingredients into a shaker with ice and shake. Strain into a rocks glass and garnish with a few dashes of bitters.

Scotch Swizzle

1¾ oz. scotch
¼ oz. lime juice
Dash bitters
Club soda

Combine first three ingredients in a glass and fill with club soda.

Scotty Dog

1¼ oz. scotch
1½ oz. lime juice
Lime slice for garnish

Shake with ice and strain into a glass. Garnish with a lime slice.

Screaming Banana Banshee

½ oz. banana liqueur
½ oz. vodka
½ oz. white crème de cacao
1½ oz. light cream
1 maraschino cherry

Shake first four ingredients well with ice. Strain into a chilled martini glass. Drop in a maraschino cherry.

Screaming Orgasm

½ oz. Irish cream
½ oz. Kahlúa
½ oz. vodka
½ oz. amaretto

Combine in a shot glass.

Screwdriver

2 oz. vodka
4 oz. orange juice

Add vodka to a tall glass with ice and fill with orange juice.

Sea Breeze

1½ oz. vodka
3 oz. cranberry juice
1½ oz. grapefruit juice
Lime wheel for garnish

Add all ingredients into a highball glass with ice and stir. Garnish with lime wheel.

Sean's Night Out

1¼ oz. Baileys Irish Cream
1 oz. spiced rum

Shake with ice and serve over ice.

Secret Place

1½ oz. dark rum
½ oz. cherry brandy
2 tsp. dark crème de cacao
4 oz. cold coffee
1 cup of crushed ice

Stir with crushed ice and serve.

Seelbach

1 oz. bourbon
½ oz. triple sec
2 dashes Peychaud's Bitters
2 dashes angostura bitters
Champagne

In a chilled champagne glass, add in bourbon, triple sec, and bitters. Stir and top with champagne.

Serpent's Smile

¾ oz. Irish whiskey
1½ oz. sweet vermouth
¾ oz. lemon juice
1 tbsp. kummel
2 dashes angostura bitters
5–7 ice cubes
1 strip lemon peel

Combine all ingredients except two to three ice cubes and the lemon peel in a shaker and shake vigorously. Place remaining ice cubes in a glass and strain drink into the glass. Twist the lemon peel over the drink to release oil and drop it in.

Serpent's Tooth

1 oz. Irish whiskey
2 oz. sweet vermouth
½ oz. kummel
1 oz. lemon juice
Dash bitters

Stir well and strain into a small wine glass.

Sex on the Beach (The Original)

½ oz. vodka
¼ oz. peach schnapps
½ oz. cranberry juice
½ oz. grapefruit juice

Combine in a mixing glass. Shake or stir. Pour into a shot glass.

Sex on the Beach

1½ oz. vodka
½ oz. peach schnapps
½ oz. Chambord
1½ oz. orange juice
1½ oz. cranberry juice

Add all ingredients into a shaker with ice and shake. Strain into a highball glass with ice.

Shady Lady

1 oz. tequila
1 oz. melon liqueur
3 oz. grapefruit juice

Combine all ingredients in a shaker and shake. Serve over ice.

Shamrock Cocktail #1

1½ oz. Irish whiskey
½ oz. French vermouth
¼ oz. green crème de menthe
Green olive for garnish

Stir well with cracked ice and strain or serve over ice. Garnish with a green olive.

Shamrock Cocktail #2

1½ oz. Irish whiskey
¾ oz. green crème de menthe
4 oz. vanilla ice cream

Mix all ingredients in a blender at high speed until smooth. Pour into a chilled wine goblet.

Shamrocked

2 oz. Midori Melon Liqueur
½ oz. Irish whiskey
½ oz. cream liqueur

Combine ingredients and shake thoroughly. Serve in a 3 oz. shot glass.

This drink is a hot bar shot in New York in March.

Shore Breeze

1½ oz. light rum
3 oz. pineapple juice
2 oz. cranberry juice
2 dashes bitters

Shake with ice and serve in a rocks glass.

Siberian Sunrise

1½ oz. vodka
4 oz. grapefruit juice
½ oz. triple sec

Mix all ingredients with cracked ice in a shaker or blender.

Sicilian Kiss

1 oz. Southern Comfort
1 oz. Disaronno Amaretto

Shake with ice and strain into a shot glass.

Sidecar

2 oz. cognac
¾ oz. Cointreau
¾ oz. fresh lemon juice

Combine all ingredients in a shaker and shake vigorously. Strain into a chilled cocktail glass.

Siesta

1½ oz. tequila
¾ oz. lime juice
½ oz. Sloe Gin

Blend or shake with ice and strain into a chilled cocktail glass.

Silent Assassin

¾ oz. London Dry Gin
¾ oz. Lillet Blanc
¾ oz. elderflower liqueur
¾ oz. lemon juice
Green Chartreuse

Rinse a chilled martini glass with Green Chartreuse and discard. Add in gin, Lillet Blanc, elderflower liqueur, and lemon juice to a cocktail shaker with ice. Shake and strain into rinsed glass and serve.

Inspired by C. Mackey, Fayetteville, AR.

Silk Panties

1 oz. Stoli Vodka
1 oz. peach schnapps

Combine in a shot glass.

Created by Sandra Gutierrez of Chicago, IL.

Silver Bullet

1½ oz. dry gin
⅔ oz. Kummel liqueur
⅓ oz. lemon juice

Shake all ingredients with ice and strain into a chilled coupe glass.

Silver Shamrock

2 oz. Bunratty Meade
1 oz. vodka

Stir with ice.

Singapore Sling

¾ oz. gin
¼ oz. Bénédictine
¼ oz. Grand Marnier
¼ oz. cherry liqueur
1 oz. pineapple juice
1 dash angostura bitters
½ oz. fresh lime juice
Club soda

Shake first seven ingredients and pour into a tall glass. Top with club soda.

Sip & Dip

2 oz. sake
3 oz. grapefruit juice
Soda water

Add sake and grapefruit juice into a rocks glass with ice and stir. Top with soda water and serve.

Inspired by M. Buscio, Jersey City, NJ.

Sixty-Ninth Regiment Punch

1 oz. Irish whiskey
1 oz. scotch
3 oz. hot water
1 tsp. sugar
2–3 dashes lemon juice

Pour the whiskeys into hot water. Add sugar and lemon juice and stir.

Should be served in a warm glass.

SLING THIS . . .

Ngiam Tong Boon, a bartender at the Long Bar in Singapore's Raffles Hotel, invented the Singapore Sling around 1915. The Raffles Bar Sling, a variation of the Singapore Sling, gets its name from the very same Raffles Hotel.

Slainte

2 oz. vodka
½ oz. Irish cream
¼ oz. green crème de menthe

Shake all ingredients and serve on the rocks.

Slim Gin

1¼ oz. gin
Diet soda

Pour gin in a glass filled with ice. Fill with your favorite diet soda.

Slippery Nipple

1 oz. Sambuca Romana
1 oz. Baileys Irish Cream

Shake with ice and strain into a shot glass.

Sloe Gin Fizz

1½ oz. Sloe Gin
3 oz. sweetened lemon mix
Club soda

Shake gin and lemon mix and pour into a glass. Top with club soda.

A popular drink of the '60s.

Smokey Cokey

2 oz. Lagavulin 16 Year Old
   Scotch Whisky
4 oz. cola

Add ingredients into a highball glass with ice and stir.

Snowshoe

1 oz. Rumple Minze
1 oz. brandy

Shake with ice and strain into a shot glass.

Social Butterfly

1 oz. Stoli Vanil Vodka
1 oz. Stoli Razberi Vodka
1 oz. crème de banana
Splash soda
Cherry for garnish

Serve over ice and garnish with a cherry.

SoCo Lime

2 oz. Southern Comfort
Squeeze of lime juice

Serve as a shot or on the rocks.

Sol-a-Rita

1¼ oz. Jose Cuervo Gold Tequila
¾ oz. Cointreau
1½ oz. orange juice
2 dashes grenadine

Combine over ice.

Sombrero

1½ oz. coffee liqueur
½ oz. half & half

Combine in a Collins with ice.

This drink is also known as a Muddy River.

S.O.S.

1 oz. Stoli Ohranj Vodka
1 oz. sambuca

Combine over ice.

South Side

6 mint leaves, plus more
   for garnish
1 oz. fresh lemon juice
2 oz. gin
1 oz. simple syrup

In a shaker, muddle mint and fresh lemon juice. Add in gin, simple syrup, and ice and shake. Strain into a coupe glass and garnish with mint leaf.

Southern Lady

1 oz. bourbon
¼ oz. Southern Comfort
¼ oz. crème de almond
1½ oz. pineapple juice
1 oz. lemon-lime soda
1 oz. lime juice

In a tall glass with ice, combine the first four ingredients. Add the soda and top with lime juice.

Southern Sour

¼ oz. bourbon
¾ oz. Southern Comfort
3 oz. sweetened lemon mix
Cherry and orange slice
   for garnish

Shake with ice and strain or serve over ice. Garnish with a cherry and an orange slice.

Spanish Moss

½ oz. Herradura Tequila
¾ oz. Kahlúa
½ oz. green crème de menthe

Shake ingredients with ice and strain or serve over ice.

Spanish Town

2 oz. Rhum Barbancourt
1 tsp. triple sec

Stir ingredients and serve straight up or over ice in a cocktail glass.

Sparkling Lemonade

2 red rose petals, plus more
    for garnish
1½ oz. CÎROC Vodka
½ oz. elderflower liqueur
½ oz. lemon juice
Champagne

Muddle two rose petals in a mixing tin. Add vodka, elderflower liqueur, lemon juice, and ice. Shake and strain into a champagne flute. Top with champagne and garnish with a rose petal.

Sparks

1 oz. Absolut Peppar Vodka
3 oz. champagne

Combine in a champagne glass.

Spearaminty

1 oz. Irish whiskey
¼ oz. spearmint schnapps

Stir ingredients and serve straight up or over ice.

Spicy Margarita #1

½ jalapeño
1 oz. fresh lime juice
2 oz. tequila
1 oz. Cointreau
½ oz. agave syrup

Cut half a jalapeño and add into shaker with fresh lime juice and begin to muddle. Add in the remaining ingredients with ice and shake. Double strain into a spicy salt-rimmed rocks glass and serve.

Spicy Margarita #2

1½ oz. Ghost Tequila
    (spicy tequila)
½ oz. agave nectar
¾ oz. lime juice

Add all ingredients into a shaker with ice and shake. Strain into a salt-rimmed rocks glass with ice.

It's the Ghost Tequila that makes this one spicy.

Spicy Mexican Mule

2–3 slices jalapeño
1 sprig mint, plus more
    for garnish
2 oz. Ghost Tequila (spicy tequila)
1 oz. lime juice
Ginger beer

In a rocks glass or mule mug, add jalapeño and one sprig of mint and gently muddle in the glass. Add Ghost Tequila and lime juice, and top with ginger beer. Garnish with mint sprig.

Spicy Paloma

1½ oz. Ghost Tequila
  (spicy tequila)
1½ oz. grapefruit juice
Club soda
Lime wedge for garnish

Add tequila and grapefruit juice into a tall glass with ice. Top with club soda and stir, garnish with lime wedge, and serve.

Spiked Arnold Palmer

2 oz. bourbon
2 oz. lemonade
2 oz. iced tea
Lemon wedge for garnish

Add all ingredients into a highball glass with ice. Stir and serve. Garnish with lemon wedge.

We prefer the bourbon variation, but it can also be served with vodka (see recipe for "John Daily").

Spinner

1½ oz. bourbon
1 oz. orange juice
1 tbsp. lime juice
1 tsp. superfine sugar
1 scoop crushed ice
Orange slice for garnish

Combine all ingredients in a shaker. Shake briskly and strain the mixture into a cocktail glass. Garnish with an orange slice.

You can also serve this one over ice in a rocks glass.

Spritzer

3 oz. dry white wine
Club soda
Lemon twist for garnish

Pour wine in a glass and fill with soda. Garnish with a lemon twist.

Spyglass

1 oz. Captain Morgan Spiced Rum
2 scoops vanilla ice cream
1 tbsp. honey
Dash milk

Blend until smooth.

St. Patrick's Day Cocktail

¾ oz. Irish whiskey
¾ oz. green crème
de menthe
¾ oz. Green Chartreuse
1 dash angostura bitters

Stir well with cracked ice and strain into a cocktail glass.

St. Petersburg

2 oz. vodka
¼ tsp. angostura bitters
Orange peel for garnish

Stir with ice. Garnish with an orange peel.

Starry Night

¾ oz. Jägermeister
¾ oz. Goldschläger

Combine ingredients in a shot glass.

Jägermeister and Goldschläger should be stored in the fridge. If they aren't ice cold, shake with ice and strain to make this shot.

Stinger

2 oz. cognac
1 oz. white crème de menthe

Add into a mixing glass with ice and stir. Strain into a rocks glass with ice.

Stoli O Rouge

2 oz. Stoli Ohranj Vodka
¼ oz. cranberry juice
Club soda
Orange slice for garnish

Shake first two ingredients and serve over ice in a Collins glass. Fill with club soda. Garnish with an orange slice.

Strawberry Caipirinha

½ lime
3 strawberries
1 tbsp. refined sugar
¼ oz. sweet lemonade
2 oz. Ketel One Vodka

In a shaker, muddle lime, strawberry, sugar and sweet lemonade. Add in vodka and ice and shake. Strain into an ice-filled rocks glass and serve.

Created by A. Vieira, Hoboken, NJ.

Strawberry Daiquiri (Frozen)

6 strawberries
2 oz. rum
1 oz. simple syrup
¾ oz. lime juice
1 cup of ice

Cut strawberries into chunks and place into blender. Add in all liquid ingredients and ice. Blend and serve.

Place half of this drink in the bottom of a hurricane glass and top with a Piña Colada for a cocktail called the "Miami Vice."

Strawberry Lemonade

2 oz. strawberry vodka
2 oz. lemonade
Lemon wedge or strawberry
　for garnish

Serve on the rocks. Garnish with lemon wedge or strawberry.

Strawberry Mule

2 strawberries, plus more
　for garnish
1 oz. fresh lime juice
2 oz. Ketel One Vodka
Ginger beer

Muddle strawberries in a shaker with fresh lime juice. Add in vodka and ice and shake. Strain into an ice-filled rocks glass or mule mug and garnish with a few strawberries.

Summer Breeze

2 oz. Ketel One Oranje Vodka
1½ oz. orange juice
1½ oz. cranberry juice

Shake and strain into an ice-filled rocks glass.

Summer Coffee

1 oz. whiskey
¼ oz. Irish cream
4 oz. iced coffee
Whipped cream (optional)

Stir first three ingredients with ice and strain. Top with whipped cream (if desired).

Sunsplash

¾ oz. Coco Lopez Cream
　of Coconut
1¼ oz. Frangelico
¾ oz. Captain Morgan Spiced Rum
5 oz. orange juice

Shake with ice and serve.

Sunstroke

1½ oz. vodka
3 oz. grapefruit juice
Splash triple sec

Pour vodka and grapefruit juice into a rocks glass filled with ice. Add a little triple sec and stir.

Super Sempé Stinger

2½ oz. Sempé Armagnac
½ oz. Marie Brizard White Crème de Menthe

Shake with ice and pour into a sugar-rimmed martini glass.

Surfer on Acid

1 oz. Jägermeister
1 oz. coconut rum
1 oz. pineapple juice

Shake with ice and strain into a rocks glass.

You can also make this as a shot.

Sweet Irish Storm

1½ oz. Bushmills Irish Whiskey
¾ oz. sweet vermouth
3–4 dashes angostura bitters
3–4 dashes Southern Comfort

Mix ingredients with cracked ice in a shaker or blender. Pour into a chilled rocks glass.

Sweet Peach Tea

½ can of hard peach iced tea or hard peach tea seltzer
2 oz. sweet tea

Add in the hard peach iced tea into a highball glass. Add in sweet tea, stir, and serve.

Sweet Tart

1 oz. Absolut Vodka
¼ oz. Chambord
¼ oz. lime juice
¼ oz. pineapple juice

Shake with ice and strain into a shot glass.

Szarburst

2 oz. Stoli Strasberi Vodka
½ oz. cranberry juice
Splash lime juice

Shake with ice. Strain into a shot glass.

Taboo

1½ oz. pineapple vodka
½ oz. cranberry juice
½ oz. sweet & sour mix
Splash triple sec
1 cup of crushed ice
Pineapple wedge and cherry
    for garnish

Blend with crushed ice. Serve in a tall glass. Garnish with a pineapple wedge and a cherry.

Tailgate

1½ oz. rum
½ oz. grenadine
½ oz. fresh lime juice
Cola

Combine the first three ingredients in a tall glass with ice. Fill with cola.

Takeaway

2 oz. Johnnie Walker Black
    Label Scotch
1½ oz. cold brew coffee
2 oz. tonic water

Add all ingredients into a highball glass with ice and stir.

Tangerine

1¼ oz. Stoli Ohranj Vodka
2 oz. orange juice
Dash grenadine

Shake with ice and serve.

Tango

2 oz. gin
1 oz. sweet vermouth
1 oz. dry vermouth
2 dashes Orange Curaçao
Dash orange juice

Shake with ice and serve.

You'll dance all night.

Tanqueray & Tonic ⓨ

1½ oz. Tanqueray Gin
3 oz. tonic water
Lime wedge for garnish

Pour gin in a glass with ice. Fill with tonic. Garnish with a lime wedge.

Tarzan O'Reilly

1 oz. Baileys Irish Cream
½ oz. Smirnoff Vodka
½ oz. crème de banana

Build in a shot glass over ice. Stir.

You'll swing from trees.

Tear Drop

1¼ oz. Absolut Peppar Vodka
¼ oz. orange liqueur or triple sec
Cherry for garnish

Combine in a shot glass. Drop in a cherry.

Not on your head.

Tequador

1½ oz. tequila
2 oz. pineapple juice
1 dash lime juice
Grenadine

Shake the first three ingredients with crushed ice. Strain. Add a few drops of grenadine.

Tequila & Soda

1½ oz. tequila
3 oz. soda water
Lime wedge for garnish

Stir ingredients with ice in a glass. Garnish with a lime wedge.

Tequila Gimlet

1½ oz. tequila
1½ oz. lime juice
Lime wheel or green cherry
    for garnish

Blend tequila and lime juice with crushed ice and pour into a glass. Garnish with a lime wheel or green cherry.

Tequila Julep

3-4 mint leaves
1 tsp. superfine sugar or ¼ oz.
    simple syrup
1¼ oz. tequila
Club soda

Crush 2 mint leaves with sugar or simple syrup in a chilled highball glass and fill with ice. Add tequila and top with club soda. Garnish with remaining mint leaves.

Tequila Sunrise

½ oz. grenadine
1½ oz. tequila
4 oz. orange juice
Orange slice for garnish

Pour grenadine into a tall glass first. Then add tequila and fill with ice and orange juice. Garnish with an orange slice.

Tequila Teaser

1½ oz. tequila
½ oz. Cointreau
1½ oz. orange juice
½ oz. grapefruit juice

Pour ingredients into a tall glass filled with ice.

Terminator #1

½ oz. Bacardi 151 Rum
½ oz. blackberry brandy
½ oz. cranberry juice

Combine in a shot glass.

I'm back.

Terminator #2

⅓ oz. vodka
⅓ oz. Grand Marnier
⅓ oz. sambuca
⅓ oz. coffee-flavored liqueur
⅓ oz. Irish cream

Layer. Pour the vodka first, then the Grand Marnier, and so on.

I'm back again.

Three Barrels of Monkeys

1 oz. Myers's Dark Rum
¼ oz. banana liqueur
¼ oz. Irish cream

Combine over ice and stir.

Three-Leaf Shamrock Shaker

1 oz. Irish whiskey
1 oz. light rum
1 oz. brandy
1 tsp. lemon juice
Dash simple syrup

Shake ingredients with cracked ice. Strain into a chilled glass.

Thunder & Lightning

1 oz. Rumple Minze
1 oz. Bacardi 151 Rum

Combine in a shot glass.

Thunderbolt

2 oz. tequila
1 oz. Dr. McGillicuddy's
Mentholmint Schnapps

Stir over ice in a rocks glass.

Tidal Shot

1½ oz. ouzo
Splash Blue Curaçao

Combine in a shot glass.

Tidal Wave

1½ oz. Laird's Applejack
4 oz. orange juice
Splash cranberry juice
Orange slice for garnish

Pour Applejack over ice in a tall glass. Add orange juice and cranberry juice. Garnish with slice of orange.

Tipperary Cocktail

¾ oz. Irish whiskey
¾ oz. Green Chartreuse
¾ oz. Italian vermouth

Stir well with cracked ice and strain into a cocktail glass.

TitoRita

2 oz. Tito's Vodka
½ oz. orange liqueur
2 oz. lime juice
¼ oz. agave syrup

Add all ingredients into a blender with ice and blend. Strain into a margarita glass and serve.

Toasted Almond

1 oz. Kahlúa
½ oz. amaretto
1 oz. cream or milk

Pour over ice and stir.

Toasted Almond Shot

1 part Kahlúa
1 part Disaronno Amaretto

Layer the Amaretto over the Kahlúa.

Tom Collins

2 oz. gin
1 oz. fresh lemon juice
½ oz. simple syrup
Club soda

Shake first three ingredients and pour over ice. Top with club soda.

Tommy's Margarita

2 oz. blanco tequila
1 oz. fresh lime juice
½ oz. agave nectar

Shake ingredients in a cocktail shaker and strain into a salt-rimmed rocks glass with ice.

Tootsie Roll #1

1 oz. Kahlúa
1 oz. vodka
1 oz. orange juice

Combine in a shot glass.

Tootsie Roll #2

1 oz. root beer schnapps
½ oz. Baileys Irish Cream

Top root beer schnapps with Irish cream in a shot glass.

Traffic Light

⅓ oz. green crème de menthe
⅓ oz. crème de banana
⅓ oz. Sloe Gin

Layer this drink in the order listed. Start with crème de menthe on the bottom and finish with Sloe Gin on top.

JOHN OR TOM COLLINS?

John Collins, a waiter at Limmer's Old House on Conduit Street in Hanover Square, England, invented this drink. The name Tom was used instead of John because the drink was made with Old Tom Gin. Today, a John Collins is made with whiskey.

Transfusion

1½ oz. Tito's Vodka
3 oz. grape juice

Combine over ice and stir.

Trinidad Sour

1 ½ oz. angostura bitters
½ oz. rye whiskey
¾ oz. lemon juice
1 oz. orgeat
Lemon twist for garnish

Add all ingredients into a cocktail shaker with ice and shake. Strain into a coupe glass and garnish with a lemon twist.

Trip to the Beach

½ oz. Malibu Rum
½ oz. peach schnapps
½ oz. Smirnoff Vodka
3 oz. orange juice

Combine over ice.

Tropical Breeze

1 oz. Coco Lopez Cream
   of Coconut
2 oz. orange juice
1 oz. rum
½ oz. crème de banana
1 cup of crushed ice
Pineapple slice for garnish

Blend with crushed ice. Garnish with a pineapple slice.

Tropical Iceberg

1½ oz. pineapple vodka
½ oz. banana liqueur
½ oz. Coco Lopez Cream
   of Coconut
1 cup of ice
Dash cream or half & half

Blend ingredients and serve in a margarita glass.

Tuaca Rocca

1 oz. Tuaca Liqueur
1 oz. peach schnapps
1 oz. vodka

Combine with ice in a rocks glass.

Tullahoma Twist

1½ oz. George Dickel Classic
2 oz. iced tea
2 oz. lemonade
Lemon wedge for garnish

Combine all ingredients in a highball glass and stir. Garnish with a lemon wedge.

Tullamore Toddy

2 oz. Tullamore Dew
   Irish Whiskey
1 lemon, sliced
2 lumps sugar
Hot water
Cinnamon stick for garnish

Combine all ingredients in a glass mug and stir well. Fill to the top with hot water. Garnish with a cinnamon stick.

The Tully-Tini

1½ oz. Tullamore Dew
   Irish Whiskey
1½ oz. sour apple schnapps
1½ oz. cranberry juice

Combine Tullamore Dew and sour apple schnapps into a shaker with ice. Shake and strain into a chilled martini glass. Top with cranberry juice.

Turbo

¼ oz. vodka
¼ oz. peach schnapps
¼ oz. apple schnapps
¼ oz. cranberry juice

Combine in a shot glass.

You can also combine the ingredients with ice in a rocks glass.

Turkey Shooter

¾ oz. bourbon
¼ oz. white crème de menthe

Shake in cocktail shaker. Strain into a brandy snifter.

This drink is also known as a Bourbon Stinger.

Tuxedo

¼ oz. absinthe
2 oz. gin
½ oz. blanc vermouth
¼ oz. maraschino liqueur
3 dashes orange bitters
Orange twist for garnish

Rinse coupe glass with absinthe and discard. Add in remaining ingredients into a mixing glass with ice and stir. Strain into a coupe glass and garnish with orange twist.

Twilight Zone

1½ oz. Puerto Rican light rum
½ oz. Myers's Rum
Splash grenadine

Shake with ice and strain into a shot glass.

Two Weeks Out

Jalapeño, cut into slices
½ oz. lime juice
2 oz. mezcal
4 oz. ginger beer
Lime wedge for garnish

Muddle two slices of jalapeño in cocktail shaker with lime juice. Add in mezcal and ice and shake. Strain into a rocks glass and top with ginger beer. Garnish with jalapeño slices and lime wedge and serve.

Inspired by T. Cocuzza from Santa Cruz, CA.

Ultimate Tea

1½ oz. Irish Mist Liqueur
Hot tea
Lemon slice for garnish

Pour Irish Mist in a warm glass. Fill with hot tea. Garnish with a lemon slice.

Ultimate White Russian

1½ oz. Absolut Vanilia Vodka
1½ oz. Starbucks Coffee Liqueur
1½ oz. half & half

Combine in a shaker with ice and strain over ice in a Collins glass.

A drink fit for the Big Lebowski. Careful, man! There's a beverage here!

Under the Volcano Martini

2 oz. mezcal
½ oz. Martini & Rossi Vermouth
Jalapeño-stuffed olive for garnish

Stir over ice in a cocktail glass.
Garnish with a jalapeño-stuffed olive.

Invented at Harry Denton's in San Francisco, CA.

The Union

2 oz. Double Cross Vodka
¾ oz. Aperol
½ oz. Bénédictine
¾ oz. lemon juice
Raspberries and lemon slice
    for garnish

Combine all ingredients and stir
with ice. Strain into a coupe glass.
Garnish with lemon slice and
raspberries.

Up Spritz Creek

1 oz. bourbon
1 oz. Aperol
½ oz. Giffard
    Pamplemousse Liqueur
½ oz. fresh lemon juice
Sparkling rosè
Orange peel for garnish

Combine all ingredients, except
sparkling rosè, into a shaker with
ice and shake. Strain into a wine
glass with ice and top with sparkling
rosè. Garnish with orange peel.

Created by Marc Filoramo, Hoboken, NJ.

U-Z

¾ oz. Irish Mist Liqueur
¾ oz. Baileys Irish Cream
¾ oz. Kahlúa

Shake ingredients and strain into a
shot glass.

Vanilia Valentine

2 oz. Absolut Vanilia Vodka
1½ oz. Chambord
Champagne
1 strawberry

Mix Absolut Vanilia and Chambord.
Top with chilled champagne.
Garnish with a fanned strawberry.

Vanilla Cosmo

2 oz. Mount Gay Vanilla Rum
1 oz. Cointreau
Juice of ½ lime
Splash cranberry juice

Combine ingredients in a shaker with ice. Stir and strain into a martini glass.

Vanilla Martini

2½ oz. vanilla vodka
½ oz. Godiva White
   Chocolate Liqueur

Shake with ice; strain.

Vanilla Pop

2 oz. vanilla vodka
3 oz. cola

Serve over ice in a tall glass.

Vanilla Root Beer

2 oz. vanilla vodka
3 oz. root beer

Serve over ice in a tall glass.

Vesper

2 oz. gin
1 oz. vodka
½ oz. Lillet blanc

Stir gently with ice and strain into a cocktail glass.

Vieux Carré

¾ oz. George Dickel Rye Whiskey
¾ oz. cognac
¾ oz. sweet vermouth
2 tsp. Bénédictine
4 dashes aromatic bitters
Lemon twist for garnish

Add all ingredients in a mixing glass with ice and stir. Strain into a rocks glass and garnish with a lemon twist.

Vicious Sid

1½ oz. light rum
½ oz. Southern Comfort
½ oz. Cointreau or triple sec
1 oz. lemon juice
Dash bitters

Shake ingredients with ice and
serve over ice.

Victoria's Secret

1½ oz. Magellan Gin
¾ oz. apricot brandy
1½ oz. fresh sweet & sour mix
¼ oz. Campari

Shake ingredients with ice until
cold. Strain into a chilled cocktail
glass.

Created by Ray Srp, Bar Manager, Bellagio Hotel, Las Vegas, NV.

Viking

1 oz. Galliano
¼ oz. Akvavit (ice cold)

Float Akvavit on top of the Galliano
in a shot glass.

Villamosa

1 part Villa Massa Limoncello
2 parts prosecco

Mix both carefully and serve in a
champagne flute.

Violetta Martini

2 oz. vodka
2 oz. cranberry juice
Splash Blue Curaçao

Stir gently over ice and strain.

You can also serve this drink over ice.

Vodka & Ginger

1¼ oz. vodka
Ginger ale
Lime juice and wedge for garnish

Combine in a tall glass filled with
ice. Add a squeeze of lime and
garnish with a lime wedge.

Vodka & Soda ⓨ

1½ oz. vodka
3 oz. soda water
Lime wedge for garnish

Stir ingredients with ice in a glass.
Garnish with a lime wedge.

Vodka & Tonic ⓨ

1½ oz. vodka
3 oz. tonic
Lime wheel for garnish

Stir ingredients with ice in a glass.
Garnish with a lime wheel.

Vodka Martini ⓨ

2 oz. vodka
Dash dry vermouth
Lemon twist or green olive
    for garnish

Stir ingredients with ice and strain.
Garnish with a lemon twist or a
green olive.

You can also serve a Vodka Martini on ice.

Vulcan Mind Probe #1

1 oz. ouzo
1 oz. Bacardi 151 Rum

Shake with ice and strain into a
shot glass.

Vulcan Mind Probe #2

½ oz. Barcardi 151 Rum
½ oz. peppermint schnapps
½ oz. Irish cream

Layer in a shot glass by first pouring
the rum, then the schnapps, and
then the Irish cream. Serve with a
large eco-friendly straw.

You drink this one by sucking through the straw in one gulp.

Ward Eight ⓨ

2 oz. whiskey
4 dashes grenadine
Juice of ½ lemon

Shake ingredients with cracked ice
and strain into a glass with finely
cracked ice.

THE ORIGINS OF THE WARD EIGHT

This drink is named after Boston's Ward Eight, known years ago for its bloody political elections. The drink is basically a Whiskey Sour with a splash of grenadine.

Watermelon

1 oz. vodka
1 oz. Midori
2 oz. orange juice
2 oz. cranberry juice

Combine ingredients in a glass over ice.

Waterwall

2 oz. Yellow Rose Whiskey
½ oz. Galliano
1 oz. Solerno Blood Orange Liqueur
Angostura bitters
Orange twist for garnish

Combine ingredients and stir well. Pour into a glass and garnish with an orange twist.

Wave cutter

2 oz. Bacardi Rum
2 oz. cranberry juice
2 oz. orange juice
Cranberries or orange slice
      for garnish

Pour rum into a glass with ice. Add cranberry juice and orange juice. Decorate with cranberries or orange slice.

West Side

3 mint leaves
1 oz. fresh lime juice
2 oz. Irish whiskey
1 oz. honey syrup

In a shaker, muddle 2 mint leaves and fresh lime juice. Add in Irish whiskey and ice and shake. Strain into a coupe glass and garnish with a mint leaf.

Wet & Wild

1½ oz. Absolut Vanilia Vodka
¾ oz. Cointreau
½ oz. lime juice
½ oz. watermelon Juice

Shake ingredients with ice and strain.

Wet Spot

1 oz. Jose Cuervo Tequila
1 oz. Baileys Irish Cream

Shake with ice and strain into a shot glass.

Where There's Smoke

1½ oz. mezcal
1 oz. Grand Marnier
¾ oz. lemon juice
½ oz. agave
2 dashes habanero tabasco
1 oz. red wine

Add all ingredients except red wine into a shaker with ice and shake. Strain into a rocks glass with ice. Top with red wine and serve.

Created by M. Filoramo.

Whiskey Collins

1¼ oz. whiskey
Juice of ½ lemon
1 tsp. sugar
Club soda
Cherry and orange slice for garnish

Shake the first three ingredients with cracked ice and strain in a glass over ice. Fill with club soda and stir. Decorate with a cherry and an orange slice.

Whiskey Smash

4 mint leaves, plus more
    for garnish
3 lemon wedges
¾ oz. simple syrup
2 oz. bourbon

Add in mint and lemon wedges with simple syrup into a cocktail shaker and muddle. Add in bourbon and ice and shake. Strain into a rocks glass and garnish with mint leaves.

Whiskey Sour

Egg white (optional)
1½ oz. whiskey
¾ oz. sweetened lemon juice
¾ oz. simple syrup
Angostura bitters for garnish

If you're adding in egg white, you must dry shake first. Add ingredients into a shaker with ice and shake. Strain into a rocks glass and garnish with a few dashes of angostura bitters.

White Bat

1½ oz. white rum
1½ oz. Kahlúa
1½ oz. whole milk
3 oz. cola

Add rum, Kahlúa, and milk into a shaker with ice. Shake and strain into a rocks glass with ice. Top with cola and serve.

White Chocolate Martini

1½ oz. vodka
½ oz. white crème de cacao

Stir gently with ice and strain into a chocolate-rimmed cocktail glass.

Invented at the Continental Cafe in Philadelphia, PA.

White Lady

1½ oz. gin
½ oz. Cointreau
1½ oz. lemon juice

Shake and strain into a frosted glass.

White Russian

1½ oz. vodka
½ oz. Kahlúa
½ oz. cream

Shake and serve over ice.

The Dude calls this drink a Caucasian in The Big Lebowski.

White Spider

1 oz. vodka
1 oz. Rumple Minze

Combine in a shot glass.

Wild Irish Rose

1½ oz. Irish whiskey
1½ tsp. grenadine
½ oz. lime juice
Club soda

Fill a highball glass with ice. Add Irish whiskey, grenadine, and lime juice. Stir well. Fill with club soda.

THE LOWDOWN ON THE WHITE LADY

FABLES AND LORE

Harry MacElhone created the White Lady in 1919 at Ciro's Club in London, England. In 1923, he took over a bar in Rue Daunou, Paris, renaming it Harry's New York Bar. In 1929, using gin in place of white crème de menthe, he altered the original White Lady recipe, and this concoction became a worldwide favorite.

Winter Maple

2 oz. Crown Royal
    Canadian Whisky
1 oz. lemon juice
3 oz. hot water
2 tbsp. maple syrup

Add all ingredients into a coffee or tea mug and stir.

Wolfhound

1 oz. Irish whiskey
¾ oz. dark crème de cacao
½ oz. half & half
Splash club soda

Stir ingredients with ice and serve over ice.

Woo Woo #1

¾ oz. vodka
¾ oz. peppermint schnapps

Combine in a glass with ice.

Woo Woo #2

1 oz. vodka
½ oz. peach schnapps
2 oz. cranberry juice

Combine ingredients over ice.

Yard Sale

1½ oz. gin
¾ oz. lemon juice
¾ oz. lime juice
1¼ oz. honey syrup
½ oz. heavy cream
1 tsp. matcha

Add all ingredients into a shaker with ice. Shake and strain into a highball glass with ice.

Yellow Bird

2 oz. rum
½ oz. Galliano
½ oz. triple sec
½ oz. lime juice

Shake with ice. Strain into a coupe glass.

Yellow Morning

1 oz. crème de banana
1 oz. Cherry Heering
1 oz. cognac

Layer this drink in the order listed. Start with crème de banana on the bottom and finish with cognac on top.

Zac-Daiq

2 oz. Ron Zacapa 23 Rum
1 oz. lime juice
½ oz. banana liqueur
¼ oz. demerara simple syrup

Shake and strain into a chilled coupe glass.

Zipper

1 oz. vodka
1 oz. Chambord
½ oz. club soda

Combine in a shot glass with the club soda on top.

Zombie

1½ oz. Jamaican rum
1½ oz. gold rum
1 oz. demerara rum
¾ oz. lime juice
1 bar spoon of Pernod
½ oz. Donn's mix (yellow grapefruit and cinnamon simple syrup)
½ oz. falernum
1 dash angostura bitters
1 bar spoon grenadine
1½ cups of ice
Mint sprig for garnish

Add all ingredients into a blender with ice and blend. Pour into a glass with crushed or pebble ice and garnish with mint sprig.

Chapter **21**
Shots and Shooters

Shots and shooters are small serves that get crowds and guests excited. Usually, shots are around 1.5 to 2 ounces, while shooters are a bit larger at 2 to 3 ounces. We feature a lot of popular recipes in this chapter, but of course, you can do shots and shooters of almost any type of spirit straight. As always, monitor your guests so you're not overserving.

TIP

Some of these shots ask you to "layer" them. To do this, take your bar spoon and place the back of the spoon into the shot glass. Slowly pour the desired liquid over the back of the spoon. This will layer the liquids on top of each other. Be sure to follow each recipe so that you layer them properly based on the spirits' densities. These layered shots not only look impressive but are often delicious as well!

Read on for some of the most popular shots. The names of these recipes have been around for quite some time, so give them a shot (literally); we weren't the originators! Remember, you will miss 100% of the shots you don't shake!

007 Shot

1 oz. orange vodka
1 oz. orange juice
1 oz. 7UP

Add orange vodka and orange juice into a shaker with ice. Shake and strain into a shot glass. Top with 7UP and serve.

You can also serve this one over ice in a rocks glass.

ABC

⅓ oz. amaretto
⅓ oz. Baileys Irish Cream
⅓ oz. cognac

Add amaretto into a shot glass. Slowly layer in Baileys Irish Cream. Finally, slowly layer in cognac, and serve.

A-Bomb #2

½ oz. Baileys Irish Cream
½ oz. Kahlúa
½ oz. Tito's Vodka
¼ oz. Tia Maria

Shake with ice, strain, and serve.

After 5

1 oz. Irish cream
1 oz. Rumple Minze peppermint schnapps

Pour the ingredients into a shot glass.

After 8

½ oz. Irish cream
½ oz. coffee liqueur
½ oz. green crème de menthe

Shake with ice. Strain into a shot glass.

Alabama Slammer

½ oz. amaretto
½ oz. gin
½ oz. Southern Comfort
½ oz. orange juice

Shake with ice and strain.

Aztec Ruin

½ oz. Jose Cuervo
    Tradicional Tequila
½ oz. lime juice

Shake with ice and strain into a shot glass.

Aztec Sky

¾ oz. Jose Cuervo
    Tradicional Tequila
¾ oz. Blue Curaçao

Shake with ice and strain into a shot glass.

B-52

⅓ oz. Kahlúa
⅓ oz. Baileys Irish Cream
⅓ oz. triple sec

Layer in order into a shot glass.

Baby Guinness

1 oz. coffee liqueur, chilled
½ oz. Baileys Irish Cream

Pour chilled coffee liqueur into a shot glass. Layer Baileys Irish Cream on top and serve.

This shot looks like a mini Guinness!

Banana Boat

¾ oz. Malibu Rum
¾ oz. banana liqueur
¼ oz. pineapple juice

Combine in a shot glass.

Blowjob

½ oz. Baileys Irish Cream
½ oz. Kahlúa
Whipped cream

Shake with ice and strain into a shot glass. Top with whipped cream.

Blue Kamikazi

1 oz. vodka
¼ oz. lime juice
¼ oz. Blue Curaçao

Shake with ice and strain into a shot glass.

Bocci Ball

½ oz. Disaronno Amaretto
½ oz. vodka
½ oz. orange juice

Shake with ice. Serve straight up in a shot glass.

You can also serve this one over ice in a rocks glass.

Boilermaker

2 oz. whiskey
1 pint lager beer

This is a pairing. Pour whiskey into shot glass and place next to beer and serve.

Buttery Nipple

½ oz. Baileys Irish Cream
1 oz. butterscotch schnapps

Add butterscotch schnapps into shot glass. Slowly layer in Baileys and serve.

Cherry Bomb

½ oz. cherry brandy
1 oz. rum
½ oz. sour mix

Shake with ice and strain into a shot glass.

Chocolate Cake

Sugar
1 lemon wedge
¾ oz. vanilla vodka
¾ oz. hazelnut liqueur

Add sugar to a lemon wedge and set next to shot glass. Add vanilla vodka and hazelnut liqueur into a shaker with ice and shake. Strain into shot glass and serve with sugar-coated lemon wedge.

Chocolate Covered Cherry

½ oz. grenadine
½ oz. Kahlúa
½ oz. Baileys Irish Cream

Layer grenadine, Kahlúa, and then Baileys in a shot glass.

You can also serve this one over ice in a rocks glass (without layering the ingredients).

Flaming Dr. Pepper

¾ oz. amaretto
¼ overproof rum
½ pint beer

Add amaretto into shot glass and top with overproof rum. Carefully light the top of the shot with a match, causing it to make a flame. Drop shot into beer.

Flatliner

½ oz. sambuca liqueur
¼ oz. tequila
2–3 dashes Tabasco

Add sambuca into shot glass. Layer in tequila and dash Tabasco on top and serve.

Four Horsemen

½ oz. Johnnie Walker Black Label Scotch Whisky
½ oz. Jack Daniel's
½ oz. Jim Beam
½ oz. Jameson

Shake over ice and strain into a shot glass.

Girl Scout Cookie

½ oz. Baileys Irish Cream
½ oz. peppermint schnapps
½ oz. coffee liqueur

Add all ingredients into a shaker with ice. Shake and strain into shot glass and serve.

Green Tea

½ oz. Jameson Irish Whiskey
½ oz. peach schnapps
½ oz. sour mix
Splash lemon-lime soda

Add Jameson, peach schnapps, and sour mix into a shaker with ice. Shake and strain into a shot glass. Top with splash of lemon-lime soda and serve.

Gummy Bear

1 oz. peach schnapps
1 oz. raspberry vodka
1 oz. triple sec

Add ingredients into a shaker with ice. Shake and strain into a shot glass.

Hand Grenade

1 oz. white rum
1 oz. Jägermeister
½ can Red Bull

Place Red Bull into a pint glass. Place both shots side by side on top of the glass. Tell the guests to take the shot of rum. This will drop the Jägermeister shot into the Red Bull glass and the guest should drink it.

Irish Slammer

1 oz. Irish whiskey
1/2 oz. Baileys Irish Cream
½ pint Guinness

Add Irish whiskey into a shot glass and pour the Baileys slowly over it, causing it to layer. Serve side by side with the Guinness.

Jäger Bomb

1½ oz. Jägermeister
½ can Red Bull

Place Red Bull into a pint glass. Drop Jägermeister shot into the pint glass.

Jell-O Shots

3 oz. Jell-O
8 oz. boiling water
4 oz. vodka
4 oz. cold water

Stir Jell-O and boiling water together in a large bowl until Jell-O dissolves. Add in vodka and cold water and stir. Pour into shot glasses or plastic cups and place into fridge. Let sit until solid and serve.

Jelly Donut

Sugar
½ oz. Chambord
1 oz. Baileys Irish Cream

Rim a shot glass with sugar. Add ingredients into a shaker with ice. Shake and strain into sugar-rimmed glass and serve.

Jolly Rancher

½ oz. green apple vodka
½ oz. peach schnapps
1 oz. cranberry juice

Add all ingredients into a shaker with ice. Shake and strain into a shot glass.

You can also serve this one over ice in a rocks glass.

Kamikaze

¾ oz. Tito's Vodka
¾ oz. triple sec
¾ oz. lime juice

Pour vodka, triple sec, and lime juice into shaker. Shake well and strain into a shot glass.

Lemon Drop #1

2 oz. Absolut Citron Vodka
1 oz. lemon juice
Sugar

Shake. Serve in a sugar-rimmed chilled shot glass with a squeeze of lemon juice.

Lemon Drop #2

1½ oz. Absolut Citron Vodka
½ oz. 7UP
½ oz. lemon juice

Serve in sugar-rimmed shot glass.

Little Beer

1½ oz. Licor 43 Liqueur, chilled
½ oz. heavy cream

Pour chilled Licor 43 into shot glass. Layer heavy cream on top and serve.

This shot looks like a mini beer!

Melon Ball

¼ oz. melon liqueur
½ oz. vodka
¼ oz. pineapple juice

Add all ingredients into a shaker with ice. Shake and strain into a shot glass.

Mind Eraser

1½ oz. vodka
1½ oz. Kahlúa
Splash tonic water

Shake the vodka and Kahlúa with ice and strain into a shot glass. Top with tonic water.

Nutty Irishman

¾ oz. hazelnut liqueur
¾ oz. Baileys Irish Cream

Add hazelnut liqueur into shot glass. Layer Baileys on top and serve.

Orgasm

⊔   ⅓ oz. amaretto
⅓ oz. coffee liqueur
⅓ oz. Baileys Irish Cream

Add ingredients into a shaker with ice. Shake and strain into a shot glass.

Oyster Shooter

⊔   1 oz. vodka
1 raw oyster
1 tsp. cocktail sauce
¼ oz. lemon juice

Pour vodka over the oyster and sauce in a small rocks glass and stir. Add a squeeze of lemon juice.

You can also add a dash of horseradish if you dare.

Peanut Butter & Jelly

⊔   ¾ oz. black raspberry liqueur
¾ oz. hazelnut liqueur

Add ingredients into a shaker with ice. Shake and strain into a shot glass.

Pickle Back

⊔   1½ oz. Jameson Irish Whiskey
1 oz. chilled pickle juice

Pour the Jameson (room temperature) in one shot glass and the pickle juice in another. Shoot the Jameson and chase with the pickle juice.

Pineapple Upside-Down Cake

⊔   1 oz. vanilla vodka
1 oz. pineapple juice
Dash grenadine

Add vanilla vodka and pineapple juice into a shaker with ice. Shake and strain into a shot glass. Dash grenadine on top and serve.

Purple Hooters

⊔   1 oz. Chambord
1 oz. vodka
1 oz. triple sec

Add ingredients into a shaker with ice. Shake and strain into a shot glass.

Redheaded Slut

½ oz. peach schnapps
½ oz. Jägermeister
½ oz. cranberry juice

Add ingredients into a shaker with ice. Shake and strain into a shot glass.

Red Snapper

½ oz. Crown Royal
Canadian Whisky
½ oz. amaretto
1 oz. cranberry juice

Add ingredients into a shaker with ice. Shake and strain into a shot glass.

Rice Pudding

1½ oz. RumChata Liqueur
1 oz. Fireball Cinnamon Whisky

Add ingredients into a shaker with ice. Shake and strain into a shot glass.

Ruby Slipper

½ oz. grenadine
2 oz. 7UP
1 oz. whiskey

In a glass, add in 7UP and grenadine. Drop whiskey shot into glass.

Scooby Snack

1 oz. melon liqueur
1 oz. Malibu Rum
1 oz. pineapple juice
Whipped cream

Add ingredients into a shaker with ice. Shake and strain into a shot glass. Top with whipped cream.

Slippery Nipple

1 oz. Baileys Irish Cream
1 oz. Sambuca Liqueur

Pour Sambuca into shot glass. Layer Baileys on top and serve.

Snaquiri

1 oz. rum
½ oz. lime juice
¼ oz. simple syrup

Add ingredients into a shaker with ice. Shake and strain into a shot glass.

A smaller version of a Daiquiri.

SoCo Lime

2 oz. Southern Comfort
Squeeze of lime juice

Add ingredients into a shaker with
ice. Shake and strain into a shot
glass.

Surfer on Acid

½ oz. Jägermeister
½ oz. coconut rum
½ oz. pineapple juice

Add ingredients into a shaker with
ice. Shake and strain into a shot
glass.

Three Wise Men

½ oz. Johnnie Walker Black Label
   Scotch Whisky
½ oz. Jack Daniel's
½ oz. Jim Beam

Add ingredients into a shaker with
ice. Shake and strain into a shot
glass.

Waffle Shot

1 oz. bourbon
¼ oz. maple syrup
½ oz. Pinnacle Whipped Vodka

Add ingredients into a shaker with
ice. Shake and strain into a shot
glass.

Washington Apple

¾ oz. Crown Royal Apple
   Canadian Whisky
¾ oz. sour apple schnapps
¾ oz. cranberry juice
Splash club soda

Add all ingredients, except club
soda, into a shaker with ice. Shake
and strain into shot glasses and
splash club soda on top and serve.

You can also serve this one over ice in a rocks glass.

Woo Woo

1 oz. vodka
½ oz. peach schnapps
½ oz. cranberry juice

Add ingredients into a shaker with
ice. Shake and strain into a shot
glass.

Chapter 22
Martini Making

Traditionally, a Martini is simply gin, vermouth, and a garnish, usually an olive or a lemon twist. Like most drinks, there are always some twists to them. Some people like vodka in their Martini, some like dirty Martinis, which include some olive juice, and some prefer a blue cheese–stuffed olive in their Martini.

Ultimately, the Martinis in this chapter are just cocktails like any other, but they're called Martinis because they're served in a martini glass. This drink is always on trend, but what style or type of Martini is always changing. Originally, it was the classic, then went to the Cosmopolitan, and now the Espresso Martini is making a massive comeback! In a few years, something else will pop up and be trendy and we'll serve it to our guests.

Overall, we tried to pick out the trendiest "Martinis" that actually taste good and are worth drinking. Cheers!

50/50 Martini

1½ oz. gin
1½ oz. dry vermouth
1 dash orange bitters
Lemon twist for garnish

Add ingredients into a mixing glass with ice and stir. Strain into a martini glass. Garnish with a lemon twist.

Alaska

1½ oz. gin
½ oz. Yellow Chartreuse
1 dash orange bitters
Lemon twist for garnish

Add ingredients into a mixing glass with ice and stir. Strain into a chilled martini glass. Garnish with lemon twist.

Angel Martini

2½ oz. Ketel One Vodka
½ oz. Frangelico

Shake with ice. Strain into a chilled martini glass.

A little Italy and a little Netherlands. (This one was invented at the Bowery Bar in New York, NY.)

Apple Martini

2 oz. Tito's Vodka
½ oz. Schönauer Apfel Schnapps
1 dash cinnamon
Apple slice for garnish

Shake with ice. Strain into a chilled martini glass. Garnish with a slice of apple.

Apricot Martini

1 oz. Godiva Liqueur
1 oz. Absolut Vodka
1 oz. apricot brandy
Cherry for garnish

Combine with ice; shake well. Serve chilled with a cherry.

It's not the pits.

Black Tie Martini

1½ oz. SKYY Vodka
Splash Campari
Splash Chivas Regal Scotch Whisky
2 cocktail onions
1 black olive

Shake vodka, Campari, and Chivas with ice and strain into a chilled martini glass. Garnish with cocktail onions and black olive.

Blues Martini

1½ oz. Ketel One Vodka
1½ oz. Bombay Sapphire Gin
Few drops Blue Curaçao

Stir gently with ice. Serve straight up or over ice.

Bootlegger Martini

2 oz. Bombay Gin
¼ oz. Southern Comfort
Lemon twist for garnish

Stir gently with ice; serve straight up or over ice. Garnish with a lemon twist.

Created at the Martini Bar at Chianti Restaurant in Houston, TX.

Breakfast Martini

1½ oz. gin
½ oz. orange liqueur
¾ oz. fresh lemon juice
1 bar spoon orange marmalade

Shake with ice and strain into a martini glass.

Cosmopolitan

1½ oz. citrus vodka
½ oz. Cointreau
½ oz. fresh lime juice
1 oz. cranberry juice
Lemon twist for garnish

Shake all ingredients in a shaker with ice. Strain into a chilled martini glass. Garnish with a lemon twist.

Cucumber Martini

2½ oz. vodka or gin
½ oz. dry vermouth
6 cucumber slices

Add three cucumber slices into a shaker with dry vermouth and muddle. Add in your choice of vodka or gin with ice and shake. Strain into a chilled martini glass and garnish with the remaining cucumber slices.

Dirty Martini

2 oz. gin or vodka
½ oz. dry vermouth
½ oz. olive brine

Add ingredients into a mixing glass with ice and stir. Strain into a martini glass.

Dry Victoria Martini

3 oz. Bombay Sapphire Gin
1 oz. Martini & Rossi Extra
    Dry Vermouth
1–2 dashes angostura bitters
1 cocktail olive and lemon twist
    for garnish

Shake or stir. Serve in a classic martini glass. Garnish with cocktail olive and a lemon twist.

Espresso Martini

2 oz. vodka
½ oz. coffee liqueur
1 oz. espresso
½ oz. simple syrup

Shake with ice and strain into a martini glass.

French Martini

2 oz. vodka
¼ oz. crème de cassis
1¾ oz. pineapple juice

Add ingredients into a mixing glass with ice and stir. Strain into a martini glass.

Gibson

2½ oz. vodka or gin
½ oz. dry vermouth
Cocktail onion for garnish

Add ingredients into a mixing glass with ice and stir. Strain into a chilled martini glass. Garnish with a cocktail onion.

The cocktail onion turns this drink from a Martini to a Gibson.

"In and Out" Martini

¼ oz. dry vermouth
2 oz. gin or vodka
Lemon twist or an olive for
  garnish

Fill shaker glass with ice and add vermouth. Swirl ice around in glass and pour out. Add gin/vodka and shake vigorously. Pour into a martini glass.

From Patrick Ford, Smith & Wollensky, New York, NY.

Lavender Orchid

1 oz. Tanqueray No. Ten Gin
¼ oz. Chambord
1 oz. sour mix
Splash ginger ale
1 orchid for garnish

In a shaker with ice, add Tanqueray, Chambord, and sour mix. Shake gently, strain into a martini glass, and add splash of ginger ale. Decorate with a floating orchid.

Limontini

1 oz. vanilla vodka
½ oz. limoncello
1½ oz. pomegranate juice
Squeeze of lime
Lemon twist for garnish

Shake vigorously, strain into a
martini glass, and serve. Garnish
with a lemon twist.

You can substitute orange-flavored vodka for the vanilla vodka.

Mayflower Martini

2 oz. Plymouth Gin
1 oz. French Vermouth
Dash angostura bitters
Orange or lemon twist for garnish

Shake with ice and strain into a
chilled martini glass. Garnish with
an orange or lemon twist.

*This drink is based on Thomas Stuart's original recipe. Modern tastes may prefer a drier
version with less vermouth.*

Mystique Martini

2 oz. Smirnoff Vodka
Dash Green Chartreuse
Lemon or lime twist for garnish

Chill, strain, and garnish with a
lemon or lime twist.

Orange Espresso Martini

2 oz. orange vodka
½ oz. coffee liqueur
1 oz. espresso
½ oz. simple syrup

Shake with ice and strain into a
martini glass.

Porn Star Martini

2 oz. vanilla vodka
½ oz. passion fruit liqueur
1 oz. passion fruit purée
½ oz. fresh lime juice
½ oz. vanilla simple syrup
2 oz. sparkling wine

Add all ingredients minus sparkling
wine into a cocktail shaker with ice.
Shake and strain into a martini glass
and top with sparkling wine.

Purple Hooter Martini

1¼ oz. Chambord
1¼ oz. vodka
¼ oz. sour mix
¼ oz. lemon-
    lime soda

Combine ingredients, except soda, into a shaker filled with ice. Shake thoroughly and pour into a martini glass. Top with lemon-lime soda.

It's not all that different from a Purple Hooters shot (see Chapter 21), but it looks classier in a martini glass.

Ruby Slipper Martini

2 oz. Bombay Sapphire Gin
¼ oz. Grand Marnier
1 or 2 splashes grenadine
Dash peppermint schnapps
Mint leaf for garnish

Shake with ice and strain into a well-chilled martini glass. Garnish with a mint leaf (set it on the edge of the drink and let it stick out).

Smoke by the Sea

2½ oz. Tanqueray London Dry Gin
½ oz. Talisker 10 Scotch Whisky
Lemon twist for garnish

Add ingredients into a mixing glass with ice and stir. Strain into a chilled martini glass. Garnish with lemon twist.

Inspired by Ryan Foley.

Tanqueray "Perfect Ten" Martini

2 oz. Tanqueray No. Ten Gin
1 oz. Grand Marnier
½ oz. sour mix
Lemon twist for garnish

Shake with ice. Strain into a martini glass. Garnish with lemon twist.

Tequila Martini

1½ oz. blanco tequila
¾ oz. blanc vermouth
¼ oz. lemon juice
2 dashes orange bitters
Lemon twist for garnish

Combine ingredients into a shaker filled with ice. Shake thoroughly and pour into a martini glass. Garnish with a lemon twist.

Thrilla in Vanilla

2 oz. vanilla vodka
½ oz. DeKuyper Peach Schnapps

Shake with ice and strain into a
martini glass.

Created by E. McNeice, Basking Ridge, NJ.

Tiramisu Martini

1 oz. vodka
1 oz. brandy
½ oz. chocolate syrup
½ oz. simple syrup
2 oz. coffee
1 tbsp. mascarpone cheese
1 egg white

Combine ingredients into a shaker
filled with ice. Shake vigorously until
the mascarpone cheese is liquefied.
Strain into a chilled cocktail glass.

Created by M. Filoramo, Hoboken, NJ.

Topaz Martini

1¾ oz. Bacardi Limón Rum
¼ oz. Martini & Rossi Extra
   Dry Vermouth
Splash Blue Curaçao
Lemon twist or olives for garnish

Stir in a cocktail glass. Strain and
serve straight up or on the rocks.
Add a lemon twist or olives to
garnish.

Invented at the Heart and Soul in San Francisco, CA.

Trinity Martini

1 oz. Bombay Sapphire Gin
½ oz. sweet vermouth
½ oz. dry vermouth
Lemon twist or olives for garnish

Stir in a cocktail glass. Strain and
serve straight up or on the rocks.
Add a lemon twist or olives to
garnish.

This cocktail is also known as the Trio Plaza Martini.

Vesper

3 oz. gin
1 oz. vodka
½ oz. Lillet Blanc
Lemon twist for garnish

Add Ingredients into a mixing glass
with ice and stir. Strain into a
martini glass. Garnish with a lemon
twist.

Warden Martini

1½ oz. Bombay Sapphire Gin
Dash Martini & Rossi Extra
    Dry Vermouth
Dash Pernod
Lemon twist or olives for garnish

Stir in a mixing glass. Strain and serve straight up or on the rocks in a martini glass. Add a lemon twist or olives to garnish.

Chapter **23**

Drinks for Special Occasions

Y ou're bound to have a few parties throughout the year, and some of those parties will probably fall on holidays. We start this chapter with some punch recipes. They'll be a hit at any gathering. Then we share a sampling of holiday drinks. Try them with your friends throughout the year.

Crowd-Pleasing Punches with a Punch

Punches of all kinds are an expected beverage at many of today's social gatherings. Whether you're an aspiring bartender or just someone who wants to be a good host (and the life of the party), you need to have at least a few of the following festive punches in your repertoire. (Check out Chapter 24 for fun drink recipes sans alcohol.)

WHO THREW THE FIRST PUNCH?

Punch may have come from the word *puncheon*, a cast made to hold liquids, such as beer. The word may also have come from the Hindu word for five. What does the number five have to do with anything? British expatriates in India in the 17th century made a beverage consisting of five ingredients: tea, water, sugar, lemon juice, and a fermented sap called *arrack*. Regardless of which history or origin is 100% true, punches are a big part of cocktail history!

Ambrosia Punch

20 oz. can crushed pineapple, undrained
15 oz. Coco Lopez Cream of Coconut
2 cups apricot nectar, chilled
2 cups orange juice, chilled
1½ cups light rum (optional)
1 liter club soda, chilled

In a blender, purée the pineapple and Cream of Coconut until smooth. In a punch bowl, combine the puréed mixture, apricot nectar, orange juice, and rum (if desired). Mix well. Just before serving, add club soda and serve over ice.

This recipe serves about 24.

Bacardi Confetti Punch

750 ml. Bacardi Light Rum
6 oz. can frozen lemonade concentrate
6 oz. can frozen grapefruit juice concentrate
6 oz. can fruit cocktail, drained
2 liters club soda, chilled

Combine the first four ingredients in a large container and chill for 2 hours, stirring occasionally. To serve, pour the mixture over ice in a punch bowl and add chilled club soda. Stir gently.

This recipe makes 8 servings.

Cointreau Punch

1 bottle Cointreau
1 bottle vodka
3 quarts club soda
6 oz. can orange juice concentrate
6 oz. can pineapple juice concentrate
Orange slices, cranberries, and cloves for garnish

Place a clear block of ice in a large punch bowl. Combine ingredients and stir. Garnish with orange slices decorated with cranberries and studded with cloves.

This recipe makes enough for 40 punch-cup drinks.

Double Berry Coco Punch

20 oz. frozen strawberries in
    syrup, thawed
15 oz. Coco Lopez Cream of Coconut
48 oz. cranberry juice cocktail,
    chilled
2 cups light rum (optional)
1 liter club soda, chilled

In a blender, purée the
strawberries and Cream of
Coconut until smooth. In a large
punch bowl, combine the puréed
mixture, cranberry juice, and rum
(if desired). Just before serving,
add club soda and serve over ice.

This recipe serves about 32.

Formula #21

1 bottle Smirnoff Vodka
1 bottle white wine
2 quarts pineapple juice
½ cup lime juice
2 quarts club soda, chilled
Sugar to taste

Mix the ingredients in a punch
bowl and serve.

This recipe serves 12–20.

Fruit Punch

4 oz. pineapple juice
6 oz. orange juice
6 oz. lemon or lime juice
1 fifth light rum
1 quart ginger ale or club soda, chilled
Fine sugar to taste
Fresh pineapple and orange for garnish

Mix first four ingredients in a
large container. Chill 2 hours.
Pour mixture over a block of ice
in a bowl. Add cold ginger ale or
club soda. Decorate with fresh
fruit garnish.

Serves 9 people twice.

Malibu Party Punch

1 bottle Malibu Rum
48 oz. cranberry juice
6 oz. can frozen orange juice concentrate
6 oz. can frozen lemonade or limeade
    concentrate
Lemon and orange slices and cloves
    for garnish

Combine ingredients in a punch
bowl and stir. Garnish with lemon
and orange slices and cloves.

This recipe serves 12–20.

M&R Hot Spiced Wine Punch

1½ liters Martini & Rossi Red Vermouth
2 dashes bitters
6 cloves
3 cinnamon sticks
3 tsp. superfine sugar
Pinch allspice
Pinch ground clove
Orange slices for garnish

Combine all ingredients except orange slices in a heavy saucepan and heat but don't boil. Strain into a punch bowl. For added effect, heat a poker and dip it into the punch before serving. Garnish with the orange slices.

This recipe serves 6–12.

Metaxa Fruit Punch

½ gallon orange sherbet
Three 2-liter bottles 7UP
16 oz. Metaxa
6–8 scoops raspberry sherbet
1 orange, sliced thin

Mix all ingredients except the raspberry sherbet and orange slices. Chill for 1 hour. Place scoops of raspberry sherbet atop the punch. Add the orange slices.

This recipe serves 10–15.

Open House Punch

750 ml. Southern Comfort
6 oz. lemon juice
6 oz. can frozen lemonade
6 oz. can frozen orange juice
3 liters 7UP or Sprite
Red food coloring
Orange and lemon slices for garnish

Chill ingredients. Mix the first four ingredients in a punch bowl. Add 7UP or Sprite. Add drops of red food coloring as desired and stir. Float a block of ice and garnish with orange and lemon slices. Note that the first four ingredients may be mixed in advance. Add 7UP or Sprite and ice when ready to serve.

This recipe makes 32 servings.

Party Punch

16 oz. orange juice
16 oz. pineapple juice, unsweetened
16 oz. club soda
3 oz. lime juice
16 oz. white or gold rum
Sugar to taste

Pour ingredients into a large punch bowl filled with ice. Add sugar to taste.

This recipe serves 12.

Patio Punch

750 ml. Southern Comfort
16 oz. grapefruit juice
8 oz. fresh lime juice
2 liters 7UP or ginger ale

Mix ingredients and add ice. Serve from a punch bowl or pitcher. Note that the first three ingredients can be mixed in advance and refrigerated. Add the 7UP or ginger ale and ice when ready to serve.

This recipe serves 15-20.

Planter's Punch

3 oz. dark rum
1 oz. simple syrup
¾ oz. lime juice
1 tsp. grenadine
3 dashes bitters
Splash club soda

Add all ingredients minus club soda into a shaker with ice. Shake and strain into a rocks glass and serve.

Makes just 1 serving, but this is a classic punch recipe. Multiply and share!

Poinsettia Punch

750 ml. orange vodka
750 ml. sparkling wine
1 liter cranberry juice
1 liter club soda
½ cup cranberries

Mix ingredients and add ice. Serve from a punch bowl or pitcher. Note that the first three ingredients can be mixed in advance and refrigerated. Add the sparkling wine right before serving.

This recipe serves 10–15.

Scorpion Bowl

6 oz. rum
1 oz. brandy
6 oz. orange juice
4 oz. lemon juice
1½ oz. orgeat syrup

Add crushed ice into a large ceramic bowl. Mix ingredients together and add in multiple straws and serve.

Serves 2–3.

Shower Punch

2 quarts orange juice
2 quarts grapefruit
   juice
1 quart light rum
3 thinly sliced oranges for garnish

Mix ingredients in a large container. Chill 2 hours. Pour mixture over a block of ice just before serving. Add orange slices.

Serves 25+ people.

Tropical Fruit Punch

15 oz. Coco Lopez Cream of Coconut
1 medium banana
8 oz. can of pineapple juice
10 oz. light rum
1 cup orange juice
1 tbsp. real lemon or lime juice from
   concentrate
2 cups ice

In a blender, combine all ingredients, except Ice; blend well. Gradually add ice, blending until smooth. Garnish as desired. Serve immediately. Refrigerate leftovers.

Makes about 5 servings.

Holiday Cocktails

Here are several drinks you can serve on holidays throughout the calendar year. Sure, you can have green beer or Irish Coffee on St. Patrick's Day, but these cocktails are a fun and delicious alternative.

New Year's Eve: Midnight Cocktail

3 oz. dry champagne
½ oz. Goldschläger

Fill a champagne flute with chilled champagne, leaving room at the top. Pour in the Goldschläger, making sure to include a few flakes of gold!

Valentine's Day: Valentine's Special

3½ oz. strawberry liqueur
½ oz. Mozart Chocolate
   Liqueur
Chocolate kisses for garnish

Shake. Serve on the rocks with chocolate kisses as a garnish.

St. Patrick's Day: Nutty Irishman

1 part Baileys Irish Cream
1 part Frangelico

Shake all ingredients and serve as a shot.

Easter: PeepTini

1½ oz. Tito's Vodka
½ oz. sweet vermouth
½ oz. fresh lime juice
1 oz. cranberry juice
Peep candy for garnish

Shake all ingredients in a shaker with ice. Strain into a chilled martini glass. Garnish with a Peep.

Cinco De Mayo: Spicy Pineapple Margarita

½ jalapeño
½ oz. fresh lime juice
2 oz. tequila
1 oz. Cointreau
½ oz. agave syrup
½ oz. pineapple juice

Cut half a jalapeño into slices and add into shaker with fresh lime juice and begin to muddle. Add in the remaining ingredients with ice and shake. Double strain into a spicy salt-rimmed rocks glass and serve.

Independence Day: Red, White & Booze

⅓ oz. grenadine
⅓ oz. white crème de cacao
⅓ oz. Blue Curaçao

This is a layered shot. Start with adding in grenadine, then slowly layer in white crème de cacao, then slowly Blue Curaçao.

Halloween: Bloody Brew

1½ oz. vodka
4 oz. beer (your choice)
4 oz. tomato juice
Dash Tabasco
Salt and pepper to taste
Lemon wedge, pickle spear,
    green bean, or celery stalk
    for garnish

Combine ingredients in a tall glass and garnish with a lemon, pickle, green bean, or celery.

Thanksgiving: Wild Thanksgiving

1 oz. Wild Turkey Bourbon
1 oz. apple brandy
½ oz. lime juice
2 oz. cranberry juice
Mint leaf for garnish

Combine over ice and garnish with mint.

Hanukkah: Israeli Sunrise

1½ oz. Sabra (chocolate-orange flavored liqueur)
1 oz. vodka
2 tbsp. softened orange sherbet

Combine Sabra and vodka. Stir into softened sherbet. Serve in a rocks glass.

Christmas: Gingerbread Man

1½ oz. vanilla vodka
4 oz. ginger beer
Cherry for garnish

Pour vodka over a couple of ice cubes in a cocktail glass. Add ginger beer, garnish with a cherry, and serve.

Chapter **24**

Mocktails and Low-Alcohol Cocktails

A good number of your guests may choose to take it easy on the alcohol or choose not to drink alcohol at all, but this decision doesn't mean that they're stuck with just water or soft drinks. A lot of drink recipes include little or no alcohol by volume (or ABV) but are still festive looking and delicious. Any of the following recipes is sure to impress.

Low-Alcohol Cocktails

Here are a few low ABV cocktails, which are growing in popularity. These are always a great add-on to any cocktail menu at your bar or at your next event or party.

Adonis

1½ oz. Fino Sherry
1½ oz. sweet vermouth
2 dashes orange bitters
Orange peel for garnish

Add ingredients into a mixing glass with ice and stir. Strain into a coupe glass, garnish with an orange peel, and serve.

Amaro Highball

1½ oz. Montenegro Amaro
Tonic water
Lime wedge for garnish

Add Amaro into a highball glass with ice. Top with tonic water and stir. Garnish with lime wedge and serve.

Americano

1½ oz. Campari
1½ oz. sweet vermouth
Soda water
Orange twist for garnish

Add Campari and sweet vermouth into a highball glass with ice. Top with soda water and stir. Garnish with orange twist and serve.

Bamboo

3 parts sherry
1 part vermouth

Add sherry and vermouth into a mixing glass with ice and stir. Strain into a coupe glass.

The first reference of this drink dates back to 1886! Modern takes on this add in dashes of bitters.

Banker's Lunch

½ oz. vodka
½ oz. dry vermouth
½ oz. orange liqueur
1½ oz. grapefruit juice
Grapefruit twist or wheel for garnish

Add all ingredients into a shaker with ice and shake. Strain into an ice-filled rocks glass. Garnish with a grapefruit twist or wheel and serve.

Botanical Spritz

1½ oz. Ketel One Botanical (your favorite flavor)
3 oz. soda water

In a wine glass, add in liquid ingredients with ice and stir.

The Spritz is becoming one of the most popular low ABV drinks.

Club Low

1½ oz. strawberry simple syrup
2-3 basil leaves
1 oz. Campari
1 oz. lemon juice
1 egg white

In a cocktail shaker with ice. Add in strawberry simple syrup and 2 basil leaves and muddle. Add in Campari, lemon juice, and egg white and dry shake hard. Add in ice and shake again. Strain into a coupe glass and garnish with a basil leaf.

Cold Snap

1 tsp. cinnamon simple syrup
2 ginger slices
2 oz. orange liqueur
1 oz. lime juice
3 dashes bitters
Orange twist for garnish

In a shaker, add in cinnamon simple syrup and ginger slices and muddle. Add in remaining liquid ingredients and ice and shake. Strain into a rocks glass with ice. Garnish with orange twist and serve.

Garibaldi

1½ oz. Campari
4 oz. orange juice
Orange wedge for garnish

Add all ingredients into a highball glass with ice and stir. Garnish with orange wedge and serve.

Kir Cocktail

4½ oz. dry white wine
¾ oz. crème de cassis

In a white wine glass, add in the dry white wine of your choice and crème de cassis. Stir and serve.

Low-Proof Julep

1½ oz. Cynar
1 oz. grapefruit juice
½ oz. raspberry simple syrup
½ oz. lime juice
3-4 mint leaves

In a cocktail shaker with ice, shake all ingredients. Strain into a julep cup with crushed ice. Garnish with mint and serve.

Perry Paradise

1½ oz. Campari
2 oz. pineapple juice
2 oz. orange juice
Orange wedge for garnish

Add all ingredients into a highball glass with ice and stir. Garnish with an orange wedge and serve.

Inspired by M. Perry, Brooklyn, NY.

Pick-Me-Up

½ oz. Ketel One Botanical Peach
  and Orange Blossom
½ oz. espresso
2 oz. tonic water
½ oz. brown sugar simple syrup
  or 1 tbsp. brown sugar
Orange wedge for garnish

Add all ingredients into a highball glass with ice and stir. Garnish with an orange wedge and serve.

Inspired by M. Michels, Sugar Mountain, NC.

Port & Tonic

2 oz. port wine
4 oz. tonic water
Orange wheel for garnish

In a highball glass, add in port wine with ice. Top with tonic water and stir. Garnish with an orange wheel and serve.

Sherry Cobbler

3 oz. dry Amontillado Sherry
¼ oz. simple syrup
2 orange wheels

Add liquid ingredients, one orange wheel, and ice into a shaker. Aggressively shake causing the orange wheel to muddle. Strain into an ice-filled highball glass. Garnish with additional orange wheel and serve.

Tropical Storm

½ oz. rum
½ oz. bourbon
¼ oz. lemon juice
¼ oz. ginger simple syrup
Soda water
Candied ginger or lemon peel
  for garnish

Combine rum, bourbon, lemon juice, and ginger simple syrup into a shaker with ice. Shake and strain into a highball glass with ice and top with soda water. Garnish with candied ginger or lemon peel and serve.

Alcohol-Free Alternatives

Check out some alcohol-free "mocktails," including a few made with nonalcoholic (NA) spirits.

Amaretti Sour

1 oz. Lyre's Amaretti
½ oz. lemon juice
½ oz. simple syrup
1 egg white or 2 tbsp.
   of aquafaba
3 dashes aromatic bitters
Lemon wedge for garnish

Combine, shake, and strain into a rocks glass. Garnish with lemon wedge.

Arnold Palmer

3 oz. ice tea
1 oz. lemonade
Lemon wedge for garnish

Add into a highball with ice and stir. Garnish with lemon wedge.

Espresso & Tonic

1 oz. espresso
3 oz. tonic water
½ oz. simple syrup
Lemon slice for garnish

Add all ingredients into a highball glass with ice and stir. Garnish with lemon slice and serve.

Chocolate Banana Colada Shake

⅓ cup Coco Lopez Cream
   of Coconut
½ cup milk
1 tbsp. chocolate syrup
1½ cups chocolate or
   vanilla ice cream
½ cup sliced banana

Mix all ingredients in a blender until smooth, pour into a margarita glass, and serve.

Chocolate Colada Shake

⅓ cup Coco Lopez Cream
    of Coconut
½ cup milk
1 tbsp. chocolate syrup
1½ cups chocolate or
    vanilla ice cream

Mix all ingredients in a blender until smooth, pout into a margarita glass, and serve.

Clamato Cocktail

1 oz. lime juice
6 oz. Clamato juice

Stir together in a highball glass filled with ice.

Coco Lopez Shake

2½ oz. Coco Lopez Cream
    of Coconut
1 scoop vanilla ice cream
1 cup ice

Mix in a blender until smooth.

CosNOpolitan

2 oz. Seedlip Grove 42
1 oz. cranberry juice
½ oz. lime juice
½ oz. simple syrup
Orange peel for garnish

Shake and strain into a chilled coupe. Garnish with orange peel.

Cranberry Collins

½ cup cranberry juice
½ tbsp. lime juice
1 cup club soda, chilled
Lime slices

Mix cranberry juice and lime juice. Stir in club soda. Add ice cubes and lime slices and serve.

Dark 'n' Spicy

1 oz. Lyre's Dark Cane Spirit
½ oz. lime juice
⅕ oz. vanilla simple syrup
3 oz. ginger beer
Lime wheel for garnish

Add ingredients into a highball glass with ice and stir. Garnish with lime wheel.

Dust Cutter

¾ oz. lime juice
6 oz. tonic water

Combine over ice in a tall glass.

Freddy Bartholomew

6 oz. ginger ale
¾ oz. sweetened lime juice
Lime wedge for garnish

Add into a highball glass with ice
and stir. Garnish with lime wedge.

Fruit Bowl

1 oz. orange juice
1 oz. pineapple juice
1 oz. grape juice
1 oz. grapefruit juice

Shake with ice. Serve in a tall glass.

Grapefruit Cooler

8 oz. grapefruit juice
3 dashes bitters

Pour grapefruit juice into a tall glass
filled with ice. Add bitters and stir.

Gunner

8 oz. ginger ale
8 oz. ginger beer
¼ oz. sweetened lime juice
2 dashes angostura bitters
Lime wedge for garnish

Add into a highball with ice and stir.
Garnish with lime wedge.

Jungle Bird

1 oz. Lyre's Dark Cane Spirit
1½ oz. Lyre's Italian Orange
½ oz. lime juice
¼ oz. simple syrup
1½ oz. pineapple juice
Lemon wedge for garnish

Shake and strain into a rocks glass.
Garnish with lemon wedge.

Kona Coast

1 oz. lime juice
¼ oz. grenadine
5 oz. apple juice
2 oz. ginger ale

Stir together and serve over ice in a tall glass.

Lyre's Tommy's Margarita

2 oz. Lyre's Agave Reserva Spirit
½ oz. agave syrup
1 oz. lime juice
Pinch salt

Add ingredients into a shaker with ice and shake. Strain into a rocks glass and serve.

No-jito

4–5 mint leaves
½ oz. simple syrup
4 oz. club soda
1 oz. lime juice

Muddle 4–5 mint leaves with simple syrup and lime juice in a cocktail shaker. Add in ice and shake. Strain into highball glass with ice and add in club soda.

Nada Colada

1 oz. Coco Lopez Cream
   of Coconut
2 oz. pineapple juice
1 cup ice

Mix in a blender until smooth.

New Orleans Day

2 oz. Coco Lopez Cream
   of Coconut
1 oz. butterscotch topping
1 oz. half & half
1 cup ice

Mix in a blender until smooth.

Orange Smoothie

2½ oz. Coco Lopez Cream
   of Coconut
3 oz. orange juice
1 scoop vanilla ice cream
1 cup ice
Nutmeg

Mix first four ingredients in a blender until smooth. Sprinkle with nutmeg.

Paloma

Black salt
2 oz. Lyre's Agave Blanco Spirit
3 oz. blood orange soda
½ oz. lime juice
¼ oz. agave syrup

Rim highball glass with black salt and set aside. Add all ingredients into a cocktail shaker with ice and shake. Strain into rimmed glass and serve.

Perrier Mimosa

⅓ cup freshly squeezed orange juice, chilled
1½ cups Perrier, chilled
4 raspberries or grapes

Divide the orange juice between two champagne flutes and top with Perrier. Garnish with two raspberries or grapes in each glass.

Enough to share!

Piña Colada Shake

½ cup unsweetened pineapple juice
⅓ cup Coco Lopez Cream of Coconut
1½ cups vanilla ice cream

Mix in a blender until smooth. Serve immediately.

Pink Negroni

1½ oz. Lyre's Pink London Spirit
1 oz. Lyre's Aperitif Rosso
½ oz. Lyre's Italian Spritz
2 dashes orange bitters
Lemon wheel for garnish

Add in a large ice cube to a rocks glass. Add in ingredients and stir. Garnish with lemon wheel.

Red Racket

½ cup cranberry juice, chilled
½ cup grapefruit juice, chilled
10 ice cubes

In a blender, combine cranberry and grapefruit juice and ice cubes. Blend on high speed till frothy. Pour into a tall glass.

Roy Rogers

6 oz. cola
½ oz. grenadine
Maraschino cherry for garnish

In a highball glass, add in cola and top with grenadine and stir. Garnish with maraschino cherry and serve.

Ruby Cooler

1 cup cranberry apple juice
1 tsp. instant tea
Lemon wedges for garnish

Mix together cranberry apple juice and tea. Pour over ice into two tall glasses and garnish with lemon wedge.

Salted Caramel Espresso Martini

½ oz. Lyre's Spiced Cane Spirit
1½ oz. Lyre's Coffee Originale
1½ oz. espresso
½ oz. salted caramel syrup

Add all ingredients into a shaker without ice and dry shake. Add in ice and shake again. Strain into a chilled martini glass and serve.

Shirley Temple

1 oz. lime juice
1 oz. grenadine
6 oz. ginger ale
Maraschino cherry for garnish

Pour ingredients over ice in a tall glass. Garnish with a cherry.

Spritz De Passione

2 oz. Lyre's Italian Spritz
3 oz. Lyre's Classico
¼ oz. mango syrup
2 lemon slices, 4 raspberries, and 4 blueberries for garnish

In a wine glass, add in liquid ingredients with ice and stir. Garnish with lemon slices, raspberries, and blueberries and serve.

Stillman

2 oz. blood orange juice
6 oz. soda water
2 dashes angostura bitters

Add all ingredients into a highball glass with ice and stir.

Inspired by S. Troullos, Philadelphia, PA.

Virgin Mary

4 oz. tomato juice
Dash Worcestershire sauce
Dash Tabasco Sauce
Dash salt and pepper
Squeeze of lemon juice
Celery stalk for garnish

In a glass filled with ice, add tomato juice. Add a dash or two of Worcestershire sauce, Tabasco, salt, lemon juice, and pepper. Garnish with a celery stalk.

Virgin Strawberry Daiquiri

¾ oz. lemon-lime soda
¼ cup sugar
1 tbsp. lemon juice
1 cup of ice
2 large strawberries, plus more
for garnish

In a blender add all ingredients and blend. Strain into a margarita glass, top with a strawberry, and serve.

Try this with other fruits as well for fun combinations!

The Part of Tens

Say cheers and offer some kind words when sharing a toast to honor friends, family, or occasions.

Try one of several cures for hiccups and hangovers.

Talk like a pro with some of the most commonly used bar slang.

Chapter **25**

Ten+ Toasts to Mark Any Occasion

Nearly any occasion that involves alcohol and a group of friends, relatives, or even strangers can be made all the more special with a few words of acknowledgment. The toasts included here are some of our favorites. Use "Cheers!" and these toasts whenever you're at a loss for words.

SAYING "CHEERS" IN TEN LANGUAGES

In the United States, toasts usually end with "Cheers!" to wish everyone well. Other countries have adapted this tradition. Here are ten different versions from around the world:

- Afrikaans: Gesondheid
- Chinese: Gānbēi
- Danish/Swedish: Skål
- Italian: Cin cin

(continued)

(continued)

- French: Santé
- German: Prost
- Irish Gaelic: Sláinte
- Japanese: Kanpai
- Portuguese: Saúde
- Spanish: Salud

Saluting Special Occasions

Birthdays, retirements, weddings, and holidays often call for someone to stand up and say a few words. Whether you're toasting the guest of honor or celebrating a new phase of life, these toasts will make you sound clever and give your guests something to think about.

Every baby born into the world is a finer one than the last.
— CHARLES DICKENS, NICHOLAS NICKLEBY

Then let us be merry and taste the good cheer,

And remember old Christmas but comes once a year.
— FROM AN OLD CHRISTMAS CAROL

May good fortune follow you all your days . . . and never catch up with you!
— OLD IRISH TOAST

May you never lie, steal or drink. But, if you lie, lie with each other at night. If you steal, steal each other's sorrows. And if you must drink . . . drink with us. Cheers to the newlyweds!
— UNKNOWN

Here's to the good time I must have had!
— R. P. FOLEY, FOUNDER, BARTENDER MAGAZINE

A Nod to Friendship

Instead of prattling on about your friend's good (or maybe not-so-good) characteristics, try one of these toasts. Everyone will be grateful that you kept your words of recognition short and sweet. After all, you have alcohol to enjoy!

May you live to be a hundred years, with one extra year to repent.
— IRISH TOAST

There are good ships and wood ships, and ships that sail the sea, but the best ships are friendships, may they always be.
— IRISH PROVERB

A lovely being scarcely formed or molded,

A rose with all its sweetest leaves yet folded.
— LORD BYRON, POET

A day for toil, an hour for sport,

But for a friend is life too short.
— RALPH WALDO EMERSON, POET

Here's to the bottle which holds a store

Of imprisoned joy and laughter!

Here's to this bottle,

Many more bottles,

And others to follow after.
— UNKNOWN

The first glass for myself, the second for my friends;

the third for good humor, and the fourth for mine enemies.
— SIR WILLIAM TEMPLE, STATESMAN

Chapter **26**
At Least Ten Cures and Lores

An important part of being a bartender is speaking with guests. You, of course, want to enrich their experience with some positive banter, but you may find yourself helping to solve issues, such as settling arguments, mending broken hearts, and curing two primary medicinal problems: hiccups and hangovers. We won't swear that all these solutions work, but if you're desperate, trying them can't hurt! Be sure to always keep an eye on your guests to not overserve them.

Hiccups

Ah, the hiccups — something that's never fun to have! Drinking alcohol irritates your digestive system, which can cause you to get hiccups. (When you put it this way, hiccups don't seem nearly as embarrassing as most people consider them.) Here's a list of possible cures:

» Slice a lemon and remove the seeds. Top the slices with sugar and bitters and eat the whole thing. This is the sure cure.

>> Mix aromatic bitters and club soda and sip slowly.

>> Drink a glass of water backward (from the opposite side of the glass). You may see this a lot at the bar, and drinking water is helpful overall.

>> Hold your nose and breathe through your mouth. Then count to 10 or 20, or count to 100 to be certain.

>> Someone scaring you always seems to do the trick.

Hangovers

It's no mystery what causes a hangover, but a cure is more difficult to reveal. Only a couple cures really work.

>> **A little prevention:** Don't overindulge or let yourself be overserved. (Someone told me [Ray] once that even in moderation, I am excessive.)

>> **Rehydrate:** Having a no-alcohol drink, like water, in-between alcohol-based drinks helps as well.

>> **Sleep:** Getting some peace and quiet always helps to reset your body and allow it to recover.

Consider a few more possible cures:

>> Drinking Sprite (and specifically Sprite) to shorten hangovers

>> Drinking 2 oz. of Fernet-Branca or any digestive on the rocks

>> Eating ginger or drinking ginger tea or ginger ale

>> Getting an IV drip — a more recent trend that's expensive but will do the trick

>> Hair of the dog: One shot of whatever you were drinking

Chapter **27**

Ten+ Terms That'll Make You Sound Like a Pro

Like most businesses, the bar and restaurant industry has its own terminology. This chapter covers some of the most popular sayings. You can sling this slang whether you're serving guests in your home or at a bar or event.

Ordering and Pouring Slang

Order up! These terms are specific to making and serving drinks.

>> **Call:** A call drink is when someone says a specific brand in their cocktail. Like "Tito's & Soda," for example, or "Jack & Coke."

>> **Bartender's handshake:** Usually a shot/drink gifted from one bartender to another.

>> **Boomerang:** A drink sent from one bartender at one bar to another bartender at another bar.

>> **Free pour:** This is when you don't use a jigger to measure your ingredients.

WARNING

We suggest mastering your craft first before free pouring. Overpouring may cause the drink to taste differently and cost the bar money because you're using more product than you're charging for.

>> **Heard:** A term used when you understand what someone is asking or telling you. For example, a server at busy bar might say, "I need three Martinis, please," to which the bartender replies, "Heard!" to confirm the drink order.

>> **Neat:** Straight spirit into a rocks or champagne flute right from the bottle.

>> **On the rocks:** A drink served on ice, usually in a rocks glass (refer to Chapter 1 for the lowdown on drink glasses).

>> **Straight up:** A shaken or stirred drink that is then strained into a glass (usually martini or coupe glass) without ice.

>> **Top-shelf:** A term talking about the "best" liquor and spirits available at the bar.

>> **Well drinks:** The opposite of top-shelf, this is a term used to talk about the lower cost spirits and liquors at the bar. These are usually housed in the *well* or area behind the bar.

Working the Bar

Nix the vocabulary from your last job. These are the new terms you will use in the bartending industry!

>> **2 or 3 deep:** Number of people waiting for a drink at the bar.

>> **86 or 86'd:** Meaning something is out/depleted or needs to be removed. This term is often used in the restaurant world to let the staff know you're out of something. You might say, "Vanilla vodka is 86'd," or "86 tonight's drink special."

>> **Behind:** When someone says "behind," they're alerting you that they're walking behind you so you don't turn around or back up into them.

>> **Behind the stick:** Getting behind the bar or working behind the bar.

>> **Corner:** Used across the restaurant industry when a staff member is turning a blind corner to make sure that you're not going to run into someone. This is a very important call to avoid spills, breakage, and physical harm.

>> **Double shift:** Working a double or double shift means you're working a morning or afternoon shift as well as an evening shift.

>> **In the weeds:** A term used when you're very busy.

>> **Last call:** A call made when there's time left to order one last drink before the bar closes.

>> **Service bar:** A part of the bar where the waitstaff picks up drinks for guests sitting at tables. A service bartender usually just focuses on the orders placed by the waitstaff.

Recipe Index

Topics Index

L

lager, 121
lambic beer, 121
last call, 359
Lewis ice bags, 12
Licor 43, 116
light beer, 121
Lillet, 112
Limoncello, 117
liqueurs, 113, 118
low-alcohol beer, 121, 137–138
low-alcohol cocktails, 337–340
low-calorie beer, 121
Luxardo, 117

M

MacElhone, Harry, 308
Malbec, 130
Malibu, 117
malt liquor, 121
malt whisky, 83–84
malted barley, 120
maraschino cherries, 25
marc, 101
margarita glasses, 13
Mariani, John, 235
Marie Brizard Liqueurs, 117
Martin, John, 54
martini glasses, 13–14
martinis, 25, 321–328
mash, 67
meal, 67
measuring glasses, 11–12
Merlot, 128, 130
méthod champenoise, 133

mezcal, 64–66

mezcal, 64–66
  popular brands, 65
  serving, 66
  storing, 66
  worms, 65
Midori, 117
mixing glasses, 11–12
mocktails, 341–347
molasses, 93
Morgan, Jack, 54
Mozart Chocolate Liqueur, 117
muddlers, 11–12, 18–19
muddling, 18–19
mule mugs, 13–14
Myers, Fred L., 286

N

neat, 56, 143, 358
99 Bananas, 114
no-alcohol beer, 121, 137–138
no-alcohol cocktails, 341–347
no-alcohol spirits, 139
no-alcohol wine, 138–139
NORMA standards, 62
North American wines, 130

O

old fashioned glasses (rocks glasses), 13–14
olives, 25
on the rocks, 358
opening bottles, 27–29
Orange Curaçao, 117
orujo, 101
Orvieto, 129
ouzo, 117

About the Authors

Ray Foley, a former Marine with more than 30 years of bartending and restaurant experience, is the founder and publisher of *BARTENDER Magazine*, the only magazine in the world specifically geared toward bartenders and one of the very few primarily designed for servers of alcohol. *BARTENDER Magazine* is enjoying its 44th year and currently has a growing circulation of more than 80,000 in print with readership of more than 250,000. The magazine can also be viewed digitally at www.bartender.com.

Ray has been published in numerous articles throughout the country and has appeared on many TV and radio shows, including *Good Morning America*, *Live with Regis and Kathie Lee*, *Lifestyles with Robin Leach*, *The David Susskind Show*, ABC News, CBS News, and NBC News. Ray has also been featured in major magazines, most notably *Forbes* and *Playboy*.

Ray is the founder of the *BARTENDER* "Hall of Fame," which honors the best bartenders all over the globe, not only for their abilities as bartenders but also for their involvement in their communities.

Ray serves as a consultant to some of the United States' foremost distillers and importers. He is also responsible for naming and inventing new drinks for the liquor industry, the most popular being the Fuzzy Navel.

Until recently, Ray owned one of the largest collections of cocktail recipe books in the world, dating back to the 1800s, as well as an impressive collection of cocktail shakers, with more than 400 shakers in all!

He is the author of *Running a Bar For Dummies*, *The Ultimate Cocktail Book*, *The Ultimate Little Shooter Book*, *The Ultimate Little Martini Book*, *The Irish Drink Book*, *Jokes Quotes & Bar Toons*, *The Ultimate Little Blender Book*, *The Best Irish Drinks*, *Vodka 1000*, *Rum 1000*, *Tequila 1000*, and his noncocktail book *God Loves Golfers Best*.

For more information about *BARTENDER Magazine*, please email barmag2@gmail.com or visit the website at www.bartender.com.

Jaclyn Foley has more than 30 years of experience in the hospitality business as a server, bartender, author, and the editor/publisher/cofounder of *BARTENDER Magazine*.

Jaclyn is a graduate of Rosemont College in Pennsylvania. She studied marketing at nearby Villanova University. She is also the author of *The Pink Drink Book, Girls' Night,* and *Skinny Cocktails.*

Jaclyn is a graduate of Absolut Akademi in Sweden, a Kentucky Colonel, judged numerous drink contests, and has traveled to nine cities around the country on behalf of Jim Beam promoting Vox Vodka and *The Pink Drink Book*. She has appeared on numerous TV shows and in many national and trade publications.

Dedication

This book is dedicated to all who serve the public with long hours, tired bodies, and great patience (and still have fun): bartenders.

And, of course, our son, Ryan Foley; his wife, Caitlin Foley; and our granddaughter.

Authors' Acknowledgments

We would like to pour out our gratitude to Tracy Boggier and the overflowing enthusiasm at John Wiley & Sons.

For mixing all the ingredients properly and adding just the right amount of garnish, Project Editor Alissa Schwipps, Senior Editor Jennifer Yee, and Technical Editor Greg Cohen.

We humbly acknowledge those at *BARTENDER Magazine* for serving this up at record speed, especially Chrissy Epp Loucel and Olivia Lipp.

And for supplying all the ingredients in this mixture and their tremendous support and help, Anne Loffredo, Chester Brandes, Jose Suarez, Peter Angus, Claire O'Connell, Jenny Manger, Jean-Marie Heins, and Kevin Pelz. And all the great folks who make, market, sell all the amazing wine, beer, and spirits around the globe.

To Jimmy Zazzali for being a great bartender and friend. And a toast to some of those we've lost — John Cowan, Matt Wojciak, Marvin Solomon, LeRoy Neiman, Peter Nelson, and the best general manager and boss, U.S. Marine, and friend, William Boggier.

To some of our personal favorite bar guests: Martha Michels, Bill McCabe, Debbie Carroll, Quinn Gibbons, Janyne Fiorelli, Kimberlee Linus Stiles, Luisa Castagna, Hymie Lipshitz, Greg G. Gregerson, John Victor Muskett III, Phoebe Getzow, Sean T. Gregory Fallon, Conor Fallon, John and Kathleen Fallon, Colin Mackey, Ted Cocuzza, William Bard, John D'Alessandro, Steve Troullos, Matt Saxonmeyer, Kevin Marren, Zach Baine, Vince and Taylor Voiro, Mike and Cat Zuppe, Alex and Chris Farrell, Drew and Katie Saine, Jayme Laurash and the Laurash Girls, and the O'Neill and Brix families.

And finally, a special tip to Howard and Delia Wilson, Caitlin Fallon Foley, Baby Foley, Emma Foley, and Ryan Peter Foley, who assisted in the fifth and sixth editions of this book.

Publisher's Acknowledgments

Acquisitions Editor: Jennifer Yee

Project Editor: Alissa Schwipps

Copy Editor: Jennette ElNaggar

Proofreader: Debbye Butler

Technical Editor: Greg Cohen

Illustrator: Elizabeth Kurtzman

Cover Image: © Brent Hofacker/ Shutterstock

Production Editor: Mohammed Zafar Ali

Take dummies with you everywhere you go!

Whether you are excited about e-books, want more from the web, must have your mobile apps, or are swept up in social media, dummies makes everything easier.

Find us online!

dummies.com

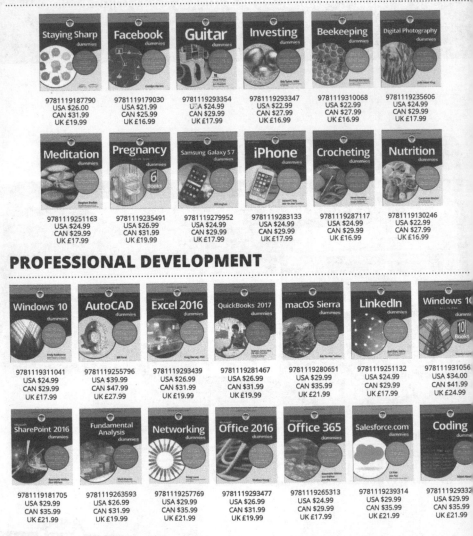